In the turbulent days of the seventeenth century,
Ireland was a melting pot of native Irish, old English
— 'English to the Irish and Irish to the English' —
and newly arrived planter.

Munster had been devastated in the Elizabethaen
wars... 'the lowing of a cow cannot be heard
from Dunquin to Cashel.'

Then in 1641, with Eoin Roe O'Neill, came new
hope. Pierce Ferriter, from a Norman-Irish family,
was expected to lead a troup of militia to resist the
rebels, but to the consternation of his friends he
joined forces with Florence MacCarthy in beseiging
the English in Tralee Castle, and he fought through
the campaign in Kerry.

After the wars he returned home to West Kerry,
to become again Pierce the poet, the weaver of love
songs in scholarly Gaelic.

Then came Cromwell, and Pierce was lured from
his retirement with a promise of safe conduct...

JOHN CABALL has a native's knowledge of Kerry,
its people and its history, and his writing is imbued
with a sense of place that brings the past brilliantly
to life.

'A man of balanced judgement, wielding a
singularly skilful as well as an admirably poetic pen.'
— Seamus MacManus.

COVER AND ILLUSTRATIONS BY TERRY MYLER.

John Caball

The Singing Swordsman

With a preface by Daniel Corkery

HAWTHORN BOOKS

The Children's Press

For an old friend
S.T.M.

This edition published 1987 by
The Children's Press
90 Lower Baggot Street, Dublin 2

First published 1953 by the
Michael F. Moynihan Publishing
Company of Dublin

ISBN 0 947962 25 5 paperboards
ISBN 0 947962 26 3 paper

Printed in Ireland by Mount Salus Press.

CONTENTS

PREFACE

THE THREE STRAINS that interweave themselves about one another in this book are, first, all that part of Kerry which lies about Tralee, that Gaeltacht stretching along the coast from Dingle to Mount Brandon and beyond ; second, the tragic figures of both Pierce Ferriter, as gallant in life as in his poems, and his wife, whose fate was no less heart-rending than his own ; while we may reckon as the third strain the uninhibited affection of the writer himself for every scrap of tradition or history that adheres to the district ; the warmth of that affection shows itself almost as ardently when it is bent upon some countryside or some valley or stream as when the tragic tale of the lovers is what it would have us share.

All the district, indeed, is given up to history. Living people are few, but there are clusters of almost, if not quite prehistoric, remains in it. There are many early Christian monuments as well, the very famous oratory at Gallarus, for instance, and from a later Christian period the ruins of churches ; the remnants of the Castle of the Ferriters tell us of a still later period, while from our own days we have the broken dwellings of the vanished people. For those who know, the remains of the Castle of the local prince is a tragic memorial, and so too, is Dun an Oir of the slaughter. Tragic, too, it is to look out at the Blasket Islands and know that human life itself is ceasing on them, even if we think that living souls should never have had to shelter themselves at all on such windswept rocks.

And the whole place is also given up to literature as surely as to history. The now silent Blaskets fashioned a book or two within the last half-century, which Ireland—the real Ireland—will not let die, any more than that Ireland will let die the story of the legendary invasion of the world's king at Ventry Harbour. From one piece of writing to the other is a far cry indeed, but of an unlettered hiatus in those centuries we have not heard.

Yet all that seaboard is a silent land, or so we have felt it as we walked the roads of it. It is, however, a silence that excites rather than assuages : there are always presences.

This book is a homely book, one that will be taken to readily by all those who are of the people of Ireland. Nor will it be judged too narrowly or too academically by other nations to whom it will have brought so much of vital history, and so much of the hills and valleys, little towns and dwellings in which history once made such stir and loud excitement.

DANIEL CORKERY.

AUTHOR'S NOTE

MOST OF THE characters are historical; a few legendary, and a lesser few imaginary. The poem: *The Land of Fál* is taken from Collected works by the late James Stephens by permission of Mrs. Stephens and Messrs. Macmillan and Company, Limited.

For reference, there are the historians of Kerry: Smith, Hickson, Cusack and King; Bagwell's *Ireland under the Stuarts*; Butler's *Gleanings from Irish History*; *Life and Letters of Florence MacCarthy Mór*, by Daniel MacCarthy (Glas); Seymour's *The Puritans in Ireland*; the autobiography of *The Reverend Devereux Spratt*; the contemporary evidence of Spenser, Davies, Moryson and Raleigh; Meehan's *The Confederation of Kilkenny*; Robin Flower's Preface to the *Danta Gradha*; the *Pacata Hibernia*; O'Heyne's *Irish Dominicans* and Byrne's *The Irish War of Defence*; Edward Bunting's *The Ancient Music of Ireland*; *The Memoirs of Edmund Ludlow*; O'Donoghue's *Brendaniana* and An Seabhac's *Triocha-cead Chorca Dhuibhne*; O'Daly's *Geraldines*; Msgr. Reidy's booklets on *Kerry* and *St. Brendan*.

For the poems of Pierce Ferriter there is the re-issue by An Gúm of Dr. Dineen's work (1934).

PROLOGUE

ONE NIGHT TOWARDS the end of the sixteenth century, Sir Edward Denny sat on a great oaken chair before the log fire in the hall of the manor of Carrignafeely in western Desmond. He was lonely as always, but that did not matter; the only thing he cared for was land, rich pasture fields with succulent green grass, huge tracts of golden waving corn, and vast acres of mountain where he might hunt the red deer or catch the gleaming salmon in the brimming pools. A few miles away, midst the little village of Tralee, rose the blackened battlements of the " Great Castel," blackened from their share in Elizabeth's wars. The Castle was now a ruin and hence the Dennys, the new planters, lived at Carrignafeely, where Sir Edward was now alone with his thoughts.

Some of the natives, when he came near them, might stare with sullen looks or sneer as he rode by; but even in peaceful England they sometimes did that. Here, however, more dangerous than England, there were ambuscades. Sometimes his finest milch cows would be sent wandering through the woods, his horses turned loose or his servants beaten, like Richard Roe his chief steward or Will Beckford, his head gardener, the other day. That, however, would soon be got over. Ireland, God be praised for it, was almost subdued at last. For any further outbreaks he knew what he would do : he would erect a gibbet near the Market Cross like that which his dear lamented wife, the Lady Margaret, placed there at the time of the Armada, when he himself was away in Dublin, attending the Council. One of the ships had been blown into the Bay. Margaret had no scruples about her treatment of traitors, foreigners or rebels; in a flash she had made up her mind and as quickly she set to work. Always used to getting her way, she was petulant and vain; but she had courage, and when he rode back to Tralee next day, twenty-four Spanish traitors were swinging in the breeze over at Gallows Field.

But to-night he was thinking mostly about the days when he first came to Ireland. After the massacre of Dun an Oir, he began to throw covetous eyes on the Desmond lands. It was in the family, this land-grabbing, and it was so easy to grab from friars ; for friars did not fight or vow vengeance. His father, Sir Anthony, at the dissolution of the monasteries, had got much loot in England, like the Priory of Hertford, a great part of Waltham Abbey in Essex, and most of the enormously wealthy Abbey of St. Albans, with the manors and advowsons of eleven parishes. That took some doing, thought Ned. Could he do likewise in Desmond, he a younger son with no prospects ? It was no use, obviously, returning to England ; it must be Ireland, then. Besides, England was too respectable—one was too restricted. True, he had written to his cousin, Walsingham, when he first arrived here that life in Ireland would suit mastiffs rather than gentlemen.

But that was before Dun an Oir, before he was dubbed a knight banneret on the field of battle, before he had seen the old Earl's waving seas of corn and pools of sparkling trout and forests of fallow deer. Also, he was becoming brave ; he was getting used to battle. Perhaps " battle " was scarcely the word for it was merely butchering some miserable natives and foreign scum, and then throwing them into the sea. One could not truly do battle with these vermin Irish ; they were likely to spring upon you out of anywhere. Indeed, they were a rum lot and the sooner exterminated the better Also, one never knew how he stood with all these tribes, some of them even claiming to be English, like the Fitzgeralds and their friends, the Ferriters. Imagine the late Earl of Desmond, " the old Earl " they called him, with his thick brogue and native ways, claiming to be English. It was a queer country, no doubt. But as bad as it was it was better than returning to Court and having to tell the old yellow pasty Queen, almost daily, that she was the most beautiful woman in Christendom.

But how to get Desmond's fair acres ? Then a plan began to unfold itself to him : he would steal away in the morning. He would get up early and even if Lord Grey or his cousin, Raleigh,

saw him he could say he was going for a canter. He would ride
into Tralee, change horses at The Golden Key—for he had plenty
of gold—his share of the Dun an Oir booty which Grey shared
out amongst them when they had the last slimy, headless
Spaniard thrown into the sea. He would ride to Cork and with
the help of his friend Boyle, perhaps get a passage on a tramp
boat to England. Then he would make his way by the most
rapid route to Whitehall. He would array himself in his best
jerkin and ruff and patent shoes, and bowing obsequiously and
smiling his sly smile, he would enter the presence of
Gloriana.

"Ah, Edward, so it's you ; and how's my brave Grey and
his faithful followers ? Has he duly avenged the numberless
insults heaped upon me by my brother of Spain ? "

But Ned would not speak for a moment or two ; he would
stand and look at her and smile—sure of himself. Then slowly
and deliberately, he would speak :

"Your most gracious Majesty, it pleases me much to tell
you that your Majesty is now freed from further trial or trouble
with as vile a nest of foreigners and Irish traitors as it was ever
a monarch's misfortune to contend. Your Majesty ! " and here
he would pause for a moment to let the full implication of the
news sink into her scheming brain, " we have captured the fort
with its stores and munitions, thrown the headless foreigners
to the waves, tortured and shot the Irish, and completed the
subjugation of all Desmond. The lowing of a cow, your Majesty,
cannot now be heard from Dunquin in the west to Cashel in
the east."

But Elizabeth was shrewd : she never gave herself away.
Although there was a slight quivering of tumultuous exultation
on those thin lips, and her eyes danced for joy in her pale yellow,
parchment-like face, yet she was silent for some moments,
and then raising her thin features, she looked fixedly at him,
and then said :

"Edward, as you are aware, we must await the official
report from my Lord Grey, but if what you tell me coincides
with the account therein, you shall return to Ireland the ruler
and lord of western Desmond."

And that is, more or less, how the Dennys first got the old Earl's Castle at Tralee and all his rolling pastures.

As the years passed and Sir Edward repaired the Great Castle, and some sort of order evolved out of the chaos in Desmond, men would sometimes walk into The Golden Key. This was the great blue tavern with the diamond-leaded panes and cross beams, and with the shining golden key swinging in front, that stood down near the Bridge at the turn of the river. Here, over their ale, they would sit and talk about the times. Often a traveller from distant parts, all dusty from the road, might come in, a lawyer's clerk, perhaps, who had ridden from Cork to get Sir Edward's signature to a title-deed, but who first turned into the tavern, as any wise man would, who wanted to sound the citizens' views.

" I wish to call at the Castle," he would say to the host, " is Sir Edward easy of access ? "

" Ah, sir, that could not be done at all, I'm afraid," the host would say with a startled voice, " you see, Sir Edward's not well now and few ever see him."

"Why, landlord ? "

" Oh, I don't know : just brooding. I suppose he thinks about the slaughter his acres cost."

" Very strange."

" And they say," his voice falling to a whisper, " that he sees strange sights."

" How do you mean ? "

" Oh, sir, that old abbey ! It isn't right to tamper with the dead."

"What did he do ? "

" He opened their graves to build houses for his servants."

" Opened their graves ! "

" Yes, that anybody will tell you ; and now the friars, in their black cowls, come striding apast him at midnight ! "

" Indeed ! "

" They walk in a solemn row with heads bowed and arms crossed."

" Has anybody else seen them ? "

"Not that I know, but many have heard the tolling of the bell."

" The bell ? "

" Yes, the bell that used to be on the spire and that the friars buried over near the river : men hear it at evening-time, sir, ringing for vespers."

" That's strange."

" We live in strange times : surely the plundering planters cannot touch the dead dust of the Geraldines with impunity."

" True, landlord ! "

" Flesh and blood may stand it, but the dead have their own law," and he crossed himself, " it's a terrible thing to be their enemy ! "

He would pause for a few moments and then continue :

" And men say, too, they hear the friars chant the midnight Mass as in the old days : the candles light up the rood ; and the murmur of the organ floats softly on the breeze. It's queer times we're living in, sir."

" Queer times, indeed, landlord."

Yes, the times were truly very strange.

I
YOUNG BLOOD
The Poet Singing

ONE DAY, ABOUT half a century after the coming of Denny, Florence MacCarthy rode from Killarney to Tralee. Few would see in the hard features, the youth who once romped with Pierce and the rest of them. That morning, a messenger came with the news of the Chieftain Ferriter's death and through his friendship for Pierce he decided to go to the funeral. He travelled the longer route by way of Tralee as he wished to call at The Golden Key on business.

His schooldays over, he had enlisted in the Spanish service and fought in the Low Countries. Because of wanderlust, he went; his father tried to keep him but it was no use. "Better let him go," he said to his lady, "let him have enough and he may come back satisfied." He had indeed got enough and returned, if not satisfied, at least content enough to take his place in the county.

Many and bitter the battles he fought for the cause of Spain and had got used, no doubt to brigandage and bloodshed. He saw, in the fields of Flanders, a cannon ball pierce the skull of Maurice Fitzgerald, and that finished him with foreign fields.

The mellow sunshine lit up the broad valley between Slieve Mish and the Stacks ; here and there were ivy-covered trees, twisted and gnarled, and crowned with the gold of autumn. To his left, were huge fissures in the shoulder of the mountain ; and beneath lay the' wood of Ballyseedy, while further onwards, under a haze, was the village of Tralee.

In a little while he cantered through the narrow streets and came to the inn.

The village lay clustering like a brood about the walls of the Castle, which stood at the loop of the River Gabhail. This was a river which ran from Stack's Mountains to the north, and arriving at the Castle, turned westwards to form a moat. Here, for almost five centuries, had been centred the power of the Geraldines. In the olden days, before Denny came, these blackened battlements had rebuffed many a foray, and as often from the parapets came a shout of defiance for the King's tax-collectors. For one could never be sure of these Norman-Irish : it depended on the exigencies of the moment whether they posed as Gaelic chieftains or else, vassals of His Majesty. They were Irish to the English and English to the Irish. Most of the great families had not yet come to look upon Ireland as their motherland ; at heart, they were devoted to the Crown, but they never would transfer their allegiance in matters spiritual from the Pope to the Sovereign. They were known as the Old English, and for centuries, though they had lived amongst and intermarried with the old Irish, yet still they looked upon theirs as the dominating culture and upon themselves as a superior race. Sometimes, when it suited their purpose, they joined with the old race in open rebellion or intrigued against the King—but that was solely for personal aims. Thus, broadly speaking, they were loyalists and were always regarded in Ireland as the upholders of the Throne.

Since the Desmond Wars the Castle had been repaired and restored, and now another Sir Edward Denny, grandson to the original, inimitable, wayward Ned, continued to hold western Desmond in his icy grip.

The town, or rather village, for so the charter of King James terms it, had changed little since the Norman Fitzgeralds had ousted the native Moriartys and built the Castle, with its tremendous bastions and towering battlements on the fork of the river—for Gabhail means " fork "—shining now like a string of silver in the morning sunshine. The Stacks from which it ran were a continuation to the north-east of the Glanruddery chain ; and the river on reaching the Castle went for some distance west, and then went directly south, forming as it did so, the moat which had ever been one of the strongest features of the Castle's defence. The main part of the village, called Burgess Street, lay mainly on the short stretch of twenty yards or so of the river that ran from east to west, on the northern side, no doubt, because the Castle and the ruins of the Dominican Priory of St. Mary lay all along to the south. Further upwards on the river bank to the north was the Parish Church of St. John the Baptist, taken over again by the Protestants when Queen Mary died.

When the good Queen Mary, or the lady Mary as they called her, sat on the throne, the old Earl would always be in his pew there on the sabbath and saints' days. There would be with him, Elinor, his Countess, with perhaps his cousin, James Fitzmaurice, or the Knight of Kerry, who lived at Dingle, or one of the Ferriters, or the Knight of Glin, who with their carefully trimmed beards, immaculate ruffs, jerkins of blue, black, brown or scarlet, pantaloons and hose of the latest Spanish fashion, and buckled shoes of patent leather, would surely give plenty of food for gossip to Tralee for some days to come. Old Dean Comane, putting aside his golden chasuble, would preach and perhaps tell them that the English schism of the late King Henry had now been healed and that his eminence, Cardinal Pole, had reconciled England with Rome. Few of his listeners really understood the issue, because during his late Majesty's reign, things went on pretty much the same ; there was Mass, and Vespers, and they told the beads as they always had done. True, some officials had to affirm the King was head of the Church, but in one way or another, they salved their consciences and so, life was little changed. Neither were the friars molested ; for one thing, Tralee was too remote and besides his Majesty had had enough of Church loot for the nonce.

But Denny surely made up for lost time on the part of his Majesty ; soon all the colour and life went out of St. John's and it seemed as if now the sabbath were a day when men should be downcast and gloomy and bandy texts with one another instead of revelling in the poetry and colour of the centuries. For the new religion said the Host was only now a bit of bread and so there was no High Mass on the great days and, consequently, nobody waxed merry or sang roundelays or skipped round the maypole as they used to do after church ; and how could men meet and gossip after vespers if there were no vespers ? And why should they light the bonfires on St. John's eve when the new religion but barely noticed St. John ? Truly it was a strange religion, the religion of her late Majesty. On the sabbath mornings there was now a plain service on a plain deal table with the minister in his plain white surplice. Some people said they liked it better but they were the few new English who always did what Denny did ; the most of the people, including " the old English Irelandised " to give them their due, would still keep to the old ways and have their Mass quietly, if not in the parish church, not very far from it, then, perhaps, in one of the great timbered houses or in Dr. O'Connell's school, or when Denny got into his tantrums, in Glen Scotia or at Curagheen on the road to Dingle.

Tralee, however, being under the watchful eyes of the Dennys lacked little in this respect. Besides the resident rector, there was the colourful character of the Reverend Devereux Spratt, tutor to Sir Edward's children. He tells us himself he was born in Somerset, where he " was religiously educated by my parents Mr. Thomas Spratt and Elizabeth, his wife, my father being a reverend godly divine whom God made instrumental in the conversion of many a soul." His father died when he was fourteen and afterwards he was sent to the University of Oxford, where he took his degree. Then he came to Ireland with his mother, whose father, Robert Cooke was pastor of the Island of Kerry or Castleisland. We next find him in Tralee where he was tutor to Denny's three sons.

Stretching from The Golden Key, which stood about a hundred yards from the Castle at the opposite side of the river,

was a line of fine timbered houses of the Elizabethan type
which Ned Denny's son, Sir Arthur, had built. Some of these
were the residences of the burgesses and other important
citizens ; others were either taverns or shops. There was a
bookshop with tiny leaded panes owned by Nathaniel Harrison,
who had fought with Denny ; there was Manuel Gabriel,
the apothecary, who spent some of his days and all his nights
with his bubbling retorts, mixing feverishly, pouring from
phial to phial, bending closer over the weird concoction,
hoping against hope for the precious transmutation—the
Philosopher's Stone. These timbered houses ran about a further
hundred yards to the east of the Castle, when the street, if it
could be called one, trailed away into a line of insignificant
cabins. Further upwards, a road went south, past the Well of
St. Mary, or Moyderwell, to Castle Morris at Ballymullen.
At the opposite end of the town the street again dwindled into
a chain of cabins, until one came to the higher ground at the
Strand Road, where there were also many fine merchants'
houses.

From everywhere in the village one could see Slieve Mish,
which had its beginnings at Gortatlea to the east and stretched
for ten straight miles across the length of Corca Dhuibhne,
rising gradually till it stopped abruptly in the stone fort of
Cu Ri, two thousand, seven hundred feet above the sea.

Three defiles or glens crossed its surface, the one being
nearest to Tralee being Gleann Scoithin or the Glen of Scotia,
called, so many say, after Queen Scotia, the " Milesian " queen
who here, in a great battle, was said to have defeated her
enemies. She was herself killed in the fray and as proof of that,
her grave is still to be seen. But whether or not Queen Scotia
ever beheld this little glen, it shall have for us more intimate
associations ; for when the time comes at last to strike a blow
against Denny and the planters, it is in Glen Scotia that the
patriots meet and plot how best to drive the huckster brood
from Tralee—from Kerry—from Desmond.

Despite its many upheavals, Tralee lacked none of the court-
liness and grace of any town of mediaeval Europe ; it had
atmosphere, dignity and colour—colour especially on market

days when all the country folk would troop in. The dealers with their stalls of taffeta, galloon and Hollands lace, with jerkins of all imaginable hues, and silks and satins from the furthest lands, would take their stand along each side of the river in front of the Castle. There, too, were the huts, with crowds about each. In one, it would be the potter and surely nothing was more fascinating than watching his deft fingers at the clay. In the next, it would be old Peter Cambridge, the cooper, and he, too, had his onlookers. He had a pair of spectacles perched at the top of his long nose, but his eyes were only for his keelers. Further on would be the weavers with their looms. Next might be a locksmith and then a turner, and near him some more mercers with stacks of lawns. A short distance from the huts were the fowls, baskets of eggs and rolls of delicious butter in snow-white linen. There, you might often hear haggling and even hard words ; it might be old Brigid, the housekeeper to Nathaniel Harrison, disputing the price of eggs, or Manuel Gabriel, who did not wish to pay more than half for a brace of chickens. There would be ballad-singers, too, singing in Gaelic to ears that did not understand, about James Fitzmaurice, or the great Sean O'Neill, or maybe about the Earls who slept in faraway Rome.

The taverns, also, would be full, and there were three or four as well as The Golden Key. Here men would discuss the latest prices or the scarcity of claret or maybe the war that had just begun between Spain and Portugal. Often you might meet an old story-teller there, who would tell you much about the town in the far off days. He would tell you also about Gerald, the Rhymer, one of the Desmonds who wrote Gaelic poetry and was called a " rimer " in derision by his enemies, the La Poers of Waterford. Back further through the centuries, the old story-teller would go, back before the coming of the Geraldines to the Gaelic Tralee that stood near the place to-day called Clonalour ; back to the Danes who mined the copper on Slieve Mish ; back to holy Brendan, who was born at Annagh, the marshy place near Tralee ; back to Ptolemy, who showed the town on his map ; back to the mythological story of how Cuchulainn rescued the fair Blathnaid from the clutches

of Cu Ri at his fort on the summit of Slieve Mish. Cuchulainn knew well the moment to attack because Blathnaid was to
pour milk into the stream which roared its way down the
mountain-side. And there is proof for this story, for to this
very day the stream is white—the fionn-ghlais. Surely no mean
pedigree for a mere town on the fringe of Europe.

This, then, is Tralee, standing at the seaward side of that
famous limestone valley, scooped out between the Glanruddery
chain on the north, and Slieve Mish on the south. All the
indefinable enchantment of the centuries is also in the vale of
Tralee, as those of us who were nurtured in its sweet shades
well know, and those of you who are exiles often, perhaps,
smile sadly to yourselves and feel your eyes grow moist, remembering the happy hours you once spent there in sweet
contentment.

Here, in this peaceful vale, happened many of the events
we are about to narrate, some of them like the siege of Tralee
Castle, showing terror, stark and naked. For one must forget
the valley he remembers in the happiness of childhood and
think of it instead full of greasy planters from nowhere, brought
in by Denny. He must visualise the old Irish on the prowl
round the mountains gazing down on that valley full of wealth,
that once was theirs and seeing the new planters with their
ruffs and cuffs and fine array, fondly thinking that life would
go on like that unceasingly.

They were soon awakened from their complacency, however,
as the dispossessed Irish soon began to band themselves together
for mutual protection and for a raid, when they could make it,
down on the plains. These bands began to be known as " tories "
and were a terror to the tyrant, so much so that the reward for
the capture of a tory was double that offered for even a priest.
Many more of the dispossessed gentlemen hied them over the
seas to France, Spain or the Low Countries, whence most of
them never returned ; but one or two did find their way back,
in whom brigandage and bloodshed had quenched all ideals,
and in whose breasts the misery of their poor broken country
in contrast to foreign climes had turned their hearts to stone.
Such a one was Florence MacCarthy.

CHAPTER II

BY THIS TIME Florence had entered The Golden Key Tavern and was sitting over his cup of wine.

" I expect a ship soon, Walter ; do you want brandy ? " he said to the landlord, after they had been talking for some time.

" At the same price, Master Florence ? "

" Thereabouts ! "

" About half a hogshead, then."

" Any wine ? "

" Portuguese ? "

" Yes ! "

" A hogshead."

" Right, Walter."

" And Master Florence."

" Yes ! "

" Mistress Ware asks for silks ; you know the Civic Ball will soon take place."

" I'll do my best ; is my horse ready ? "

" Waiting for you, Master."

" Good-bye, Walter."

" Fare you well, Master Florence : my sympathy to Master Pierce."

Soon he reached Cathair Mhor Abhann, now called Blenner-ville.

I wonder if that ship from Lisbon has come, he mused. Yes, but the funeral ? Almost forgot I'm going to a funeral ; a good riddance, old Eamon. What a relief to Pierce ; a good fellow Pierce. Clean ! Not a goody-goody though : a fellow with a conscience. Too sensitive ; should have gone to the Lowlands. Thinks he loves Ireland ; but what's Ireland ? A mixture of clans, all quarrelling, and sometimes uniting to fight the Norman. Damn the Normans ! What a cancer they are ; but why am I going to the funeral of this Norman ? Because of Pierce, I suppose ; but I hate Normans : why don't I hate him ? I suppose it's the earnest way he talks about

Caitlin Ni h-Uallachain ; as if there wasn't enough of talk about her. Maybe there's something in what Ferriter says ; but how many of the O'Briens and O'Sullivans think of Caitlin Ni h-Uallachain ?

Ferriter's before his time ; I wish I could agree with him, though. I wonder what he'll do now ; get married, I suppose. Why am I not myself married ? But then I don't intend to stay in that stuffy castle all my life. No, war's my trade. The more cruel the better. God be with the good old days in Flanders. How I'd like to slit the throats of these greasy new planters from ear to ear. I wouldn't do it for Caitlin Ni h-Uallachain : I'd do it merely because Denny is Denny, and Browne is Browne. Sly Ned Denny, the supreme ruffian. Some day I hope to make the Dennys pay to the last farthing, to the very last farthing.

By this time he was at the top of Curragheen. The sky was a deep blue and cynic though he was, the beauty of the landscape almost took his breath away. Mountains sprawled on every side ; to the right, the sandy Maharees stretched into the Atlantic and behind, rose mighty Brandon.

When he came near Gleann na nGealt, Florence dismounted and walked. I wonder what was the herb those crazy travellers found here ? Likely as not there's no truth to the rigmarole ; but still, there are more things——.

There was more truth to the " rigmarole," however, than Florence imagined, for in this beautiful little glen were two wells to which mad folk from the furthest end of Eireann came to drink and also to eat the sorrel and the water-cress ; then the rage of their madness would leave them and they would return to their loved ones calmed in body and in soul. They came to Gleann na nGealt, the Glen of the Lunatics, by instinct ; something urged them in their search for solace to keep on tramping the weary roads till at length they arrived in this haven.

A lot of good we ever got from foreigners, a fat lot ; only left us worse than they found us. Us ! What do I mean by " us " ? I thought I'd hardened myself against sentiment ; that's what comes of listening to Ferriter and his nonsense. There's no such thing as " us " : we're but a few warring tribes

—warring with the half-Irish Normans and bastard planters
and worst of all, with ourselves. God, what a country ; wouldn't
it make the angels weep ? It isn't even a country : it's a back-
water, a morass, a quaking bogland, anything you will : a
cursed spot that the thousands of cut-throats and robbers from
everywhere and anywhere carved and recarved between them.
If a man still sees a sobbing Caitlin Ni h-Uallachain beneath
this misery, I pity him. Why can't men forget Caitlin, the
daughter of Houlihan, as I've done ? Why can't they steel
themselves, prove to their friends in the taverns she didn't
exist. How foolish to suggest those delicate white hands could
girdle a man with steel, could put lightning in his blood. Damn
those delicate, white hands ; why can't I forget them ? It
should be easy to forget a thing that didn't exist.

He was nearing Aunascaul. Hell, what was that ? A shoe
gone. And in this wretched place ; as bad as Flanders was, it
was better than this. I suppose I must walk to the village ;
there's a smithy there, I think. I remember once when returning
with Pierce we stopped at old Dan Duggan's ; at least we
left our horses at Dan Duggan's, but we waited at Con Curtin's
tavern. A decent sort, Con, though his wife never stopped
talking ; but they keep good ale.

Sometime afterwards, he sat in the tiny taproom with a
cup of beer, while Mistress Curtin eyed him in her traditional
way. She was low-sized, dark and past middle age and her
eyes were grey and hard with something of magnetism. She
sat in the opposite corner, her white features in sharp contrast
to the tawny wine-barrels and casks. Evidently, Con was
not about. Mustn't give her an opening ; whatever I do, I
must avoid religion.

She, in turn, wondered who he was. Going to the funeral,
no doubt ; what a dour aspect he had ; surprising he wouldn't
speak. And that scar in his cheek ; he must have been in the
wars. Perhaps she'd better say something : an innkeeper
usually did.

" A nice fresh day."

" Not bad."

Not very encouraging, but she tried again.

" We've had a poor summer."

" Yes."

She stuck to her guns.

" Too bad about the Chieftain Ferriter."

" Yes ! "

" A great and a good man he was ! the poor indeed will miss him."

" Will they ? "

" 'Tis well I know it : many's the beggarman and widow will weep for him."

" Is that so ? "

" I hear that Pierce, the heir, is a dreamer," she continued undaunted.

" Madam, we're all dreamers."

She was pleased : talk of any kind pleased her.

" Yes, but there are dreamers and dreamers : most of us dream about things that matter ; but young Ferriter has his head in the clouds."

" But, Madam, real things are dreams when dreams are as realities."

He hoped that would be beyond her : attack is the best defence ; but she didn't intend to be put on the defensive. She had fought too many campaigns for that. Like an old strategist, she came back :

" It all depends upon what one considers real things : what do you, for instance ? "

So she was trying to put him into a corner.

" Equal and indifferent justice, madam, is a real thing."

" That is what the Chieftain always said."

" He said it, Madam : it's easy to say things. Talk is cheap. Justice for him meant Norman justice : he threw a few coins to the poor but he despised them."

" Sir, that's strange talk : of the many that went this way yesterday and to-day, few spoke like that."

" They are mostly the county gentry, Madam, made up of planters and half-Normans. I'm of Gaelic stock, so much the worse ; to me a Norman will always be a Norman, an ulcer on the body of the land."

" If the Normans are thus, what are the new planters ? "

" The less said the better."

" I agree ; but you aren't fair to the older stock : the Desmonds and Ferriters have had many centuries to level themselves to the Gaelic race."

" No, Madam, late or early, they're all planters. The Gaelic clans failed because they never united against the common foe. Besides, I don't know quite what you mean by " levelling." I'd rather not continue the topic : enough has been said about that, goodness knows. Would you mind telling me the hour of the funeral ? "

" Mid-day, to-morrow."

" Thank you."

That was satisfactory ; he could afford to take it leisurely. Besides the inn was comfortable and the beer good. Mistress Curtin wasn't too bad when kept at bay ; but she required careful handling.

" Have many gone westwards ? "

" Yes, since dawn, everybody and anybody, even Tomás Rua, the harper."

" Tomás Rua ! "

" He was with, of all people, Mr. Spratt from Tralee."

" Who's Mr. Spratt ? "

" You don't know the Reverend Devereux Spratt ? He's tutor to Sir Edward Denny's children."

That was a treacherous move : she had veered round to her favourite topic, religion.

" And what has Mr. Spratt got to do with me ? "

" Nothing, I'm sure, except that he is a canting old hypocrite."

" We're all hypocrites : why pick on him ? "

" Because he is never done quoting texts."

" And what did you say to him ? "

" Oh, nothing much : talk is wasted on his likes."

That was a bold admission ; so there were times when she was silent.

" I wonder why he was with Tomás Rua ? "

" He likes it to be known he patronises the arts and also Christian charity demands he should help a lame dog."

" Where does Tomás come from ? "

The question put no strain on her omniscience.

" Cashel ! "

" What brought him here ? "

" When Desmond made him his harper."

" Those old fellows deserve our sympathy more than the bloodthirsty chieftains."

They were becoming quite friendly. The beer was good ; but still he never believed in too much talk in taverns.

" I suppose Tomás travels little now."

" More than ever : he's got to. He told me he'd recently been staying with Lord Muskerry at Blarney."

There was a clatter of hooves on the cobbles and in a moment, a traveller entered. He was in his middle twenties and about average height and he had frank features and blue, intelligent eyes. His good humour contrasted sharply with Florence, the pessimist.

" Ah, welcome Finian," said the hostess, " and what good fortune brings you this way ? "

" Scarcely good, Mistress."

" Has anything happened ? Some trouble at the school ? "

"Well, yes and no : it isn't easy to avoid trouble these days."

He looked at Florence who returned his glance ; here was an opportunity for Mistress Curtin.

" This is Finian O'Shea, a schoolmaster from Listowel," she said, " but I'm afraid, sir, I don't know your name."

" My name's Florence Mac Carthy from Castle Loch."

" I'm glad indeed to know you, sir. Now that you both are acquainted, won't you drink to the house ? "

They sat down. Finian looked tired she thought ; he was generally in trouble with that school ; for the " visitors " gave him little rest.

Perhaps it may be wondered how in those days of strife it was possible at all to conduct a school under the eyes of his Majesty's minions. By law, no schools were permitted save those which taught English and the English way of life ; and solely for this purpose Henry the Eighth set up parish schools. A further act of Elizabeth established a free secondary school

in every diocese ; there the master had to be an Englishman,
or else " of the English birth of this realm." As well as these
schools there was Trinity College in Dublin, founded " for
breeding up the natives of that kingdom in civility, learning and
religion." By " religion " was meant, of course, the Protestant
religion.

Nevertheless there were Catholic schools in all the towns
and cities. The authorities made considerable efforts to suppress
them. English power in Ireland greatly feared these schools
because the teachers trained the scholars in " superstition and
idolatry," and as soon as they came of age sent them beyond
the seas to become priests.

Thus by no means as drastic as the penal code which began
towards the end of that, the seventeenth century, yet the lot
of masters was not an easy one, and it took a man of endurance
to found and carry on a school. Such a man despite his youth
was Finian O'Shea.

Besides these urban schools there were others, one or two
of the great Gaelic academies of leechcraft, letters and of law
which had somehow survived into these troubled times. One
such was the school of Flann Mac Aodhagain or Mac Egan,
situated in the Mac Egan territory, which formed a triangle
to the north of Loch Derg where the Brosna met the Shannon.

CHAPTER III

" ARE YOU GOING FAR, sir ? " Finian asked, laying down
his glass.

" Yes, to the funeral of Eamon Ferriter."

" I hadn't heard of his death."

" He was a good age and his day came ; did you know him ? "

" No, but Pierce is a friend of mine."

" Ah, so you know Pierce : a fine fellow. Might I ask if
you've known him for long, Master O'Shea ? "

" Yes, we were at school together at Doctor O'Connell's."

" Another scholar from Tralee :   you're a patriot, then, like Pierce ? "

" Patriot, Master Mac Carthy ? "

" Yes, patriot : what a joke."

"Why ? "

" Because Ireland's finished, my friend, absolutely finished : a man of your energy should leave the sinking ship ;   should get out of it."

"Where to ? "

" Oh, anywhere ; Flanders, France, Spain."

" But my work calls me here."

" Work ! schoolmastering ! a sorry trade : besides, they'll hang you in the end."

" They hanged many a better man than me."

" You wish to become a martyr, then, Master O'Shea ? "

" I wonder what has made you so sour : the wars, I suppose."

" Yes, I've been in the Low Countries and seen a thing or two. I was by the side of Maurice Fitzgerald when a cannon ball blew him to pieces."

" How extraordinary ! poor Maurice. An idealist if ever there were one : have you seen Ferriter's poem on his death ? "

" My dear man, I haven't the slightest interest in poetry : poetry is thrash ; many's the time I said it to Ferriter ; but what's the good ? I suppose there's a fool born every minute."

" I agree with you in your last comment : if I weren't one I wouldn't try to keep my school open in the face of such odds."

" Then why do you try ? You'd make as much money in a day peddling, as a schoolmaster makes in a month."

" Oh, I don't know : handing on the torch, so to speak."

" Waste of time : this country is finished. What did that poet say the other day ? A Blessing on the Soul of Ireland. The Dennys, Crosbies and the rest of the wolves have torn her asunder. Heavens, man, where's your common sense ? Why carry on against such odds ? "

" No, I haven't given up hope : you've been a cynic so long that such talk comes natural to you ; but there are still some left who will never acknowledge defeat, Master Mac Carthy."

" Like yourself ? "

" My friend, I know too well my shortcomings as a soldier and as a patriot. I realise too how black everything looks. Perhaps, as you and many have said, Ireland's finished ; but you and they forget that we've friends abroad. In the Courts of Europe, in the Court of His Holiness, they're true to our cause. Eoin Roe and Preston are preparing a fleet ; and there are rumours of trouble in the north. I can't explain why I speak so frankly but I feel that with all your brusque exterior your heart is in the right place : you're a patriot gone wrong."

" Thank you : I suppose my heart, as you term it, was once in the right place, but service in the Spanish army taught it the futility of patriotism. Patriots generally have an axe to grind, present company excepted, of course."

" Thank you."

" You can keep your thanks till you're at least my age, and have an opportunity of seeing how true my remarks are : I've never yet met a self-seeker who didn't fall back on patriotism when all else failed."

" Would you call Eoin Roe a selfseeker ? "

" You've got me to a favourite topic. There are people here who are never done talking about Eoin Roe : he grows daily in stature. He'll fight the foreigner and throw him into the sea ; he'll break the fetters of the pale, forlorn Caitlin. Isn't that so ? "

" Yes, to a certain extent."

" But my dear fellow, don't you realise that cows far away have long horns. I met Eoin Roe in Flanders : he was full of Ireland, of course, but spoke about her in such a way that anybody could see he had never lived here, had never trudged through the dreary bogs, had never spent a winter in this muddy, windswept wilderness. He saw the cause of Ireland in a rosy hue, with the last rays of a setting sun showing a sobbing, melancholy queen, who nevertheless, still smiled through her tears. Not at all an unpresentable picture ; but I tried to tell him things were far otherwise. That there was as much enmity between the rival native clans as there was between Gael and Planter : that the tradition of good government had disappeared centuries ago : that a restoration of the Gaelic, aristocratic system which went down at Kinsale, would benefit only a few petty kings and chiefs ; and that thus the common people cared little how the wind blew."

"A bold speech, my friend, and not altogether incorrect in parts. I'm well aware that Eoin Roe has lived too long abroad to understand Ireland's case ; but what else have we ? we must clutch at any stray straw, must use everybody and anybody to bring peace to this distracted land. Eoin Roe's name counts for a lot among the people : he appeals to their imagination. However, our great obstacle is, as you said, the rivalry and jealousy among the clans. The other day, Ferriter wrote a few lines asking Eoin Roe to accept the leadership of the Gael ; but Donnchadh Maol O Suilleabhain retorted that the poet went beyond all bounds in his readiness to transfer his allegiance from Munster to Ulster ; what can you do with that sort of thing ? "

"You prove my point : that's why I've given up Ireland and everything Irish as a bad job : it's a dreary topic. What about some more wine ? But I see our hostess has disappeared."

He tapped the table and Mistress Curtin came bustling from an inner room. She beamed on them. When she had refilled the cups, she said :

"You must not think of going, Finian ; I'm preparing a meal and you must join us ; and you too, sir, if I might make bold to ask you."

Getting quite friendly she was ; anyway, he rather liked young Finian. He might as well accept, he thought.

"Yes, Madam, I shall be delighted."

When they finished their beer, they went inside to the dining-room. It was small and snug. There was a wooden partition halfway about the walls ; and a large hearth of red brick upon which a pile of logs blazed cheerily.

Altogether it was a pleasant meal ; there was venison pie followed by sweet savouries and they spoke little at first for both were hungry. Mistress Curtin realised she would hear more gossip by biding her time.

"Excuse the absence of my husband, gentlemen, but he's gone to Dingle."

" Madame, we lack nothing when we have you as hostess,"
answered Florence, with a stiff bow.

I wonder if he means that, she thought. He isn't as bad as I
imagined.

During the meal they exchanged vague pleasantries, but
afterwards as they sat by the fire smoking the new tobacco,
she ventured to remark :

" You two seem to agree very well."

" We agree to differ, Madame, on many essential points,"
said Florence.

" For instance, Master Mac Carthy ? "

" Hundreds ! Education, for example."

" In what way ? "

" Finian believes in education : I don't."

" Why not ? "

" Because I believe the people of this country always gave
too much time to book learning : they want, if you please,
to be ollamhs, brehons and physicians. There are schools of
poetry here and schools of poetry there—."

" But the ollamhs are very learned men," chimed in Finian.

" Learned to a point, I agree, but a queer, out of date learning :
a learning neither of benefit to themselves nor to anybody
else. Rannuiocht mhor, rannuiocht bheag, deibidhe ! fiddlesticks ! They are as archaic as the Fianna. That's the supreme
fault of the Gael : he can't see that the whole Gaelic system,
literary and political, is finished."

" Still you yourself seem to be well acquainted with Gaelic
letters, from the manner of your speech."

" I agree I picked up a lot of useless knowledge from Doctor
O'Connell at Tralee ; but it proved of little use to me on the
fields of Flanders."

" What then should boys learn ? How to use muskets ? "

" Don't misinterpret me, please : I'm not so foolish as to
believe that boys can do without some kind of mental training ;
it's the system I condemn. You've two kinds of school, Doctor
O'Connell's, for example, where the main subjects are useless
Latin and still more useless Greek, and old Flann's school with
its Gaelic poetry, which is even more useless still. Why can't

we have a school where boys will learn the art of self-defence
and how to handle a piece of ordnance ? When I first went
to Flanders I had to begin all over again."

" Why are you so anxious to throw overboard the Gaelic
system which has lasted so long ? "

" Listen, my good fellow : on my way from Flanders, I
spent some weeks in London town. There's a school of poets
there who don't waste their time in a hair-splitting endeavour
to write poetry to archaic rules : they don't for ever seek
internal rhymes and concordance of syllables. No, they just
sing like the blackbird, the linnet, the thrush. What ollamh
could talk about glorious mornings flattering the mountain
tops with sovereign eye, or like old Herrick, sing of his Julia
midst the lilies and the roses ? "

" It is unfair to compare languages and literatures thus : each
language has its own particular merits, its own style, its own
facility for expressing the thoughts of those that speak it. Despite
what you say, our poets possess plenty of initiative. Have you
never heard of Sir Thomas Wyatt and his experiments with
English metres ? "

" But, my dear man, Sir Thomas Wyatt is merely a name in
English poetry. He established no tradition."

The conversation had got far beyond Mistress Curtin. It
was about time they came down to earth.

" Tell me, Finian," she said, " on what charge they closed
you last time ? "

" They make charges easily, Mistress ; but as you put the
question, here's the order."

He took from an inner pocket a roll of parchment.

" Perhaps any of you would care to read it."

Florence took it and glanced down the neatly-written page.

" Whereas a native of this Kingdom, one Finian O'Shea,
being generally addicted to popery, does train up children
in superstition and idolatry. So soon as they come to
age, he sends them beyond the seas, from whence they
return either Priests, Jesuits, or Seminarists, enemies to the
Religion established and pernicious members to this State

and whereas the said Finian O'Shea, in violation of 28
Henry VIII, doth deceive many and persuadeth unto them,
that they should be as it were of sundry sorts, or rather
of sundry countries, where they indeed be wholly together
one body, whereof His Highness is the only head under
God, the Lord President of Munster, under our hands,
prayeth and requireth him in his Majesty's name to cease
from the exercise of teaching and instruction of youth.

(Act of Parliament, Dublin, 1537 : 28 Henry VIII.
C. 15, ss. 1, 9.)

" So that's that," he mused, " but tell me, what'll you do
now ? "

" God knows ! Go on the run, I suppose."

" Do you intend opening your school again ? "

" Certainly ! this will blow over in a short while : I've
been in similar trouble before. I'll stay in Corca Duibhne
for some time—perhaps even stay with Pierce for a day or two."

" Why not come now ? "

" That's kind of you ; but I think it would be safer to avoid
crowds for the present. However, I'll be with you as far as
Dingle."

" Mistress Curtin " said Florence, " I wonder if Dan Duggan's
my horse ready ? "

" I'll send a messenger, sir," she said, going to the door.
She was disappointed at the scholastic turn of the talk : she'd
have preferred gossip about the gala nights at Tralee Castle ;
even falconry would be better than poetry.

In a few moments she was back ; yes, the horse was ready.
Florence and Finian stood on the cobbles as Dan Duggan
bustled forward. Finian untethered his mare ; and as they
mounted, Mistress Curtin smiled from the doorway ; both
doffed their plumed hats and bowed and in one gallop rode
down the hill.

CHAPTER IV

ON EVERY SIDE were the mountains, covered with ash, oak, rowan and pine and sometimes as they rounded a horse shoe bend, they caught glimpses of the distant sea and beyond it, the cloud-capp'd peninsula of Iveragh. The Skelligs seemed like lost solitary temples. On the riders went, past gurgling streams, with sometimes an old water-mill looking like an ancient fortress. At last, coming to the top of a hill, they saw Dingle below.

A little later their horses were ambling through the hilly streets. At length they halted at the Red Rose Tavern placed about mid-way in a row of stone houses, each having a balcony in the Spanish fashion. Over the entrance was a stone on which two roses were carved and beneath were the words : AT THE ROSE IS THE BEST WINE. Nearby was the Church of St. James with its fine steeple. On the opposite side was the ruin of a castle, destroyed like that of Tralee, in the Desmond wars, and on each side of it stretched further rows of houses. At either end of this long street stood a gateway on which swung enormous gates of wrought iron : through that on the east came the road from Tralee : the other opened on that tremendous sweep of mountain and lake, bog and pasture, for centuries the home of the Ferriters, the last left in Desmond of the proud old Norman race.

In Dingle men still sometimes spoke about the Armada. Also Spanish ships constantly sailed in and out past the small fort over at the bottle-neck entrance to the harbour ; and in the hills about the town lived many a Spanish sailor who sailed the seas no more. Many pilgrims, too, left the Bay for the Shrine of St. James of Compostella in northern Spain, which next to Rome, was the greatest mediaeval place of pilgrimage in Europe. It was a proud boast indeed of Dingle that it was called the Parish of St. James—all now the more tinged with sadness that the Protestants had taken over the fine church and read their strange services there on the Sabbath mornings— there where St. James used to smile and bless his beloved Dingle and where he was patron for longer than any man or any scribe could remember.

Even its very name—Dingle—seemed to conjure up visions of mediaeval splendour and rustling silks and Spanish grandees. It was an old town, and like all old towns, had its moods. It could be gay, indeed, when gaiety was in the air but it had a brooding melancholy when disease or famine stalked the land. That indeed had often occurred in the long years of its experience. Sometimes the corn would fail or there might be smallpox ; or it might even be war—war with its rotting corpses, and festering putrid sores, and robbery and lust. That was not so easily got over. Corpses might be buried and wounds in time might heal ; but it is the ruin to all that ennobles and uplifts that is war's most treacherous legacy. For Dingle had heard the rattle of the sabre and the roar of the cannon ; had heard the heavy studded boots of Grey's soldiery pounding on the cobbles and the jingle of his cavalry, and had seen too the cruelty and the lust to kill in men's eyes. Men—if Grey's hirelings could be called men. For men would not have done the deeds which they did, nor slaughtered powerless old men nor tossed little children down jagged cliffs into the seething waters. It was not however, so much the killings nor the rape, nor the famine that the people minded : it was the frustration, the want of cohesion, the confusion. If the old Earl had been James Fitzmaurice—if San Sebastian had not commanded Dun an Oir—if the Spaniards had held out but four days longer—if—

There were enormous crowds in the town when the travellers arrived ; for besides the stir caused by the Chieftain's death it was also the great autumn fair of Michaelmas. There were tinkers with thin, bony nags, jennets and donkeys, trick-o'-the loop men, players and mummers, maskers and minstrels, fortune-tellers and jugglers all thrown haphazard together. Prime and pretty maidens, arm in arm, past by each other in Green Street or the Dykegate ; shrill-voiced women haggled over the latest Spanish shawl or maybe an Indian necklace of gaudy beads. There was much laughter and gaiety despite the death of the old Chieftain ; for men rarely heed the tolling of the bell unless it tolls for their own near and dear ones.

Away down on the Fair Green, men, some old, some barely out of their teens, haggled also over prices. When the bargain was made they would go into The Red Rose or the other taverns and clinch the bargain with a glass of wine. The Rose would be always the busiest ; its wines had the reputation of being amongst the best in Desmond ; and that is indeed no wonder as Dingle kept for itself the choicest of the produce of French and Spanish vineyards which sailed into the Bay on Spanish galleons of white, belly-filled sails, and in quaint old French vessels that sailed from the many ports from Bordeaux to Brest.

CHAPTER V

THE ROW OF stone houses, amongst which The Red Rose Tavern was, were all two-storied, large and the balcony windows had marble frames. They stood well back from the road.

"What ho ! John Tapster, what ho !" shouted Florence as he dismounted.

A stockily-built lad in a green apron ran out.

"Good evening, my masters," he said, bowing obsequiously, taking charge of their horses.

Just then the rubicund countenance of Tom Trant, the host, appeared at the doorway.

"Ah, good Tom, but I'm glad to see you," said Finian.

"Welcome, my friends," he said, bowing, "but I'm afraid I'm not acquainted with this gentleman," he replied, looking at Florence.

"This is Florence Mac Carthy from Castle Lough, Tom."

"A good old name, a good old name, Master Finian : but won't you come inside."

Dusk was already falling and the lights began to twinkle in the town. The sound of good cheer came towards them as they followed the host across the small courtyard, and at the threshold they were met by a glow of warmth. Then Tom, with many apologies, left them to fend for themselves.

The taproom was full to overflowing and with difficulty they reached the fireplace. Here and there somebody greeted Florence with a nod but that was all; there were no smiles or handshakes. A difficult, distant fellow, this Mac Carthy!

"Few friends here, Finian," he said as he cast his eye around, "but wait, I think I see Walter Hussey."

Just then, he caught Walter's eye, who rose and came towards them.

"I'm very glad to see you, Florence: it must be years since we met."

"Yes, quite a bit."

"You've travelled?"

"A little. You're going to the funeral, I suppose?"

"Naturally!"

"Oh pardon me, this is Finian O'Shea, a schoolmaster."

"Finian O'Shea who once taught at Tadhg O'Corcoran's?"

"You've guessed it," answered Finian.

"I've heard of you: won't you join my friend and myself?" said Walter.

"If you wish."

They forced their way to where his companion sat.

"Henry, some friends of mine."

The gentleman thus addressed looked up. He had a refined, pale face and hair just going grey; he screwed his dark eyes in a quizzical way and with a friendly smile, said in his English drawl:

"Allow me to introduce myself: I hate formal introductions. I'm Henry Lawrence from Oxford: you're Florence and this is——?"

"Finian," added Walter.

"Finian, how do you do? Now that we're all acquainted, why not join me in a glass of wine?"

"Certainly!" said Florence.

It was difficult to catch the eye of the host; but eventually Lawrence succeeded and Tom, with his oily smile, came over.

"Welcome, my masters: going to the funeral, no doubt?" he said to Walter and his companion.

"Yes, Tom," said Walter.

" Ah, poor Eamon," he continued, " and just at this critical moment."

" What critical moment ? "

" Why, haven't you heard ? "

" Heard what ? "

" About Master Pierce."

" What about Master Pierce ? "

" His marriage ! "

" His what ? "

Florence looked as surprised as Finian.

" Haven't you heard about it ? " said Walter, " he abducted a maiden from Galway."

" Abducted a maiden ? "

" Yes ! "

" You mean Pierce, our friend, the dreamer ? " asked Florence.

" Yes, Pierce the dreamer."

Tom bustled away.

" Bravo Pierce ! Bedad you are a man at last," exclaimed Florence, slapping his thigh.

" That certainly is news," said Finian slowly.

" What are the details ? " enquired Florence.

" He went to visit a relative in Galway, laid his eyes on this lovely maiden, and straightaway abducted her."

" Incredible," said Finian, " when did it happen ? "

" Yesterday : yesterday, too, was the wedding day."

" Where are they living ? "

" Nowhere : they have left on their honeymoon."

" Did Eamonn know of this ? "

" That was why he died," answered Lawrence.

" My friend Henry and I were shooting near Marthain when Tom Trant's message arrived," said Walter. " We intended calling on the old man that evening, and were on our way, when we heard he was dead."

" How did they break it to him ? " asked Finian.

" A few of the servants wanted to hush it up " continued Walter, " but Robert, the steward, thought it his duty to tell the tale : he went to the old man and told him his son had brought with him a beautiful bride from Galway."

" What mean you by a beautiful bride ? " he asked, " why marriage is the last thought in my son's head."

" Nevertheless, he was married this day in Dingle town," reiterated Robert.

Gradually, the old man pierced the story together. A son of his to act thus ! His Norman pride and apoplexy did the rest and he was dead within the hour."

" Did he disinherit the runaway ? " asked Florence.

" He raved about cutting him off with a penny and all that, but he was in no fit condition."

" The old ruffian," said Florence.

" So that Pierce doesn't know his father is dead ? " asked Finian.

" Presumably ! "

" Extraordinary ! "

" Yes, extraordinary," continued Walter, " but things will right themselves in a short while : after all, it was high time Pierce married."

" Yes, I suppose so."

" Well, gentlemen, what are your plans ? " enquired Florence.

" We stay here to-night and go on to the Castle in the morning," answered Walter.

" That suits me, then," said Florence. " Ho, landlord, ho ! "

" Coming, my masters."

Thus they whiled a few hours away. Henry Lawrence, knowing he was among friends, told them why he had come. He was there, he said, to put the King's cause before the Chieftains ; for in England, the ruffian Puritans gained daily in strength and a clash must come soon. What would the Chieftains do ?

" I'll tell you what they'll do, if I can help it, Mr. Lawrence," Florence replied, " they'll fight for neither King nor Parliament ; they'll fight for the their own sod, and above all, they'll fight to drive the planters from Ulster."

By God, that would be the way to get revenge on Denny ; train men, arm them. If all Ireland rose together, if it only did ! Train them to march ; show them how to carry a gun ; take Tralee, by God, and wipe away that veneer of foppery which

the Dennys brought with them ; take their castle and rule
again like old Desmond used, with his brehons and his bards.
Nominally it would be in the King's name ; and Mr. Lawrence
could tell His Majesty how his beloved Irish subjects were
ready to die for him ; but it would be for ourselves, for our
lands, for our wealth. No poetry or high notions about that ;
leave the poetry to Ferriter. And talking of Ferriter, would
he join ? Could he be got away from the divided loyalties
of the centuries ? But Ferriter, evidently, had sufficient to
occupy his attention for some time at least.

CHAPTER VI

JUST THEN AN old harper bearing a small instrument entered.
He was dressed in a darkish green cloak with gold braid about
the edges. He was well-nigh four score years and his white
locks gave an added dignity to his brow. His fine, intelligent
eyes encircled the tap-room and with a smile he bowed cour-
teously many times in acknowledgement to greetings. It was
Tomás Rua the renowned harper spoken of by Mistress Curtin.

Tom immediately poured him out a flagon of wine for in
those days in Desmond it was thought a privilege to entertain
a musician or a poet.

" That is old Tomás Rua," said Finian aside to Henry
Lawrence, " he was harper to the House of Desmond."

In a few moments the host called for some music.

" And perhaps a song, too," said Walter.

" Aye," replied Tomás in deep, well-bred tones, " but my
years of music are now almost at an end. Well I remember
when I could indeed play and sing too ; many the happy
hour I spent playing before the old Earl, God rest him, and
before James Fitzmaurice and many more of the Desmonds
besides ; that was in the great hall of the Castle at Tralee and
all the old Norman nobles would be there and many of the
Gaelic chieftains as well. But that great family, the patrons of
poetry and song, have now gone forever."

" Gone for ever," echoed many of his listeners.

By this time all eyes were on Tomás.

" Music, music," they cried unanimously.

" I'll do my humble best," he answered, taking his instrument from the floor on to his knee. His long, delicate fingers touched the strings caressingly and soon that lovely air, " Eibhlin a Ruin," in liquid notes of exquisite tenderness encircled the room. After a few bars his old, enfeebled voice began to sing. It was a remarkable song, one about the changes of raiment which Caitlin the daughter of Houlihan assumes according as she is in sorrow or in joy. She casts aside her shining cloak of silken sheen when sorrow and suffering come upon her ; many a child that loved her dearly, many a son that stood by her in her misery, she has lost. She is helpless, her wealth gone from her, her children scattered. Gone, too, are her nobles who were the support of her poets. Her wounds smite her to the quick : they are almost incurable. But he will go the ailing one, to his beloved Eibhlin a Ruin, and share the disease with her, so that her enemies may not know which of them suffers the more.

The music and words intertwined as ivy clinging to a ruin, and the deep emotion of the old man's faltering tones coupled with the wistful beauty and gentle pathos of the verses made many eyes to flash in gleams of hope and admiration. There was loud applause from everybody but Tomás did not seem to hear it ; he gazed fixedly in front of him.

" Ah," he exclaimed, as if to himself, " the old Earl, God rest him ! he loved that song and many's the time I sang it for him."

Tomás Rua slowly sipped his wine and mumbled away to himself. There was a poem of his own which he used to repeat over and over to himself, especially in his cups. They were verses he wrote when, years afterwards, one dark night four faithful followers opened the grave again and took the Earl's remains across miles of countryside to Castle Island, and beyond that again to Cill an Ainme, the Churchyard of All Souls, the special churchyard of the Geraldines, reserved alone for those bearing the proud name of Fitzgerald, or their relations by blood. And there in the flickering torchlight they said a last prayer over the once proud lord of the Palatinate of Desmond, whose power was almost that of a monarch, whose Countess used to wear the very gowns which the Queen's sacred Majesty had worn.

Tomás was muttering away :

> To Cill an Ainm' they brought him by stealth
> In the winter's piercing blast ;
> And dry-eyed they watched in the flick'ring light
> As the clay on the coffin was cast.
>
> Tears ! 'twere idle to shed them now,
> Idle too were the caoin :
> In Desmond's acres the stranger hath sway,
> The wolf walks abroad o'er the green.
>
> Abroad o'er the green banks of Leamhain and Lee,
> The stalking wolf snarls o'er his prey ;
> The clairseach is silent, the pipes too at peace
> No bard at the board with his lay.

"Aye !" he said, turning towards them, "the wolf indeed walks abroad o'er the green. But tell me," he said to a young man beside him, "do you know what they did with his head ?"

"I'm afraid I do not, sir," he replied.

"Well, the Queen stuck it on London Bridge, and would you believe it," he continued, his voice becoming infinitely more tender, "they say the place where the blood was shed remained red for long afterwards."

He took a sip from his glass and continued his mumbling.

"More wine for Tomás, landlord, more wine," said Finian.

When the wine was served, Henry Lawrence, turning towards Tomás, said good-humouredly :

"Give us some more music, Tomás, lively music."

The harper began again, but this time it was an exquisite fairy dance that he played. Tiny elves with little shoes of blue and gold and jackets of red seemed to patter about, and with

magic spells bring a sparkle into the eyes even of Tomás himself.
Tom, the host, who with flustered, perspiring face leant by
the side of a large cask, was glad of a short respite. He was not
a musical man, but he understood the moods of his customers.
With all his quips and smiles, Tom Trant was deep ; being in
an inn made one so reticent and shrewd. There was Finian
O'Shea over there with that strange gentleman who had the
scar on his cheek. What in heaven's name did they keep on
discussing war for ? And the refined English gentleman telling
them all about the King and how he would soon have to fight.
Yes, and they mentioned Denny a few times ; no, they didn't
seem to like him from the turn of the conversation. Why
couldn't they leave Sir Edward alone ? Why not let byegones
be byegones ? Tom would not say that openly, of course ;
he never committed himself. Neither used he open his mind
to Lord Grey and his officers and soldiers, when as a young man,
he served them with many a glass of ale, wine and usquebagh,
fifty years ago. They were a rum lot if ever there was. He
remembered Grey hiccoughing and trying to stand on his
sagging feet, but with faultless English, exclaim : " Landlord,
to our Virgin Queen, Gloriana ! " and raising his glass, he
would smile and quaff it at one gulp. Very few would take
notice of the toast for by this time Grey would be drunk, and
besides who cared about a Virgin Queen hundreds of miles
away ? Every man had to get what he could : you either
robbed somebody of gold or land—or even virtue—or else
were left yourself on the bogs of Brandon or, perhaps, at the
slimy depths of Smerwick. There were no half-measures, no
compromise. It was funny the fortunes of war, thought Tom.
Here to-day and gone to-morrow, but a landlord, with a bit of
luck, lasts through many a change. The Geraldines had gone
and that was that ; the Dennys now ruled the roost and a
landlord never knew when he might want a favour. Tom,
however, must keep his mind to himself.

By this time Tomás had finished playing. After the applause,
there was a general movement within the tavern. Some had
finished that flagon of wine which had sealed their bargain and
were making for the door ; others signed to Tom to replenish

their pewter cups. Tom, however, was busying himself, snuffing the candles ensconced in bronze brackets on the oaken walls and calling Mat, the tapster's boy, to put more logs on the hearth. The red plush curtains had been drawn across and all within seemed as cheerful as any tavern in the Kingdom, especially now as a slow drizzle had begun. Customers were still coming and going, and over by the fire was a group standing about old Tomás.

" A little more music, Tomás, please," said a voice.

" Yes, some more, Tomás," added a few.

" Please play the Lament for the Lady Hoare, Tomás," said a voice from the far corner.

The harper, who was tuning his instrument, stopped. A slight smile came over his features, but almost immediately he became passive again.

" It's all very well for you, young men, to ask me for the Lament for Gregory Hoare's lady, but how many of you would scorn the jackals as she did ? How many, I say ? Everywhere now there's treachery and deceit. Ah, but my young friends," he continued, his voice becoming softer, " there was no deceit or treachery in Desmond when the Geraldines held regal court in the Castle at Tralee."

But shortly he commenced to play and thus whiled a few hours away. Next morning with crowds of others they took their leave of Dingle.

CHAPTER VII

LITTLE WINDING ROADS ran out from the town in many directions, some towards the hills, others to a country that became wilder at every step. One such road went due west through bog-land and mountain and after a mile or so rose gradually to the summit of Baile na n-Ath. It was along this road that our travellers went. From Baile na n-Ath a new panorama came into view, more beautiful even than the rest of the wild beauty of Corca Dhuibhne. Away to the right, lay the gleaming blue of the

harbour of St. Mary Wick, shortened to Smerwick, surmounted
by the Three Sisters. To the left, was the pinnacle of Cruach
Marthain, where the patchwork of well-tilled fields reached
almost to the summit. In the centre of the picture, there was
a small peninsula stretching into the silver sea. Here was the
Castle, known locally as the Dun, the home of the Ferriters
for more than four centuries. It was a day when mighty stretches
of cloud, driven by a crisp breeze, swept across the sky, and
all about in the gleaming sunshine lay the golden stacks ready
for the winnowing. Here, at dark, vessels laden with spices,
silks and brandy anchored unknown to the King's tax-collectors
at Dingle, while others brimful with hides and wool glided
seawards to France, Spain and the Lowlands. Often standing on
the bows, waving farewell to their loved ones, were youths
like O'Daly and Moriarty, who somehow preferred the halls
of Louvain, Salamanca, Paris and Bordeaux to the late Queen's
protégé, her College of the Holy and Undivided Trinity in
Dublin Town.

The old Gaelic name of the district was Dunurlin; but
for many a day men had called it Ferriter's Towne. It was
a countryside that for sheer magnificence must have few rivals
—an amphitheatre encircled by mountains and hills and surrounded on three sides by the waves crashing on rocks and
crags. Sweeps of golden sand curved about the sunlit bays;
immense stretches of marsh teemed with wild duck, snipe and
woodcock. There was good land, too, and the succulent green
grass gave as rich a produce as any in Kerry.

Dunurlin had fathered the Ferriters since the thirteenth
century; so the old chronicles say. They held under the Earls
of Desmond, Dunquin and the Blasket Islands (also called
Ferriter's Islands); most of Dunurlin; and some each of
Marthain and Killmallkeder. But when Desmond fell and Denny
came they lost all except alone Baile Uachtarach, where the
Castle stood and which scarcely amounted to five hundred
acres. This tiny remnant then on the very rim of the ocean
was all that was left to Pierce. And Pierce, now that he was the
new master, which side would he take? It was all very well
to write poetry and to love Ireland—in theory—but when it

came to a decision it was only then one saw the real man. Would he be like his old father, Eamon, who would do anything and everything to hold on to his remaining few barren acres. Often strange travellers used to come to Smerwick; they might be spies from King Philip or priests dressed as sailors; but Eamon cared little what winds blew them thither; his only desire was to hang on somehow. It had taken deep diplomacy indeed to keep in the Queen's good graces when she declared Desmond's lands forfeit. From the doings at Dun an Oir, he had kept carefully aloof; for he was crafty or compliant according to the needs of the moment. It was surely no age for honest men.

When Denny came he dared welcome him to the lands of Desmond. Yearly he used to send protestations of loyalty to the Queen—do not the old chronicles say he was pardoned in 1574, 1601 and 1602 for minor breaches of the law? When King James came running from Scotland to sit on the English throne he again pledged his loyalty. Of later years he had been much perturbed by the whisperings of an insurrection in the north; Eoin Roe O'Neill was to sail across the seas, and God alone knew what would happen then; most probably he would lose even Baile Uachtarach. But it was then that death came and closed his tired old eyes in a last long sleep.

The Ferriters were typical Normans, ruthless and cruel, especially in those early days when they hounded the O'Falveys, once the most distinguished clan in Corca Duibhne, out of the lands of their fathers, so that even to-day the once proud name O'Falvey is even rarely heard in the peninsula. As time went on, and as necessity demanded, the Ferriters allied themselves with the native MacCarthys, O'Sullivans, O'Donoghues; but as quickly changed sides again. They were ever jealous of their prerogatives and privileges, and, generally, upheld the authority of the Crown as far as they thought it politic to do so. Whatever the Earl of Desmond did, they did; he was their sun in the heavens and they reflected his glory; and now that their patron was gone life looked black indeed.

Yes, it was surely a relief to poor old harassed Eamon, playing his interminable double game, thought Florence as he watched the red clay tumble on the coffin. A relief indeed. His poor

tired bones surely deserved rest, a long, long rest. Not that
Florence blamed him much ; many of the native chieftains
could scarcely be trusted, not to mind the semi-Gaelic ones.
No, in a civilised age Eamon would have made an excellent
citizen ; but Elizabeth's planters were not civilised. They gave
no quarter nor asked for any ; there was no honour, no mercy ;
it was for each to get what he could and how he could.

Yes, Eamon had indeed seen the lights of Desmond go out
one by one, and he, one of the last of the Norman " middle-
race " had seen doom before him. He had been worried about
Pierce, for he well knew how unpractical and how given to
the metaphysical he was. If he would only be more friendly
with Denny, and marry a Browne or a Herbert, perhaps, all
might yet be well. But no, all he wanted was poetry, endless
poems about Nuachar Chriomhthainn, Cro Chuinn and Achadh
Airt. Only a few days before he died, all propped up between
a pile of pillows, he sent for his son.

CHAPTER VIII

" I HAVE SOMETHING important to say to you, Pierce."

" Yes, sir."

" Have you ever thought of marriage ? "

" Might I ask the reason for your enquiry, sir ? "

" Well, it's high time you got yourself a wife, or rather
that I got a wife for you, since you yourself appear to make no
move in the matter."

Pierce said nothing.

" Yes, it is high time, indeed. This morning I got a letter
from one of the Brownes who has heard of your prowess in
many quarters and would not be averse to joining both of our
families in happy wedlock."

Pierce shifted uneasily.

" Might I ask the lady's name, sir ? "

" What does that matter ? "

" Her age then ? "

"He doesn't say : from what I've heard, she is well past her prime—a little thing when you remember she has five thousand crowns."

"You mean, sir, that you expect me to marry a lady merely for her fortune ? "

"What I mean, or do not mean, doesn't matter. The important thing to note is that I cannot possibly keep up this castle and estate without further funds. Even Sir Edward finds it hard ! You know yourself it takes every guinea to pay the taxes ; and what with the rising prices and the depreciation of money, I don't know how we can stand it much longer. Besides, this woman will make you a good wife : I hear she is extremely competent."

"But she is far older than me, sir."

"Fiddlesticks ! Your own mother was older than myself by many years and we were very happy."

"But, sir, I never believed in marriages of this kind : I want to marry a woman I can love."

"When you get to my age, young man, you will realise how little there is in this love business : the secret to a happy marriage is sound common sense."

"If you will pardon me, sir, that for me is out of the question : the younger generation has other views."

"That is only your inexperience : I thought the same when I was your age. Besides, you would be better off married to any kind of a wife than moping about Dun an Oir from morning till night. I often wonder where you brought this introspection from. I saw some verses of yours about the house : it wasn't by poetry your ancestors held these lands in the teeth of opposition."

"Opposition from the Irish, sir ? "

"From the Irish and English ! Are you going crazy, young man ? "

He tried to raise himself : the blood rushed to his withered cheeks as he nodded with vehemence.

"Yes, in the teeth of opposition," he continued fiercely, "for both of them hated us. To the Irish we were English : to the English, Irish ! Why, do you think, they left us alone at the time of Dun an Oir ? Because, young man, my old father made his peace with the Queen. Why didn't they attack us after Kinsale ? Because I took good care to keep the Dennys on my hands. And now you talk about your own Dun an Oir, Goll Mac Morna and the rest of them. You're crazy ! " and with that, he banged his fist on a small side-table, almost overturning it.

Neither spoke for a few moments. The Chieftain made himself more comfortable among the pillows but his gaze had not left his son's face. Pierce looked at him straight.

" Then why did you send me to the School of Flann Mac Egan ? "

" Many's the time I rue it. I sent you to Baile Mac Egan because I wanted you to take your place with O'Sullivan Mor, O'Sullivan Beare and O'Donoghue of the Glens. Half-Norman that you are, I feared lest you might lack self-confidence when amongst them, but I didn't mean you to come back here the sorry spectacle you seem to be. In Heaven's name, man, pull yourself together : go about the land and see what the men do. Even if you did nothing but count the sheep on Binn Dhiarmada, you'd be, at least, sensibly occupied."

" But I am taking an interest in the land, sir."

" Nonsense : don't fool yourself. But for Robert, I don't know what I should do. When you left the Doctor's, you were some good : you could fish and row with the best of them. But now—"

He threw up his hands in despair and turned to gaze through the narrow window that looked out towards the Blaskets. The waves broke on the cliff-face with a muffled roar. Raising his hand, he pointed to Inis Tuaisceart like a monster riding the billows.

" Do you see those islands ? " he said slowly, a little wistfully. " They are called Ferriter's Islands. Why ? Because they belong to us, the Ferriters. We are a proud family : none prouder in all Desmond. For centuries we held this little corner : we watched it, tilled it, guarded it, fought for it. In all the confiscations we clung to it. Time on time again, these old walls heard the clash of steel on steel and beat back the tribes who thought they were better than we. But, by God, we battered them, and crushed them to pieces, and ground them in the dust beneath our feet."

" But where has this crushing in the dust got us ? "

" Got us ? Got us ? " the chieftain hissed. " I'll tell you where it has got us—pride of place in Desmond, the equal of Sir Edward himself."

" But what is Denny but a land grabber ? "

That was the last straw. His jaw dropped, and he turned towards his son, with his mouth still open, and a hard look in his red eyes. But in a moment, he had himself under control.

" It is indeed a bitter pill that a son of mine should so speak— more bitter still that he is my heir. Since I came into my birth- right, I slaved and toiled for you. When your mother died, I got the best tutors for you that Desmond could provide. At an early age, I sent you to the Seminary in Tralee, the finest school in the four provinces. Then to fit you for that wily MacCarthy Mor and O'Sullivan Beare, I sent you to the ablest master of Gaelic verse in the Kingdom. And you thank me by coming home a bookworm and a good-for-nothing."

" I am sorry, sir, you see it like that, but you and I seem to speak a different language."

" I am afraid so, Pierce, a different language. I am afraid, also, that that is what your forebears away back would say about you. Yes, it was a different language they spoke when they first came here as tenants of the Desmonds. It was a different language my father spoke when he kept away from those filthy foreigners down at Dun an Oir. And it was a different language I spoke, when suspected in the wrong of being on the side of O'Neill, I went on my knees to Denny. I did it for you and to hold on to these old walls ; but now I see it was in vain."

He bowed his head and was silent for a moment. When he looked up again, the old fire was still there.

" You can take it or leave it : either you marry the daughter of Sir Valentine Browne, and eventually become the owner of these lands, or else—"

Pierce rose, and with a slight bow, left the room. After

that tirade he wanted to be alone. He walked along by the cliffs to the end of the peninsula : there he stood for a long time gazing on the blue-green, sparkling sea.

Yes, he would try and think more of the work in future. But the marriage ? That rotten marriage ! If it was Honoria whom he often saw at Lady Kerry's, then it was out of the question, money or no money. What should he do ? To go on living with the old man in his present state was next to impossible. God ! the things men do to hold on to their few acres.

What should he do ? The old man would want an answer almost immediately. Would he go and ask Lady Kerry's advice ? Was she, in her fat complacency, the one to give it ? No, she was too self-centred. There was Sir Edward, with his bluff fox-hunting manner. No, besides he would not trust him with a secret. What a pity they had sent Father Dan O'Daly abroad again ! Then he thought of Brian O Loingsigh, an old family friend, who lived far away on Loch Corrib. He would go to Galway to Brian, and ask his advice.

CHAPTER IX

HE RODE TO TRALEE, changed horses at The Golden Key and was quickly away again to Lixnaw, thence to Listowel and along by the old straight road that ran to Carrigafoyle ; soon he came to the little village at the ford over an inlet of the Shannon. Here, there was a good harbour with two Spanish galleons unloading casks of wine. He went into a tavern and asked for a glass of Bordeaux and after a very pleasant talk with the landlord was away again. Yes, he liked the little place, and what a beautiful name, the Town of the Ford of the Stronghold, Ballylongford, the stronghold being Carrigafoyle Castle, once the home of the proud O'Connors and also disastrously destroyed, like so much more of Desmond, in the Geraldine Wars. He turned to the right and rode past the ruins of Lislaughtin Friary and soon came to Tarbert and thence along

by the Shannon. Shortly, he sighted the battlements of the
Knight of Glin's Castle, close-by the greenish-blue waters ;
on the other side was Clare—gently rising ground with golden
patches of gorse. There were pigeons cooing about the battlements as he rode up the narrow road towards the drawbridge.
For he would remain that evening with the Knight of Glin—
himself a Geraldine—and like all the Geraldines ever fast friends
of the Ferriters.

Next morning he got a fresh horse and was away early,
and soon past the sweeping majesty of the River at Foynes ;
next he galloped through castellated Askeaton with its merry
boisterous millers, and holy ruins which, until Elizabeth's
day were full of solemn, chanting friars ; then on to the limestone
walls of Mungret and at length arrived at Limerick. That
night he stayed at a tavern in the city.

On the third day he rode to Ennis and thence headed straight
for Galway. Then the land began to get stony and poor ;
but accounts said it was poorer and stonier still away to the
west in the Burren, where there was nothing for miles and miles
but white limestone ; not even a blade of grass. Truly, it was
well said that it hadn't wood enough to hang a man, water to
drown him, or earth to bury him.

He soon reached Galway where he remained the third night.
He waited until the afternoon before re-commencing his
journey next day as he had not now far to go. Soon he was
cantering from Galway City, through the flat countryside with
its stone walls running here, there, everywhere ; it was so
different to his own Kerry and yet so much the same ; one
would think he was in Kerry almost but on looking round,
the preponderance of those walls of stone would make the
difference apparent. He would nod now and then in acknow-
ledgment to a salute ; people passing him by wondered who
was the handsome stranger. In a short while he saw the turrets
of the Castle and was soon trotting up the main avenue. Most
of the windows were lit up and near the drawbridge was a
man-at-arms. Hearing the sound of hoofs, he stood stiffly to
attention, holding his sword upwards in front of him. Pierce
saluted and the man-at-arms having acknowledged it, called

out in a loud tone as if in warning to somebody inside : " A
visitor to this House ! " Immediately, an official in gold braid,
the major domo, came forward with a stately walk, and bowing
low with his right hand on his breast, said in a deep voice :

" My master, Brian O Loingsigh, bids me welcome to his
House, the noble and illustrious Pierce of the princely house of
Ferriter ! "

Pierce wondered how he knew his name ; but most likely
Brian himself sighted him from inside. But there was little
opportunity to let his thoughts wander, for the major domo
making a sign, a groom immediately came forward and taking
Pierce's horse, immediately undid the small portmantle which
was fastened on the saddle and handed it to still another servant.
In his greatest day the old Earl probably never had half this
ceremony, thought Pierce ; but Brian was ever a one for all
the niceties of ceremonial procedure ; besides, living here
remote from the world, the Gaelic chieftains were able to keep
much of the old feudal splendour—for Connaught, being less
influenced by the Normans, had kept to the old ways more
than any other of the provinces.

Pierce then followed his guide towards the great door from
which a ray of light spread itself across the broad courtyard,
till it lost itself in the shrubbery opposite. Brian himself was
now standing on the threshold ; he descended the few short
steps and catching both of Pierce's hands in his, smilingly said :
" A thousand welcomes, Pierce." Pierce's father was indeed a
very old friend of his : they had been school-fellows together
in Galway at Master Lynch's Academy ; and many a tale of
fun and frolic went round when they met.

They had entered the main hall with its air of spaciousness
There was a ceiling of magnificently carved oak, high panelled
walls and a broad, sweeping staircase ; there was a sense of
remoteness and of the mediaeval in this great hall, here so
secluded amidst the groves and shrubs, and so close to the
gently-lapping waters of the island-studded Loch Corrib.

Down the broad carpeted staircase a lady was coming—a
lady all in white. She tripped gracefully from step to step
with a sense of ease which emphasised her fine carriage all the

more ; her head she held high but it was not in a haughty
way for the gentleness of her lips gave the lie to that ; it was
somehow a nobility, a dignity of presence, a stateliness, which
lent to her whole person a graciousness and a regal bearing
which Pierce had hitherto never beheld.

Her gaze rested on his frank, open features for a moment
or two as she came towards them. " Sybil," said her father,
" this is our friend and guest, Pierce Ferriter." She raised her
eyes once more and her silvery voice rippled out some words
of welcome, but what they were he could not remember ;
he was confused, a confusion hard to understand in one usually
so self-possessed, and his heart seemed to beat a little faster,
but that might only be his imagination. He seemed lost in
a strange world, a world of shining minarets and crystal palaces
beneath the glitter of golden sunshine, a world in a far off faery
land. But he felt instinctively some danger ; some innate sense
warned him that to return from such isles of mystery one had
to cross perilous seas and wander amidst forlorn lands. However,
this overwhelming change which had come on him could not
be ignored ; it must take its inevitable and perhaps futile
course. All Pierce knew was that he was conversing with Sybil ;
that they were walking to the left of the hall, she on his right
hand ; that her eyes were on his most of the time and that he
was mumbling replies to her questions. When did he leave
Galway ? did he meet any friends there ?—how long did he
think he might stay ?—it must be a week surely—but soon
they were at the drawing-room ; and Brian who was behind
stepped forward and opened it.

At dinner that night in the great oaken dining-hall, with
its carved heads and escutcheons, and its huge open fireplace,
they spoke of many things—of Corca Dhuibhne, of Desmond,
of the new planters, of the old, raddled Queen, of stuttering
awkward Jamie. The prospects of more Spanish help were
considered and Brian concluded that the sooner it came the
better as all the North, by what he could hear, would soon be
in arms ; any day now in Ulster a match would be set to the
powder and then the King's writ would not run very far. Yes,
the times looked bad, and besides money was getting scarcer

and scarcer ; or rather its value was depreciating every day, due to the gold of the Americas that was flooding Europe. In spite of the outward show, he had been finding it hard of late to make ends meet.

As they were about to say grace, a servant entered and announced the arrival of another visitor. When they had finished Brian said :

" I'll leave you two together for a few moments."

" I don't mind in the least, sir," said Pierce, smilingly.

Soon he returned, saying a neighbouring chieftain wished to see him on business, but that having already dined, the newcomer would await his host's pleasure till afterwards.

During the course of the dinner, Pierce was glad to observe his shyness had almost completely disappeared.

" Well, au revoir, and Sybil will talk to you. I'll see you shortly, my boy," said Brian at the end of the meal.

The door closed.

CHAPTER X

" IT'S NICE of you to come to see us," she said playfully.

" Not exactly," he replied, taking the cue, " I came only because I wanted something."

" It's kind of you to say that, Pierce."

" Thank you."

Her eyes sparkled ; she was fascinating—a woman one could love very much.

" Why don't you come often to see us, Pierce ? "

" Busy, I suppose, though I thought of riding over when I was at Baile Mac Egan."

" Hm ! so you're full of poetry, then ? "

" Poetry is useful when pretty damsels are by."

" Oh ! "

" Yes, I mean it : when one's emotions get the better of one, they sometimes break into verse."

" Have your emotions been ever thus ? "

" Perhaps ! "

" Hm ! "

He was reminded of the moth circling nearer the light ; but he had had his experiences.

" What is your castle like in Corca Dhuibhne ? " she asked.

" Like most other castles, Sybil."

" Like this one ? "

" No, nothing like the tranquil Corrib."

" You are by the sea, then ? "

" Yes, as a Viking I naturally prefer it."

" Vikings are rare these days, Pierce."

" What do you mean, Mistress ? "

" I'm thinking of the days when men were men."

" But I don't understand."

" It will again take a woman to lead you, decrepit men, just as it took a Grace O'Malley a century ago."

" You flatter, indeed."

" No, I'm just telling the truth : I'm tired of father bemoaning the times. How could the foreigner keep his grip on the land if it weren't for the spineless chieftains ? "

Pierce laughed.

" Oh, it isn't such a joke, I can tell you. If you had to listen to a dolorous litany from morning till night."

" What kind ? "

" Every kind, but mainly financial ; and now to crown all, father tries to betroth me to a merchant from Monaghan."

" Why ? "

" Lack of money ; he says he can't carry on much longer."

" So does mine, Sybil."

" And what are you doing about it ? "

" Looking for a rich heiress."

" Like me ? "

" A pity you haven't got money, else you might do."

" Thank you, Master Pierce."

" Though I should say you would be difficult to manage, Sybil."

" Really ! "

" You'd take a lot of taming."

" Perhaps I might be a Grace O'Malley."

" You flatter yourself, my dear Mistress."

" Yes, we flatter ourselves there may be Grace O'Malleys still left in Connaught."

" But men don't want warriors for wives."

" Men have to take what they get, Master Ferriter."

" Yes, unfortunately, sometimes."

After a pause, she said :

" You don't seem to like women."

" I'm too busy."

" Or burnt fingers ? "

" Again you flatter your sex."

" Still the damsels of Desmond are beguiling, I hear."

" Not so beguiling as the colleens of Connaght."

" What do you know of the colleens of Connaght, Master Ferriter ? "

" They're extremely provocative."

" Don't you like that ? "

" Yes and no ; I like a maiden to be original but not to have the ambitions of a Grace O'Malley."

" I never said I had such."

" You implied it."

" We won't argue."

" Better not, Sybil, it would be a recantation."

She threw him a suspicious look ; but he saw that with her bravado, she was a helpless creature forced to live in outlandish times—times that frustrated all her woman's sense of delicacy. In other lands she might be a gracious lady tripping daintily through the minuet at the Courts of King Philip or King Louis.

" How do you while away the hours, Sybil ? "

" Thinking ! "

" Thinking, you say ? "

" Yes, I've a lot to think about."

" For instance ? "

" There's my betrothal."

" That shouldn't worry you."

" It does."

" Why ? "

" Because, as I told you, I don't like the merchant from Monaghan."

" You couldn't try to love him ? "

" Love him ? "

" How often does he come to see you ? "

" Whenever a wineship wanders into the bay ; you see he combines work with pleasure."

" When is the betrothal, might I ask ? "

" Some time at Christmas ; but let's forget unpleasant things. Father charged me to have a care for you ; some liqueurs, Master Pierce ? "

" If you wish, Mistress Sybil."

She rang the bell, and then went over and sat by the spinet. Softly she began to play the old tune, " Cailin og a stuair me."

The servant entered with decanter and glasses. The melody kept on ; now in one key, now in another, sometimes almost lost in concord of sweet sound, its tender melancholy echoed round the room.

Pierce remained seated. Opposite were two windows in the Spanish fashion, with a balcony ; and he could see the moon glide through the clouds, lighting the lake with a silver sheen ; the breeze sighed mournfully through the sedge. He walked across and looked out, and then opening the window, stepped on the balcony.

He was thinking. A woman is always so helpless, that is unless she were a Grace O'Malley ; and Sybil was no Grace O'Malley. A little dangerous, perhaps, but not as dangerous as he first thought. He looked at the fitful moon and again at the silver waters ; the music still rippled out into the night. Why did all things to-night speak to him in such harmony ? Why was he so happy ? Was it because he loved her, loved her the moment he saw her in the hall ?

He re-entered the room and stood listening to the music for a few further seconds ; and then Brian returned bringing a friend with him, the Chieftain Joyce from the Joyce Country. For the rest of the evening they sat in the withdrawing-room, where over the wine their host continued to complain of the times.

CHAPTER XI

NEXT MORNING as he was strolling about the lawns which stretched downwards towards the lake, he saw Sybil on the pathway that led to the boathouse. She bade him a greeting with an assumed nonchalance which did not deceive him ; and it was then he realised that she, too, loved him. They walked slowly onwards to the hazel copse where there was a seat. They spoke, as on the previous night, of airy nothings for some time and then, quite suddenly she began to speak of her fiancé. He was a middle-aged merchant she said, extremely wealthy and from Monaghan, who, with the help of her father's persuasion, had made her consent to accepting betrothal to him very shortly. She did not say she had no love for him—that was self-evident. Money was her father's chief interest in the marriage, for besides the devaluation of money, gentlemen of their sort had been seriously embarassed, and often almost impoverished, by the rebellions and wars.

During the days that followed they were rarely apart, and even the servants began to whisper. Sometimes they went boating on the Corrib ; Pierce would have the oars and sitting opposite him would be his beloved, her golden ringlets softly fanned by the summer breeze, with perhaps a bonnet of the whitest silk dangling in her hands.

" Pierce, will you sing for me ? " she would say.

Of course he would sing—he'd do anything for her ; he would dive to the bottom of the deep, or, indeed, scale the blue air for her. What was there he wouldn't do, or at least try to do, for her ? Sing ? She had only to ask. What would the lady Sybil like ? Why, naturally, the tender words of *Cailin og a stuair me*, the one she played a few nights ago, that sweet tune that Master Shakespeare couldn't resist, and who with his English awkwardness when dealing with things Irish, spelt it : Calen o Custure me.

And that night when they were again alone for some little time after dinner she played it once more on the spinet. He was again outside on the balcony looking on the silver ripple of the water amidst the reeds, when suddenly the music stopped and she came towards him. He could see she had been crying. Then she stood by him silently, and they looked at each other for a long time. In loving Sybil he loved all women, in all climes, of every age—the eternal Eve. The tautness of his nerves relaxed and visions of fairy fancy floated before him.

It was a paradox, no doubt. A young man whom his father wished would find a wife, had fallen in love, but with the wrong woman. It was against logic, against reason ; but life is far larger than logic. Truly do our courses lie in the stars. His heart pounded against his breast ; he wanted her with his whole soul.

" Sybil ? "

" Pierce ! "

" Is this wise ? "

She said nothing. The fire in her sent his blood tingling through his veins ; he took her hands in his.

" You know, dearest, your father has other plans for you."

She still said nothing.

Slowly he put his arms about her ; her upturned face was very pale ; he looked at her earnestly. The plaintive cry of the plover rang over the lake.

" You realise I love you ? "

" Yes, Pierce."

" Do you love me, Sybil ? "

In answer, she put her face nearer his, and then he bent and kissed her softly on the lips.

They stood thus for a long time ; the moon still cast fitful shadows and the plover called her lonesome cry but the lovers were wrapt in the wonder and timelessness of the great mystery.

When he was able to think, Pierce wondered what he should do. Bring Sybil to Corca Dhuibhne ? They could scarcely go to his father—at least not now. Stay in The Rose, perhaps. Boyhood memories came back to him, those happy times in Trant's Tavern and roaming on the hills round Tralee. What would his friends day ? Florence, Walter—he daren't think of O'Daly or Moriarty. Safe in their monasteries, they wouldn't understand. Or would they? But that train of thought he couldn't follow now.

"You were thinking, Pierce?"

"Yes, my darling."

"About?"

"About going to Duibhne."

"Is it difficult?"

"Yes: but suppose we talk about other things."

"About what, Pierce?"

"The music you played just now, my darling."

"You liked it?"

"I'll always remember it."

"That's no answer to my question, Pierce."

"Do you wish me to say again that I love you, Sybil?"

"Yes!"

"I love you, my dearest. Are you satisfied?"

"Yes, Pierce; but I'll also associate that air with my rescuer."

"Your rescuer!"

"Yes, immediately I saw you in the hall I made up my mind that you'd rescue me."

"You don't mince matters, my dearest."

"I never do."

"So I'm to be your rescuer; nothing else?"

"Unfortunately, Master Pierce, I love you as well."

"Why unfortunately, Sybil?"

"Because it's going to mean trouble, all kinds of trouble."

"You think so?"

"Without any doubt."

"But the course of true love never did run smooth."

"That depends."

"On what?"

"The age one lives in"

"There are difficulties in every age, Sybil: Naoise and Deirdre: Diarmuid and Grainne: and ——"

"Pierce and Sybil."

"Yes, Pierce and Sybil, my darling."

They were silent; then she said:

"But we can't take to the hills like Diarmuid and Grainne."

" Naturally ; we must first be married ? "

" But where, Pierce ? "

" We'll discuss that in the morning."

" Why not now ? "

" Because I want this night to be a night of memories, to look back and think of us two under the moon, while the lake ripples at our feet. Beautiful isn't it, my darling ? Look at those clouds."

" Full of trouble."

" But life's full of trouble ; what are our myths and legends, with their weird echoes reaching to the infinite, but a symbol of man's fight against the unseen ? See the sense of frustration in Celtic legend ; but I'm wandering."

" Yes, slightly."

" I always want to remember you sitting there in the soft candlelight——"

" There are things I also want to remember, Pierce."

" What ? "

" The tall stranger talking in the hall."

" Hm ! "

" He looked different."

" Let me finish it."

" You're selfish, Master Ferriter."

" Perhaps, but I want to tell it."

" Tell it, then."

" The lady looked at the dark stranger and the dark stranger looked at the lady and ——"

" And ? "

" The dark stranger saw that the lady had beautiful eyes, soft hazel eyes——"

" And ? "

" He knew he would always keep the memory of those eyes with him."

" Memories fade, Pierce."

" Some, yes ; but such memories, never."

" But I thought such things only happen in books ? "

" Life is stranger and more complex than any book. If, for instance, the dark stranger goes away without the lovely lady,

those eyes will draw him back again ; that's why he's going
to bring her to Desmond with him."

" Suppose the lady waits for a little while ? "

" Afraid ? "

" Nonsense ; I would go to the ends of the earth with you."

" Why, then ? "

" Because I don't want to compromise you."

" What about yourself ? "

" It doesn't matter about me ; but you're a scholar and
a poet and have powerful friends. What will they say to bringing
a bride back like this ? "

" But I *am* bringing you back ; the powerful friends can
say what they will. Besides, my father insists that I get a wife."

" But we're poor, Pierce."

" You're coming back with me in the morning."

" How ? "

" That remains to be seen. I said to-night is going to be a
night of memories—for both of us."

" Let's drink to our happiness."

They returned to the room ; and Pierce poured the wine.

" To our love, Sybil."

They touched glasses and she smiled at him.

" Won't you play again, Sybil ? "

" What ? "

" *Cailin og a stuair me ;* then anything you will. May I
watch you ? "

" Yes, Sir Knight."

Many times she played the sweet air, each time a different
way ; then she changed to the lament of the lover for Una
Bhán.

" Why so sad, Sybil ? " he asked.

" I like it, Pierce."

" You like to think of maidens pining in great castles."

" Why not, Master Ferriter ? "

" But Una they laid in the cold earth."

" True, but don't you agree the music is so very beautiful."

Her fingers gliding gracefully over the keys fascinated him ;
her auburn hair swept backwards shone gold in the soft light.

For a long time he remained motionless, looking at her and listening. Then the door opened and Brian bustled in.

"Sorry for being away so long Pierce, but I trust Sybil has had a thought for you."

"We've got on quite well, sir, thank you."

"One can never be sure how Sybil will take a stranger."

"Really, father!"

"Quite true, my dear: sometimes you never speak a word."

"I can assure you, sir, Sybil has not been so with me."

"Glad to hear it, Pierce, glad to hear it."

"You said, I think, you had something to say to me, my boy. But to-night I'm expecting an old crony to smoke tobacco and so, with your permission, we'll postpone our discussion till to-morrow. Won't you join in our little tete-a-tete?"

"Certainly, sir, thank you."

"Sybil, bid our guest goodnight, my dear."

She made a curtsey.

"Good-night, Master Pierce, and please don't let father keep you talking into the small hours."

He smiled.

"Good-night, Mistress Sybil," he said softly as he bowed.

CHAPTER XII

NEXT MORNING at breakfast Brian said:

"I'm sure you'd like a walk before lunch, my boy, as the morning's so fine. Sybil will go with you as usual—that's if you're not getting tired of her company. In the afternoon we can have a long talk."

"Thank you, sir."

"Take a boat if you wish."

"Very well, sir."

"Well good-bye; take care of him, Sybil," he said, waving them down the pathway.

With all his faults, Brian had a good heart, thought Pierce.

He felt guilty in deceiving the old man, and while talking to him had avoided his gaze as much as he could. How would he take the elopement ? Or were it worth considering his feelings since he was willing to sell his daughter to the trader ? And his own father ? Well, let him rave as he would ; relations could hardly be worse between them. If he wished to disinherit him, let him do it : five hundred acres of bog weren't much use to anybody.

In his new role he scarcely knew himself. He was about to abduct a woman ! Gone were all the precepts of the past ; his common sense warned him, but what is common sense at such times ? Sybil he must bring with him ; Sybil he shall bring with him. Otherwise Christmas would be upon them and her betrothal would take place and then she would be committed to marry her merchant ; for betrothal in those days constituted a diriment impediment. There was no way out ; she was coming then to Desmond. Besides he knew he never again would or could give to anybody the love he bore her. That love was a pure, a holy, a beautiful thing,

The great lovers of the ages to whom the gods have given abundantly, taste something of the fire of genius and in the contemplation of their love tread silver pathways through shining stars ; but there is always a price—the price the gods ask. Between these lovers was a love like silver, gold, emeralds, call it what you will, something written by the stars in their courses. Eternity had planned that a tall, dark stranger should look into the hazel eyes of a lovely lady, and that the gods should then play with them as wanton boys do with flies, and perhaps even kill them for their sport.

" Do you really wish to row on the lake, Sybil ? " he said.

" Yes, if you want to, Pierce."

" To the boathouse then," he answered.

In a little while they were gliding down the lake, Pierce scarcely dipping the oars. She sat facing him in the stern, and her eyes when they caught his had all the tenderness, the hazel softness of all women, in all ages—in love. They scarcely spoke as they skimmed the sparkling waters.

" Happy, my darling ? "

" Yes, Pierce ! I wish this would keep on forever, gliding softly out, softly out to——."

" Hy-Brassil ? "

" Yes, away to Hy-Brassil, away, away——."

And now Galway, with its towers and steeples, like a bit of old Spain, was coming towards them. Pierce remembered that evening exactly a week ago when he arrived in the grey melancholy of that autumn evening he could not keep from thinking that Spanish sailors passed him in the narrow winding streets or that Spanish grandees came down in state from those great houses with the family arms proudly emblazoned on their walls. Beautiful, dark-eyed maidens seemed to trip ever so lightly by and one could almost hear the swish of their silks and the rustle of their gowns.

Thus past the towers and turrets of the beautiful old city they went, past the scores of swans near the Claddagh, past the old bearded fishermen patiently mending their nets ; away towards Arran, towards Arran and the wild waves. There along that broken coast if one looked carefully one might see the ghosts of Grace O'Malley and her ship, she the proud queen of the west who never bowed to a higher earthly sovereign.

" Pierce, have we gone too far ? " Sybil asked.

" You'll see the Corrib no more, Sybil," he replied, looking straight at her.

" Where to, then ? " she asked pretending not to know.

' To Corca Dhuibhne in Desmond, my darling," he softly answered.

CHAPTER XIII

ROBERT O'KELLY, the steward at Castle Ferriter, glanced over the accounts ; the new master would surely want to see them sometime, if and when he returned. Not indeed that such matters ever much troubled him ; but now that he had authority, perhaps like Prince Hal in Master Shakespeare's play, he might become most prim and proper. One could never tell what some people would do.

The steward looked at the book again and tried to concentrate, but it was difficult. Thoughts of all kinds kept crowding in on him, particularly thoughts about the Lady Sybil. I wonder what she's like, he mused. Is she a scheming wench who never leaves a man alone till he's safe in her net ? Or is she merely trying to escape from an awkward situation ? A wench that would run away like that with a man could scarcely be a paragon of the drawing-room ; most maidens have a say in their abduction—they like to put up a convincing struggle as the abduction then seems all the more romantic. And this hussy is probably like that.

But it's strange there's no word from Galway ; for they say the Galway people never forget a wrong : they bide their time. And what business is it of mine ? None, I suppose, except I love the young master as much as I ever loved anybody. To think that the little boy whom I used to carry on my shoulder up to the battlements, and who gave hopes of such promise, should give all these gossip-mongers so much to talk about, and perhaps even hint at darker sides to his character. Not, of course, that there was any real disgrace in abducting a woman, but it contrasted so completely with the dignified way which the Ferriters, in common with the best of the county, always conducted their affairs. As a young serving-man he remembered the marriage of the Chieftain Eamon : it was a grand affair lasting seven days and seven nights and all the people from Moorstown to Marthain, and Dunquin to Dingle still spoke about the wine and the beer flowing like water and the carcases of roasted oxen in the courtyard. And to what would Master Pierce return ?

For one thing everything was in a state of chaos since the funeral yesterday : the crowds ran the small number of servants off their feet, and as the castle would have to be turned inside out for the reception of the new mistress, he decided on extra temporary help. There was no doubt the young master would return immediately he heard of his father's death ; if he didn't yet know it he wouldn't be long so for stories travelled fast in Desmond. Robert heard a rumour that he had left for Killarney after his marriage in Dingle ; he would probably show his bride the wonders of the lakes and the mountains and then hearing the sad news, come post-haste back. At any hour they might come riding up from Baile Uachtarach ; the accounts could wait—so putting them back in the drawer he turned to more immediate things.

He would also have to postpone the sorting of the personal possessions of the late Chieftain and of the disposing of some of them ; also the distribution of the funeral baked beans to the needy would have to wait ; the men would have to carry on themselves with the threshing—everything must be put aside to prepare for the new mistress, for it was many years now since the presence of a lady had graced the old walls.

Funeral or no funeral the young master must celebrate the bringing of his bride back to Duibhne—in a quiet way of course. In a few days' time when the new mistress would have settled down, Robert would hint that perhaps it might not be any harm if a few of the neighbours like the Fitzgeralds from Gallarus and Minard, and maybe the Knight of Kerry and his lady, and one or two more, would come and drink to the health of the bride and groom. There, over across the stone passage, in the barrel-vaulted banqueting chamber, he would prepare the feast. He would re-arrange the French tapestries on the walls and lay the long table with plates of various kinds of sweet bread and rows of trenchers and pewter cups. He would light the innumerable candles in the crystal candelabra and see to it that the oaken cupboards were well stocked with wine, beer and uisce bheatha. He would put two chairs at the head of the table for Pierce and his bride and forms down the sides for the others. In the alcove behind the red curtain he would roast the meat—the best mutton from Binn Dhiarmada and tender beef from Killmallkedar ; and as well there would be fowl, crayfish and lobster, as well as the many vegetables and savouries. And as the meal went on and the wine began to flow these half-Gaelic chieftains would become more and more rebel, for in truth since the coming of Denny and the new English, their loyalty began to lay all the more lightly on them. They would toast the House of Ferriter, of course, and the new mistress, and the old Earl, God rest him, and James Fitzmaurice ;

and then into the small hours they would sing of the royal Pope ; King Louis of France and of Spanish ale bringing hope to the little black Rose—their Roisin Dubh.

This Robert had planned to do.

*　　*　　*

The steward at Castle Ferriter saw that his new master had changed, and for the better. He was alive with the joy of living and had become more refined, gentler even, than the sensitive scholar from Baile Mac Egan. Apparently he was much in love with his bride, a bride Robert had to admit, that did not answer to his previous conceptions. Her eyes were the eyes of one used to command ; and she had the bearing of a great lady. He went out to meet them.

" Welcome home, Master Pierce."

" Thank you ; and here, Robert, is your mistress."

He kissed her hand.

" I am honoured to receive you, my lady."

" Thank you, Robert : your master told me how much the house of Ferriter is indebted to you."

" The house of Ferriter means everything to me, my lady."

" You've had a dreadful time, Robert," said Pierce.

" Yes, Master Pierce ; but as you know, the old master had been wretched for so long that it was better for him to go."

" Had he a quiet end ? "

" Very ! He scarcely spoke : most of the time he was in a coma. Then on Monday night after supper, he fell asleep and never awoke."

" It was hard on you."

" True, I admit, Master Pierce, it was a responsibility for me, a mere servant, with no relation to rely on, but everything passed off well enough."

" I'm sorry, Robert, there was nobody to assist you. Was the funeral large ? "

" A hundred coaches rode down to Dunurlin."

" Who was there ? "

" Lord and Lady Kerry, the Knight of Glin, the Knight of Kerry, Fitzgerald from Gallarus, O'Donoghue of the Glens,

Mac Carthy of Castle Lough, Hussey of Castle Gregory, and——."

" You certainly had your hands full : did anybody stay the night ? "

" Only Lord and Lady Kerry and the Knight of Glin : the others stayed at The Rose."

" Hm ! Robert, we've a lot of work to do."

" Of all kinds, Master Pierce : I put aside the accounts till your arrival. I've been trying to get the place into shape for your homecoming."

" Thank you, Robert : you'll stay on, of course, and serve me as faithfully as you served my father."

The steward smiled.

" Master Pierce, I held you on my knee : I've spent my life here in the service of your father, and do you think I'm now going to leave you ? "

" I never want you to leave me, Robert ; but I thought, I thought that——."

Robert only smiled again.

" Thank you, Robert : well that's that. Now, my love, you must see your new home. We'll arrange about a requiem in the morning and see about mourning clothes and the rest. My father, for all his brusqueness, had no interests but mine at heart ; and it would be a poor tribute from me, Robert, if I didn't mourn him befittingly."

*   *   *

That night, from the battlements, they looked out to sea.

" It's different from the Corrib, Sybil."

" Yes, Pierce : what's that island out there ? "

" Inis Tuaisceart."

" Shall we go there sometime ? "

" Of course, my dearest : we'll go everywhere."

She gazed at the broken coast : while the waves crashed on Cuan a' Chaoil with a roar like distant thunder.

" Pierce, sometimes I wish I were Grace O'Malley."

" But I thought you were."

They both smiled.

" Why do you want to be Grace O'Malley ? "

" Just a vague fear."

" But my darling, I'll never again leave you."

He took her in his arms.

" Pierce, there's been no word from father."

" Why worry ? Aren't you happy ? "

" Of course, Pierce ; but you know——."

" Yes, I know, but I also know he kept you in prison."

" If only I could hear how he's feeling about——."

" Hush, Sybil, thoughts like that are natural : you may be sure he has heard of our marriage."

" But Pierce——."

" No more fears : you belong to me always. You'll reign like a queen from Coomeenol to Cam na Cuaile Thuaidh."

The stars began to twinkle in the deep blue ; and the silver tip of the moon rose behind Marthain.

" Do you remember, Sybil, our betrothal night ? "

" Yes, Pierce."

He kissed her softly.

" Again, my darling, to-night is a special night, the night of our homecoming ; and of your beginning as mistress of the castle. It, too, is a precious night. In our old age we ll remember gazing at Inis Tuaisceart sharp against the dappled sky, and watching the moon come over Marthain."

" That's beautiful, Pierce."

" What ? "

" The way you speak."

" But not as beautiful as you."

She smiled.

" You like watching the waves, Pierce ? "

" Yes, such a contrast to Loch Corrib : which do you prefer ? "

" I once thought there was nothing more beautiful than moonlight on the Corrib ; but the grandeur of Corca Dhuibhne takes my breath away.

" Truly ? "

" Yes, it takes my breath away ; still such things are merely external."

" How do you mean ? "

" I mean I would follow you no matter where you went."

" I thought I was but your rescuer."

She smiled.

" Yes, but when a potential rescuer looks at a maiden with those eyes of his."

" I didn't know my eyes were different from others."

" They are."

" And you, my darling, have eyes of fire."

" I thought it was eyes of hazel."

" It isn't easy to get the word ; people with eyes like you are dangerous."

" Why ? "

" You set traps for the unwary ; little did I think when on my way to the Corrib——."

" That you'd abduct me."

" I don't like that word ; we were married immediately, weren't we ? We didn't roam like Diarmuid and Grainne."

" Or suffer the pangs of Naoise and Deirdre."

" That's because we've never been parted."

" Pierce, do you want to be parted from me ? "

His arm tightened round her.

" Sometimes Sybil, you ask queer questions."

" I didn't mean to startle you : to be parted for a short while only, I mean."

" I never want to leave you, beloved. Look at the sky : do you see the Milky Way ? In our love you and I shall always tread that shining path."

" Your imagination runs away with you, Master Pierce."

" When you are near."

" You must learn to curb it."

" Why then, I must curb my love for you."

" Pierce, how shall we spend the rest of our honeymoon ? "

" Roaming in our kingdom, my lady."

" Well put, Sir Knight ; but where in the kingdom ? "

" Oh, everywhere : do you like mountains ? "

" At a distance."

" You must learn to follow the sheep tracks : we'll climb Binn Dhiarmada and see the ocean roll beneath us."

" It looks steep."

" You'll soon learn : but first you must see Dun an Oir where Grey massacred the foreigners."

" How dreadful."

" Haven't you heard of Dun an Oir ? "

" I suppose I have : one hears so many things."

" I must tell you about Dun an Oir."

She put a finger to his lips.

" No massacres, if you please, Master Pierce—at least not during our honeymoon."

" Right : probably it's good for me, too, because I took these things too seriously as a boy. Talking of stories, you must visit my friend, Seamus, the seanchai, at Clochar."

" Of course."

" And roam along the sands of sweet Béal Bán, when the white horses ride the waves."

" Yes ! "

" And wander among the golden-hearted people of Ard na Caithne."

" How delightful."

" And lead in the dance at a wedding in the village."

" Yes ! "

" And stop the coach to chat with Father Micheál."

" Of course."

" And see a thousand years of history at Gallarus."

" History again ! "

" Believe me, Sybil, I'll teach you to like history."

" But not during our honeymoon."

" No, of course not. What would you like me to teach you ? "

" Never to forget the first night I saw you."

" That would be impossible."

She looked up at him.

" I'll never forget your coming to the Corrib."

" My darling, we always seem to return to the lady in white with the hazel eyes."

" Or the tall stranger with the dark eyes."

" And the faery music, *cailín og a stuair me.*"

" And the stranger listening under the moon."

" There we are back again, my dearest, to where we started."

" But you didn't finish : where else do we go on our honey-moon ? "

" Where did I stop ? "

" A place called Gallarus."

" We'll wander amidst the red ruins of Cill Maol Cheadair."

" Yes ! "

" Next on to Baile na nGall of the golden sands, and see the fishermen go down to the sea at Duinnin ; then we'll talk to the dark maidens at the Feothanaigh."

" No more maidens, please."

" Jealous ? "

" Very."

" In that case you must climb some of Brandon for maidens are rare on its steep sides."

" Agreed ; but how about the people, Pierce ? How will they receive me ? "

" They'll come out and make a neat curtsey, and offer you little gifts."

" Beautiful : you know I am going to be very happy in Desmond."

" Of course you are ; and some day we'll go in state to Dingle in the old blue coach ; we'll have a royal time—not quite as rushed as the last."

She smiled.

" And The Rose will receive us royally ; and Tom Trant bustle more than ever."

" How lovely."

" Next day, we'll drive the thirty miles to Tralee. We'll stay at Walter Ware's who used to tell me the ghost stories and then call at the old school and see what changes the years have brought."

" I'll like that."

" Did I tell you about my friends, Thaddeus Moriarty, Florence Mac Carthy, Walter Hussey, Daniel O'Daly ? "

" A little : where are they now ? "

" Scattered, scattered everywhere. O'Daly and Moriarty are friars in Spain. A pity we hadn't Tadhg Moriarty at our marriage : he was a fine type of lad ; but they were all good fellows at that school."

" After Tralee, what shall we do, Pierce ? "

" Ride out to Ardfert : thence on by the Feale to Lord and Lady Kerry's. I wonder if Lady Kerry will still call me ' honest Pierce ' ? "

" Why used she call you that ? "

" Don't know : I never thought I looked honest."

" Neither do you : you look exactly what you are, a scheming daredevil who plucks a helpless maiden from the bosom of her father, and brings her to a lonely castle on the rim of the ocean."

" Do you want to leave the lonely castle ? "

" My darling, I'll stay here always—with you."

He kissed her.

CHAPTER XIV

TOWARDS THE SMALL hours a loud knocking awakened Pierce : it was Robert.

" Master Pierce, some of the servants coming in late, saw men disembark at Cuan a' Chaoil."

" How many, Robert ? "

" About a score and ten."

" How many men here ? "

" A dozen in all."

" Any muskets ? "

" Yes, about one for each man."

" Any powder and shot ? "

" A fair quantity."

" Right ! Call the men : arm them and order them to stand by. I'll first bring your mistress to safety and then return."

Sybil was awake.

" My darling, you heard the news : I'll bring you where you'll be safe."

" Where, Pierce ? "

" To a cave close by. Get yourself dressed : put on warm

garments. I'll be back in a few moments. Now," he said when he returned with a lantern, " please follow me."

They crossed the courtyard. The men had barred the main gates and were now getting ready on the battlements. He opened a side door, from which stone steps led down through a cavern in the cliff side.

" This is steep, Sybil : give me your hand."

When they descended halfway, it became more difficult, and a false step would mean a fall of twenty feet. The angry lash of the waves came nearer. Their ghostly shadows danced on the gloomy walls ; but at last they reached the shingle. He led the way for about twenty yards till they came to the inner wall, from which ran two tiny caves.

" In that one to the right there's a flat stone where you can rest if you wish ; but remember the opening to the left brings you to the sea ; there's no need to remind you to avoid that. You won't be lonely I hope, but why should I ask that of a Grace O'Malley ? "

He looked at her and she smiled, and then he put the lantern on the ground.

" I'll leave you this ; but don't show the naked light. Good-bye, my darling," and he caught her in his arms.

" Good-bye, my husband : I know you'll beat them back."

He returned quickly.

" I'm sure it will be nothing, Robert."

" I hope so, Master."

The steward posted eight men on the battlements and on the ground there were four besides Pierce and himself.

" They're coming, sir " said Tom, the groom, at length.

" How many ? "

" They're scattered, sir, but I should say a few dozen."

" Right men, keep a close watch ; and remember, I'll well reward your services for this night."

" Our greatest reward, sir, is in serving you," answered Tom."

" Hear ! hear ! " echoed the others.

" Thank you men ! I'll not forget this."

They waited.

" Only for that moon, Master Pierce, it would be well with us."

" You forget, Robert, that our enemies probably say the same."

" Yes, but——."

" Here they are, sir."

There was a rap on the gates.

" Is Pierce Ferriter within ? "

" Yes ! "

" This is Brian O Loinsigh seeking his daughter."

" His daughter is the wife of Pierce Ferriter."

" The harlot of Pierce Ferriter."

" You'll regret that."

" And you your treachery."

" Charge the gates, men."

In a moment Pierce was on the battlements ; he saw that a group of men with a battering-ram were about to rush the gates.

" Take aim, men," he said, " Ready ! Fire ! "

Four of them rolled over and the rest dropped the beam and ran. All was quiet.

But they came on again. From the bushes shots rang out ; and a bullet struck one of Pierce's men.

Over a doorway to the left heads appeared ; in a matter of seconds six men dropped into the courtyard.

Pierce shouted : "Robert, Pat Sullivan, Sean Lynch and Con Connor will attack to the rear : follow me ! "

It was a hand to hand fight. Pierce made for a huge fellow who, holding a musket by the barrel, tried to strike Con Connor with the butt-end, but Pierce drew and hit him on the chin, knocking him over. But he was up in a moment and rushed at Pierce. For a few seconds they swayed, then fell and rolled over. He was a heavy brute and could not stand up to Pierce's light muscular frame, who in a few moments had his fingers on his throat.

" Lynch, come here and truss up this fellow."

That finished one. The others were pomelling each other and two rolled on the ground. Pierce went to the aid of his man. That was another prisoner. Meanwhile, more came over.

" Fire men ! he shouted to the battlements.

A few bodies hit the cobbles ; but the battering on the gates continued. Still more came over the wall so he called to three more men to come with him. They rushed at the raiders. Pierce had his musket raised to strike when lights danced before him ; and a weight like tons of metal crashed on his head.

*   *   *

When he came to he still lay on the courtyard. It was daylight and a strong wind blew and leaden clouds crawled in from the sea. His head seemed on fire ; he licked his parched lips and for an instant, hoped that it had been a nightmare ; but there was little doubt it was real for he could see bodies about him. One, a few yards away, gaped at him.

With an effort, he stood up and then he saw Robert lying near the gates with his hands tied behind him and a gag round his mouth. He undid him.

" I kept shouting to you, Master," he said, " that's why they gagged me."

" I'm glad you're alive, Robert : God, what a night ! "

" Nasty enough, Master Pierce."

" But hurry, Robert, let's see to these men : that's poor Fuller on the battlements ; and who've we here ? Lynch and Spillane ! Also dead."

" There's Flaherty yonder, Master : dead, too."

" Master Pierce, you'd better see about the Mistress : I'll take charge here."

" Very well, Robert : I won't be long."

He quickly wrenched the door open and ran down the steps ; the seaweed glistened on the shingle. I wonder she doesn't come to meet me ; she probably thinks her father and his rotten crew are still here.

A flock of gulls made the air lonely with their cries.

At last our fears are at an end : there's nothing ever more to cloud our love. Still I wonder she doesn't come to meet me ; it's no time for jesting.

He sang softly " *cailin og a stuair me*," as he turned into the darkness and the cave was filled with sound.

" Sybil, where are you ? "

But only the drip from the roof answered him.

" Sybil, Sybil, you must be here ! Sybil, can't you hear me ? " he called out several times as he ran quickly along the wet sand.

He continued to the end ; but there was nobody there. He turned left into the smaller cave that led to the sea. No, not there, either. Perhaps she was in the tiny cave in the cliff opposite. He waded across the outgoing tide and peered in ; but no, that too was empty.

He returned. Robert was talking to Connor and Lynch.

" Robert, there's nobody below."

" Not below ! "

" No, nobody : God, what has happened ? "

" Please keep calm, Master."

" Oh God, Robert, where is she ? "

" I'll get some of the villagers and make a search."

That day they found nothing ; but during the night the tide laid the body on the sands of Cuan a' Chaoil.

CHAPTER XV

TRULY THE GODS play many a cruel jest.

" Sybil ! " he muttered, as bareheaded, he tramped the hill-country near Cill Maol Cheadair, " Sybil, my darling, forgive me ! " The gale from Marthain blew the fiercer and he tightened his riding-cloak about him.

" You know, Sybil, I did it for the best : I thought you'd be safe there. How was I to think of the incoming tide ? Why didn't I leave you with your father ? What if you did marry that merchant ! Wouldn't you be better than lying in Dun Urlan with the grey clouds and the scream of the gull and the lonely tombs about you ? What must your last moments have been in the grip of the icy waves ? Oh Sybil, I'll go mad, go mad."

He walked slowly down to Gallarus. There were sheep grazing near the oratory and over against the entrance an old man sat on the low wall; he wore a round, green hat and his grey locks reached to his shoulders. His cloak was of faded saffron and by his side lay a cruit. Hearing somebody approach, he turned his head, and there was an expectant smile on his white, withered face but his eyes were the eyes of the blind. It was Diarmuid Dall, the harper.

"Pierce Ferriter bids you good day, Diarmuid."

"Surely not Pierce of the princely house of Ferriter," he answered as his withered cheeks broke into a smile of welcome.

"Yes, Diarmuid."

"Ah, it's Pierce indeed, my good boy. It's many a day since I played at your parents' wedding; but what's this I hear about you? I know it opens the wound afresh, but my heart bleeds for you, *a mhic*. It's hard to be parted forever from a lovely wife: harder in such awful circumstances; but you must know that time will slowly but surely throw a veil over it."

Pierce sat beside him and for a while he was silent. Then he said simply:

"For me, Diarmuid, that can never be."

"I expected you'd say that. My thoughts were yours when many years ago, the gallowglasses of the Lord Deputy butchered my own son before my eyes; they saw him digging in a field and beckoned him.

"'That's a pretty house you've got', the commander said. 'I'll post a half-dozen men with you for three months'.

"'You'll do nothing of the kind', my son replied, 'for we've scarcely room for ourselves'.

"They were in a bad mood that day for many gave them sharp words; this was the last straw, for the commander shouted:

'Seize him, men; and if he resists, run him through'.

"He fought tooth and nail; but one burly fellow coming up behind, ran a dagger through his ribs and he died before I reached him."

Both were silent for some moments and then the old man said in a brighter tone:

"But there was one thing that helped me to forget, and

that was my music, my beautiful music. Often when everything looked dark, the sweet sounds coming to life in these strings soothed me and gave me hope. I used to put my whole sorrow into my playing ; despair alternated with melancholy. The howl of the wind and the piercing sweep of the sleet—the crash of the waves—the echoing roar of the thunder—that I tried put into my playing. At first I failed but soon there were moments when it seemed as if at last I had mastery over my instrument. It became as docile to my touch as a steed that has served a man through the years, and it was then I composed many airs, laments full of the same, sad thoughts. Everybody's woe seemed my woe and everybody's burden mine. I composed a lament for the death of Sean O h-Uiginn's only child ; I wrote another on the drowning of the four fishermen from Dunquin ; and my boy, I composed a lament, too, for you when I heard of your tragedy."

" I'm grateful, Diarmuid."

" Would you like to hear it ? "

" Not here, Diarmuid ? "

" Why not ? "

" I don't like the sky."

" True : I always feel in my bones when rain is near."

" Then let's go over to the ale-house at the bend of the road."

" Right, my boy," he answered, as he groped for the harp ; but Pierce forestalled him, and taking harp in one hand, gave the other to the old man.

" Now lean on me, Diarmuid, and we won't be long."

Soon they sat before a blazing fire in Casey's tavern, a half mile down the road. The host fussed more than usual ; for it was not often that a Ferriter drank his ale.

Strange to say, the music was sweet and calm like moonlight on a lake, with sometimes the ripple of the water and the whispering of the breeze through the sedge. There was in it, at times, a wild despair and weird sounds filled the room, but quickly it became soft again with a little melody that spoke of the cooing of doves and the folding of linnets' wings at the close of day.

The old man smiled when he had done.

" It would comfort me if that air sometimes helped to lighten your sorrow. I named it : ' The Lament for the Lady Sybil.' "

As the years went by, the people called the bare, lonely promontory, Sybil Head, and the castle beneath, Castle Sybil. Often in the winter nights, when the winds howled and the rains beat against the panes, they told again the sad story. Sometimes, a wandering harper would lift the latch and, bowing to the company, seat himself by the fire. Then, taking his instrument, he would slowly caress the strings.

" Silence ! " the host would say, " and listen to The Lament for the Lady Sybil."

II
SWEET VENGEANCE
The Poet Fighting

FLORENCE HEARD the news of the drowning at his home
at Killarney on the shores of Lough Leane, where his castle
stood. One knowing Florence by now can make a pretty guess
at his thoughts : " a nice mess poor Ferriter finds himself in ;
should I go down there again ? What could I do in any case ?
Better leave him alone. Time, I suppose, will heal it ; but most
of us are optimists when condoling with others ; not at all
so optimistic regarding ourselves." Very true indeed.

So he left " poor Ferriter " alone as most of Pierce's friends
rightly did ; they left him alone with his acres of bog, his men
and his boats. Sometimes his Viking-French blood would hear
the call of the sea again and like his forebears of old he would
exult in the crash and roar of the waves, in the heave of the tide,
as he rowed round the islands with the salt on his lips in the lash
of the gale. He would talk with the crews of Spanish wineships
and learn how they had run the gauntlet of the pirates who
infested the southern coast ; or listen to the captain of a French
frigate talk of John Jennings the bold buccaneer who ruled the
main.

Then rumour began to come that trouble was brewing in

the north. The old Irish wanted revenge for the planting of
Ulster at the time when O'Neill and O'Donnell sailed over
the seas to exile. Often there were rumours of their return,
but that was all. Once the English Ambassador at Venice
wrote that while O'Neill expressed his good wishes for the
King's Grace, yet in his cups " he doth declare his resolute
purpose to die in Ireland."

But O'Neill and O'Donnell never came back to strike a
blow for their beloved Ulster. But there were others left
to do it ; if not for any ideal, then simply for revenge, like
Florence. Surely this was wonderful news, this news from the
north ; it's good they're going to pay back the old score.
How many men could I raise in the county, he asked himself ?
How many in Killarney ? About a hundred, and for Tralee,
say about two hundred, with the same from Corca Dhuibhne.
That would make five hundred men in all ; with luck I might
raise six hundred.

In Ulster there was little trouble in raising men—thousands
of them—for most of the original owners remained near their
old homes. They lived on the hills and bogs, or else became
nomads ; their hands were itching to root out the scum for
ever from royal Ulster.

The rebellion was to begin with a plot to seize Dublin Castle
which the insurgents knew had but a small guard. Eoin Roe
was ready to join them from the Continent and he had got
promises of help from Cardinal Richelieu. However, at the
last minute, Owen O'Connolly, one in the confidence of the
conspirators, let fall some information in a tavern and this
gave sufficient warning to the English. Thus the attack on
Dublin failed, but all the north rose, and much of Ireland as
well.

CHAPTER XVII

IN MUNSTER, the President, St. Leger, looked worried as
he talked with Lord Kerry ; for reports said that the rivers of
Ulster ran red with blood.

"But, Your Excellency, we've weathered many storms," Lord Kerry said.

"Nothing like this, Lord Kerry."

"True!"

"What officers have you?"

"It depends on whom I can trust."

Whom could he trust? If it were a straight fight, as in England, then it were easy enough to pick one's men; but here there were the old Irish, the new Irish, the old English, the new English, the Ranters, the Levellers, the Anabaptists and God knows how many more. Denny, of course, was the backbone of his defence; what of the Ferriters, the Husseys, always King's men when the King's writ went far?

"Can you depend on these half-Gaelic chieftains, Lord Kerry?"

"Ferriter's honest enough, I think; he's been brooding a bit over the loss of his wife, but a taste of war will bring him round; nothing like the roar of a cannon to stop brooding."

"Very well, if you say so. What of the others?"

"The Husseys, perhaps."

"Please yourself; I leave the county in your hands. Here's your commission for martial law—that's if it's necessary. I'm not able to spare much arms, so do your best. How many rebels in the field?"

"Oh, hundreds. That rat, Florence MacCarthy, calls himself Governor of Kerry, and MacElligott, O'Sullivan Mor, O'Don-oghue and MacGillycuddy have joined him. But we'll soon make short work of them, Your Excellency."

"I hope so. Well, I must take my leave, Lord Kerry. Limerick and Tipperary look serious—but nothing like the North, of course. So, do your best and don't spare them."

When Pierce heard he was a Captain in the King's Militia he knew well what trouble it boded. Lord Kerry might think he would take arms for the Crown: time would tell how well Lord Kerry could judge a man.

He thought of the alternative—to go over to the Irish. Who or what were the Irish? Excepting a few chieftains, they were his own tenants, Sir Edward's and Lord Kerry's; at worst a rabble from the four quarters of Desmond. It wasn't easy to leave his life of semi-leisure for the mess-tent and barrack square ; harder still to become an outlaw on the mountains. But one thing was sure : if he drew his sword against Denny, he could throw away the scabbard.

If he could see Florence ! He trusted him ; Florence for all his cynical ranting, loved Ireland more than the adventurers ; for it is idealists who become the sourest cynics.

Immediately Pierce received the news he decided to ride to Tralee. When he stopped at Aunascaul to change horses he scarcely spoke to Mistress Curtin, and she in turn wondered why the young chieftain seemed so serious ; it was time to be getting over the death of the Lady Sybil, so it was. However, he was quickly away again.

As his horse ambled up Gleann na nGealt he thought of the enigma created by the clash of his ideals with those of the class to which he belonged. Which would it be, the old Irish, the savage old Irish, or the society represented by the refinements at Lady Kerry's and Sir Edward's ? The savage old Irish, yet so kind of heart ; no courtly graces, none at all. What did the sound of the lute or books of pricksong mean to them ? Nothing. Or the graces of European living ? None. Leaping over their wild mountains they'd sooner, chattering their uncouth speech, snarling like dogs—yes, like dogs—with their glibs and glaring eyes and a knife between their teeth. Wasn't that the picture Lord Kerry, St. Leger or the Lord Deputy had of them ?

Knowing the old race as he did, Pierce smiled. Truly a bad report travels far. The Gaels were outlandish in many ways ; but whose fault was it ? Whose now ? If they succeeded in the Rebellion would they reform ? Would they lose their easy-going ways ? At what terms would they fight for the King ? Was there any bridge between them ? Could the King be trusted in his promises ? See the way he signed the death warrant of Strafford ; but that's the way with kings : they'd promise you heaven and earth.

Away in Plantagenet times the Ferriters fought for the Kings, the Harrys and the Richards. Proud they were to send men to Bosworth, and in the Wars of the Roses, too, they wore the White Rose of York with their lords, the Desmonds. Then came Eliza and she ravaged and burned all Desmond from Dunquin to Cashel and afterwards her planters held up their hands in horror at the natives crawling on their bellies to find watercress. Next, old Jamie, babbling his Scots-Latin with his swollen tongue as he carved up Ulster, lovely Ulster. Then there was Charlie, Charlie and his Parliament ; but Parliaments are like cats, they grow more sour with age. Your Most Gracious Majesty, the Long Parliament is surely getting very sour ! But we really think your royal father of lamented memory went a little too far with his plantation of Ulster. Six whole counties he took. All well and good ; but where did the rabble go ? Nowhere—just wandered round and round. Your royal father should have sent them out to the Barbadoes, or Bermuda, anywhere but leave them roaming about Ulster gazing on the acres that once were theirs. In truth, we wouldn't have expected much more from your nosey old sire ; but you're in a nice mess yourself ; for we really think some of them have a grievance. Not that your royal father shouldn't have taken their lands ; but that many of the new planters weren't the right type : they were a mixed lot—plebians—not of our Florentine birth or breeding. And we fear they will side with the Scots against your throne ; for after all, half of them came from Scotland. That's loyalty for you : they got their lands from your royal father only to turn against his royal heir. Like us, Your Majesty, they themselves are the arbiters of what loyalty means.

Only the stubborn Old Gaels know where they are and what they want ; Ireland is simply theirs and they want it for themselves. They look on and bide their time ; seeing the planters come and go ; seeing monarch succeed monarch ; seeing their lovely Clar Fodhla torn to bits by the Norman-Irish, Elizabethan planters, King Jamie's jailbirds, and now those Presbyterians and Nonconformists and Independents and Heaven knows how many more. The old stubborn proud Gael was as stubborn as ever. No use before this rushing headlong into a fracas—but now with all Ulster in arms—yes, by God, all Ulster—all Ireland. And at the Court of St. James' they profess to be filled with horror at the "Bloody Diurnail from Ireland." They themselves filled the barrel with powder, set the fuse burning and then were horrified at the explosion. What a pity Dublin didn't fall ; that Owen Connolly wretch, who gave away the secret to drinking companions in a tavern, boiling in oil would be too good for him. But the old race have Ulster ; the hucksters were on the run, as they would be soon in Desmond. Ulster is ours ; our lovely Ulster is ours again. Now the rabble from nowhere know somewhat of the Red Hand, the Red Hand of the royal Ulster of King Conor.

But to come back to present problems : I've been appointed a Captain in the Militia of His Most Gracious Majesty. What am I to do ? What would my father have done ? Only one thing : keep in with the county ; play a safe game, like the Ferriters did with the Plantagenets and the Tudors ; like they did at Dun an Oir ; a very safe game. And now it's my turn ; only a short hour to decide. Sir Edward will be all fuss, of course ; and all his Baptists and Anabaptists will be shivering for their lives, their mean rotten lives. Why should I join that gang ? What way out is there ? If I desert now where shall I find Florence—or anybody else for that matter ? Suppose, at any rate, I report at the Castle and see how matters stand ?

CHAPTER XVIII

WHEN AT LENGTH he came to the Castle at Tralee, he found Sir Edward feverish with excitement. His little moustache bristled with self-importance, and he darted through the court-yard shouting order and counter order. Servants raced about and riders rapidly crossed to and fro over the drawbridge.

" We must stifle these damned rats, Pierce : we must smoke them from their verminous haunts. Have you heard about Ulster ? "

" A little."

"Do you know they're not going to leave a single Protestant alive up there?"

"Nonsense, Sir Edward, I don't believe it."

"This is no time for flippancy, my boy; you'd better get into uniform. Florence MacCarthy and MacElligott with a blood-thirsty gang are somewhere on the mountains; I want you to take fifty men and scour the country for them."

"You can't mean——"

"Yes, I mean it, and mean every word of it; and what's more, you'd better get your men ready immediately; for you leave first thing in the morning."

So that was it; he expects me go and fetch Florence. How droll—if it weren't so urgent. I'm glad he picked me though. But there must be some way out of it. I suppose it would be better perhaps to don the uniform and march at the head of the company in the morning. What else can I do? Perhaps Florence will recognise me; I wonder if he has a perspective glass. If he recognises me, it may be easy to make signs to him to surrender—and bring him back with me—then we could both escape—escape to where?—with whom else? Would there be many deserters in the Castle? How could one pick them out, but I'd better leave that to Florence. Am I counting my chickens too soon? Suppose Florence doesn't recognise me, or suppose we have to use our muskets, or suppose again that he's killed? What's the use of trying to puzzle it out? With a bit of luck it may go well. But I'm thirsty; a cup of sack, maybe. Where? Yes, I remember, the great dining-hall, where I used to dance with Meg Russell. But why think of her, that scheming jade? Like all her sex! For true love they return deceit. Never believe what a woman says; neither take her hand as a pledge. Do not choose a woman for her beauty until you find out her faults; for even though the berry is beautiful yet it is bitter to the taste. Maeve fled from the King of Cruachan through pride and sensuality; also Gerald, the great Earl, lost his Countess of the chestnut hair, because through her guile and deceit she was seduced from him. With much trickery and cunning, the wife of David the King left him; even Fionn's own wife went away. It's foolish to attempt a remedy. From now till Judgment Day if each man told of the deceit of woman, he wouldn't be able to tell half the story. Perfectly true. All except one—and she sleeps in a lonely grave in Dun Urlan. Only one of all the tribe of Eve who has rooted her name in my soul. But three days of marriage. And then? She was so different; so different from the scores of flighty females one meets from time to time; so different from Mistress Russell as a painting of a master differs from a daub—a master like that Rembrandt Van Rijn whom Florence was always talking about. But enough of that. As I said, a cup of sack. This is the door, I think. I wonder if there's anybody inside.

There were. It was a number of officers and civilians drinking in a group, and Pierce paused for a second as he looked at them. There were some of his old acquaintances there whom he used to meet at the levees, the physician Elkanagh Knight with his white goatee beard nodding and talking rapidly; burly Richard Jackson, the chief steward; Peter White the Provost of the town, with his grey hair swept backwards and a great jewel flashing on his finger as he toyed with his glass; Sir Thomas Harris, prim and dapper as was his wont; his friend Nathaniel Harrison, the bookseller and, of course, Manuel Gabriel and Walter Ware. The officers, and there were about a dozen of them, were as travel-stained as himself; for they had been riding round the county all that morning calling up the men Denny had been training for several months. He was on a nodding acquaintance with a few of them but one he recognised before he had gone a few paces; it was Richard—Richard Hussey, who instantly he saw Pierce edged his way forward.

"I was wondering if you'd ever come," he said, "Sir Edward told me he sent for you."

"Though I didn't expect to see you," and lowering his voice continued, "It looks as if we're both in a bit of a mess, doesn't it?"

"Yes, it's a bit difficult, Pierce; I wonder what's to be done?" But before Pierce could reply, Sir Edward came striding in.

"Now gentlemen, to your tasks, to your tasks; I suppose you know there's a war on."

"Yes, Sir Edward," said old Elkanagh Knight, "but I was

just explaining here to some of our new arrivals how the situation stands."

"Simple enough, Doctor, simple enough," replied Sir Edward, "I'm going to Castlemaine in the morning to take over from Captain Spring who will replace me here for the time being. I think Castlemaine needs strengthening."

"That's true enough, Sir Edward," said Sir Thomas Harris, "in fact the rebels may attack at any moment."

"Damn them, yes, God knows what they'll do next. The refugees are still coming in ; if they keep on like this I don't know how we'll feed them. It's the same in the Short Castle. They're coming from as far away as the Shannon. But drink up, gentlemen, drink up ; you know as well as I do what's to be done. By the way, Captain Ferriter, the chief steward will show you where to get your uniform."

They finished their glasses in silence and then each went about his business. There was indeed much to be done. The town had to be ransacked for every loaf of bread, sack of flour and bushel of wheat ; cattle and sheep had to be collected and driven into the bawn ; spinning wheels and looms to be gathered ; leather ; beds ; fuel and the hundred other things that a be-sieged garrison would need. All that afternoon there was ceaseless coming and going over the drawbridge—men on horseback, men driving cattle, two men bearing a quern ; a few more bringing scaling ladders, rosin, pitch and kettles of scalding oil ; women rushing forward with huge bundles of clothing, followed by scared children ; more women running home again for their pewter cups and crockery—for the Irish, the wild Irish, were on the hills and God alone knew what would become of them. Why didn't they themselves stay in peaceful Devon or in beautiful, slumbering Warwickshire ? Why come to this wretched, this forgotten land, this Ultima Thule where the uncouth, the dirty natives, jabbering their hideous language, ever waited their chance to rob and rape ?

He had no clear idea as to what his duties were ; Sir Edward told him to get his men into shape—but where were the men ? There was nothing on all sides of him but a seemingly endless stream of refugees going backwards and forwards and running about the courtyard or wandering through the upper stories of the Castle, seeking somewhere to deposit their few possessions; then running out again only to return with another motley assortment.

After a while, he saw Sir Edward who did not seem very pleased to observe that Captain Ferriter had not yet found any labour worthy of his attention.

" It's impossible to find anybody in authority, Sir Edward," he said.

Still the same dreamer thought Denny ; I wonder if I've made a mistake in granting him a commission from his Majesty. Of course everybody knows he associates with the lower orders and has even been to one of their schools of poetry ; yet, for one reason or another, I like him for I think he's at least straight —he wouldn't pretend to be your ally if his conscience would'nt allow him—unlike many more of our so-called friends.

" Here Ferriter," he said, getting a flash of inspiration, " will you please go into the back courtyard where Peter Cambridge is erecting a gallows ; perhaps you may find Captain Hussey there who will show you your regiment ; and if not perhaps you'd supervise Cambridge and his workmen."

" A gallows, Sir Edward ! Pray for what ? "

" For what ? I'll tell you for what : to gladden the hearts and lift the minds of the Irish rats towards their last end," and looking at Pierce he smacked his lips and rubbed his little fat hands.

In life, generally, one is not often called upon to make momentous decisions ; one continues in the same routine from day to day, from year to year, perhaps, without being obliged to take sides in any issue ; but sooner or later the time comes when judgment can no longer be postponed. Even then the issue is doubtful to the last second ; it may be something said, or a shrug of the shoulders, raised eyebrows or a sneer—one of those " tremendous trifles " that alters the whole course of men's lives. In this case it was not so much what Sir Edward said, for no doubt he was entitled to hang any of the unfortunate " lower orders " who would stray into his clutches ; but it was the diabolical way he smacked his lips and rubbed his little fat hands as he spoke; there was evil in that man, thought Pierce.

"Sir Edward," he said, "I resign my commission."

Looking back on it afterwards he never knew why he said those words; he never really meant to; but now that they were uttered, there was no retreat. For a moment Sir Edward was too surprised to say anything by sensing that the situation required most tactful handling, tried to bring his quick temper under control.

"What do you mean, Captain Ferriter?"

"I mean that I resign the King's commission."

"And what then?"

"That is none of your business."

"It certainly is my business: I'm in command here."

"In command of the English, yes."

"Have you taken leave of your senses, Captain Ferriter?"

"Not that I'm aware of."

Denny's temper was, however, fast getting the better of him, but yet he saw it was no time for raising a quarrel and smothered down his wrath as best he could.

"Captain Ferriter," he said, "it's well for both of us that Lord Kerry's not here."

"Why, might I ask?" enquired Pierce, icily.

"Because he'd have charged me with neglecting my duty of putting you in the pillory."

That only aggravated matters; it was now Pierce who had need to control himself. He was struck speechless for a moment by the studied insult and would have hit the little pompous man full in the jaw but that his common sense warned him; that indeed would have been the end of all his plans for surely he would have been thrust into a dungeon and there left to rot. No, whatever the insult, he must keep his head and when the opportunity was ripe join the Irish; for he had decided the very moment he resigned the King's commission that that was the only course open to him—at least the only honourable course, and the course to which his intellect as against his emotions gave sanction. Though he liked the English and understood their ways yet he felt that his place lay after all with the Tadhgs and the Diarmuids ; he was now convinced that environment was a powerful antidote to heredity, frequently overcoming it in the end.

" The pillory indeed, Sir Edward, how thoughtful of you ; it's almost as thoughtful as the gibbet which you say you're building," he said, forcing a smile.

" Captain Ferriter," he said, " do you see the plight of all these poor people ? "

" Well, Sir Edward ? "

" And you resign your commission thus in the hour of England's greatest need ? "

" But it's not the hour of Ireland's greatest need, Sir Edward ; on the contrary and if you'll allow me to say so, it's the hour of Ireland's greatest triumph," and with that he turned on his heel, leaving the little man to recover as best he could. He knew he was safe for some time ; but not for very long. Sir Edward would at first scarcely know what to do ; there seemed to be nobody in sight whom he could consult ; if he ordered Sir Thomas Harris or Jackson or any of the others to arrest Captain Ferriter they would merely tap their foreheads and blame the turn things had taken for their commander's sudden derangement.

CHAPTER XIX

PIERCE CROSSED the courtyard, intending to take a walk through the town so as to think out his future movements and as he neared the portcullis he saw Richard Hussey descending the stairway nearby, bearing an armful of old rusty muskets.

" Drop those somewhere, Richard," he said, " and come outside for a walk ; I've something to say to you."

As they went down Burgess St. he quickly told his friend what had happened, adding that he was about to go and search for Florence in the Glen of Scotia.

" That's if you can take your horse from under Sir Edward's eyes," said Richard.

"Anything is possible in that mob; and besides I don't think anybody would dare arrest me."

"Not even under orders from Sir Edward?"

"No, not even under orders from Sir Edward; you see they have such implicit faith in the loyalty of the Ferriters that it will take a lot to shake it."

So there and then he said he would return, get his horse and leave the town with as little fuss as possible.

"Very well, Pierce; I'm with you," said Richard taking his hand.

"You mean that you'll come with me?"

"Yes, I'll come with you."

Pierce was glad he had a friend like Richard, a real sincere friend, and as he shook his hand he felt this to be the greatest moment in their friendship; he had always felt that he could tell Richard the deepest secrets of his heart and that his confidence would be respected. They were alike in many ways, a long line of Norman and Saxon ancestors, a similar childhood and youth, the years at Baile Mac Egan, but above all it was the mutual love of books which bound them together. Richard, on his side, looked up to Pierce as to nobody else; in his eyes there was scarcely anything he could not do, and now seeing that his hero had thrown down the sword of state he would do likewise. Not that he didn't feel uneasy wearing the King's uniform—on the contrary, he had spent many an hour debating with himself as to what he should do; most of his friends were with "that rat" Florence on the mountains and he, too, but waited for the least likely excuse to join them.

They walked further onwards, crossed the river at the bridge near The Golden Key and walked back towards the Castle on the other side. They paused for a moment at Nathaniel Harrison's; all the books had been taken in from the window and through the leaded panes they could see Nathaniel feverishly filling a large box with richly wrought old vellum volumes.

They went in. Nathaniel, courteous as usual, greeted them, but did not cease from what he was doing. Pierce was sorry for him, really sorry; Nathaniel was a kind little man and if all the English who crossed the Irish Sea had but a tenth of his humanity or his scholarship there would be little need of rebellions or wars. How different to Denny indeed, thought Pierce ; Denny was typical of English officialdom in Ireland —narrow, ruthless, tactless—tactless to a degree that in the end, after centuries of misrule, forced him and his likes to re-cross the Irish Sea—a failure.

Pierce and Richard, saying nothing, lifted bundle after bundle of the books and handed them to Nathaniel who safely stowed them away in the box. Where was he going to put the box, they wondered to themselves ; but as if divining their thoughts, he said briskly as he hammered on the lid :

" Now gentlemen, I'd be so grateful if you'd both help me in bringing this rather cumbersome object across to the Castle ; you see it contains all I have in the world—some valuable first editions of Master Chaucer and Master Spenser, and also a little money."

Still saying nothing, each of them bending, lifted the box between them and shuffled out ; they rested for a few moments on the side of the bridge that ran over the bend of the river almost in front of the drawbridge, but were soon away again. Still the crowds passed backwards and forwards. Soon they were in the courtyard and put their load on the cobbles and waited for their friend. When he came up with them he simply said : " Thank you," evidently thinking they would be his companions inside those grim walls. They would have liked to have told him but it were better perhaps to tell nobody. Instead they made their way to the stables at the end of the bawn and, taking their horses, walked through the courtyard and thence out through the main entrance. As they were about to step on to the drawbridge, whom should they see stumbling towards them but poor old Manuel Gabriel with his ill-kempt locks starting from beneath his velvet skull cap, the pockets of his jerkin bursting obviously with bottles, and bearing a few retorts and iron stands beneath each arm. He gave them a nod and was gone.

This England never did, nor never shall,
Lie at the proud foot of a conqueror—

noble words, indeed, Master Shakespeare, the words which Tralee of the Dennys, this little Britain beyond the seas, tried to bear now in its breast ; but it was not easy, for panic having once set in, it was difficult indeed to shout :

> Come the three corners of the world in arms,
> And we shall shock them . . .

On the contrary, an observer might be inclined to agree that the shock was far more plainly to be seen on the faces of these poor men and women running with their pots and pans. Pierce had pity in his heart for them—that is for most of them—but the Dennys, the Crosbies and others of their ilk richly deserved all that the future would bring.

They quickly mounted and rode down by the river and thence away to the mountains. The air was clear and frosty. The bare furze fringed the gurgling stream and they could hear the twittering of the robins in the fallow fields fronting the road. Slieve Mish was a radiant blue but had snow on its summit. Down yonder was the town and beyond the blue of the Stacks. As far as the eye could see were the stolen acres of Denny.

Further upwards the trees thinned out. To the right was the roar of the river, carefree and joyous beneath the banks of holly and firs. Suddenly a white flag waved over a thicket on the opposite side.

Looking very puzzled both of them came to a halt and Pierce signalled the figure which had now appeared from amidst the thicket to approach. A man bearing a white flag came down the hill. When he crossed the river and began to climb upwards Pierce recognised him : it was Florence. What could he mean ? In a short while, however, he had reached the road and stood at the horses' heads.

"Pardon me, gentlemen," he said, "I recognised you both from our dugout and the white flag was the only means by which I could halt you : would you mind telling me, please, where you got those uniforms ? "

"Not at all," answered Richard, "a very old and dear friend of ours, Sir Edward Denny ; you've heard of him, probably ? "

"Slightly," replied Mac Carthy tartly, "but the question wasn't so much addressed to you, Captain Hussey, for my spies have informed me that you have been hob-nobbing with the aforesaid Sir Edward for the past week ; my main purpose in halting you is to ascertain if Captain Ferriter is also of your frame of mind and wishes to retain permanently the King's jacket ? "

"But I'm not retaining permanently the King's jacket," replied Richard, "I've quitted, I've left—I mean we've both quitted."

"And where might I ask are you going now ? "

"To join the rebels."

"Rebels, Captain Hussey ? "

"We mean Major Mac Carthy," said Pierce, "that we've both resigned our commissions in the planters' army, have come to join the forces of our own country—that's if we may."

"Oh, I see," he said, looking at them in turn for a moment or two ; then, turning suddenly around he began waving his arms as if he were signalling to somebody across the ravine, whereupon figures began to emerge from amidst the shrubs and trees.

"You see we can't be too careful, gentlemen," said Florence, turning towards them, "my men had you covered all the time ; but come on, let's go up the glen to headquarters."

They had still a mile to go, uphill the whole way, so both of the riders dismounted and led their horses while Florence walked beside them. Their vivid scarlet jackets were in sharp contrast to the buff coat of their companion. A strange situation. no doubt, but not quite so strange in that century of turmoil for with the many interests involved it was impossible for the issues to be clear cut ; the new English and the old Irish were perhaps the only groups who had little doubt as to where their place lay ; the old English were otherwise, and the predicament of Pierce and Richard amply illustrate this seemingly Gilbertian situation. Not that the wearing of the red, either, irrevocably tied one to the King, for there again there was a division, the King against the Puritans. Many on the "rebel" side still protested their loyalty to his Majesty, as the Stuarts had always counted for much even in the eyes of the old natives.

As they went along, Pierce told their friend the whole story of that morning's events; it was the predicament of Ned Denny, however, when confronted with Pierce's change over that appealed to Florence's sense of the grotesque; " sly Ned Denny, the supreme ruffian."

" But Denny's going to Castlemaine this morning to take command of the garrison," continued Pierce, " and has appointed Thomas Spring to Tralee. Crosbie is in Dublin. Most of the English have fled to the Great Castle: others of them have taken Ballymullen. White the Provost and Sir Thomas Harris are in the Great Castle as well as people like Jackson, the chief steward and old Elkanagh Knight, the surgeon. Of course, half the town is there as well, with among them many of our old friends such as Harrison, Gabriel and Ware. They've a good supply of arms but scarcely any powder."

" Have they much arms, Pierce? "

" A fair supply."

" Ours are scarce enough but we've a good supply of gunpowder."

" I'll tell you what," said Pierce, full of enthusiasm in having shaken off the shackles of the planters, " there's a powerful piece of ordnance, 'Roaring Meg' at Castle Sybil; Richard and I might fetch it some day."

Soon they sighted the large thatched hut where the officers had their rendezvous.

CHAPTER XX

WHEN LORD KERRY heard of Pierce's *volte face*, he ordered Denny to return to Tralee, and Spring to resume command at Castlemaine. Two days later, Florence attacked the latter fortress and captured it. Pierce was not present at this siege as he had returned to Ferriter with Richard to supervise the bringing of " Roaring Meg."

The taking of Castlemaine was the patriot's first victory. Many more flocked to them, and the whole force then set out for Tralee. On their way they met Joe Haly, one of Denny's rent collectors, whose bag of illgotten gold and silver made a welcome addition to their coffers.

Then St. Leger sent word to Denny to join him with some men. At least so Denny afterwards said; but many thought he merely invented the excuse to get away. He brought with him a hundred men as well as his wife and children; but before he went he appointed the Provost and Sir Thomas Harris joint governors of both castles; Richard Jackson, steward of his house; and Elkanagh Knight to oversee his goods.

By this time the English in the county had become frantic with fear; many joined St. Leger; others tried to go to England Even Lord Kerry, seeing how completely the rising had swept the country, retreated to his castle by the Feale.

In a little less than a week, Pierce and Richard rejoined their comrades in Glen Scotia, the gun and carriage being pushed in their train by a few serving-men.

That evening there was a council of war. Florence felt no little pride as he appraised his men. For two years he had planned and hoped for this day.

Pierce was chatting with Richard Hussey. Talking poetry as usual, thought Florence. On the form behind sat O'Sullivan Mor listening to O'Donoghue of the Glens; in the corner to the right stood Finian O'Shea, Henry Lawrence and Mac Elligott. For an Englishman, he liked Lawrence. His thin, rather donnish features made him incongruous in this cabin on the mountainside. An idealist; one of those rare Englishmen with a soul. Finian was talking earnestly about something. A good fellow, Finian; depend on him to fight to the end. With Ferriter and he, and one or two others, there should be enough. Mac Elligott can be relied on, too: you could trust your life to a man from the country of the Mac Elligotts. To the left, near the door, were Garrett Fitzmaurice from Listowel, with Donagh MacGillycuddy and James Browne, both from Killarney. He didn't know much about them; but their inclusion meant more muskets, more men. It was ironical, no doubt, that Elizabethan planter Browne with the insurgents;

but no man need hide his ancestry, no man that was willing to take a pike against the planters.

Again Florence looked at Ferriter : with those tiny wrinkles about his eyes, he seemed older. He trusted him before everybody, and never did Pierce prove this trust more than on the night before. He first made sure Denny's men drank their share to celebrate the " victory." Next he opened the cells ; but it was in directing the " prisoners " to the magazine and, then, in lowering the drawbridge that one saw his courage and coolness. Yes, Ferriter was made for war but that damn poetry sometimes befuddled him ; it made him too sensitive ; what did soldiers want with poetry ?

Florence began to talk. He summed up the situation for them. The President of Munster, St. Leger, he said had appointed Lord Kerry governor of the county for the King, sending him arms for a hundred men. It was an unfortunate choice on the part of St. Leger for Lord Kerry had turned about and fled to England. Florence further reminded them that Denny called a council consisting of Peter White, the Provost, and the other burgesses. They collected what arms they could about the town. Then calling all the able-bodied men they exercised them twice a week. Next the President ordered Denny to join him with a hundred men. On the eve of his departure, Denny appointed the Provost and Sir Thomas Harris joint governors of both Castles ; Richard Jackson steward of his house and Elkanagh Knight, the surgeon to oversee his goods. Most of the English and renegade Irish had fled to the Great and Short Castles. Florence concluded by asking his fellow officers for their views on the taking of Tralee.

Some suggested storming the town and taking as many prisoners and capturing as much ammunition as possible. Where, however, were they to put prisoners ? Ferriter suggested they attack the planters still left in the countryside, forcing them to seek shelter in the Castles and thus swell the numbers. This Florence thought an excellent idea : O'Donoghue, however, considered it too slow but Ferriter replied that a siege was always slow and generally had little drama. Besides he could not afford to use too much shot. Florence put the matter to a vote and

Ferriter's plan carried the day. They were thus to force more of the Englishry into both Castles and hasten surrender by this means. Six hundred men were ready and waited but for the word.

Then Florence proposed a discussion on the various commands. He asked whom they should suggest as supreme authority. Himself or nobody was the reply. They gave him the rank of Major. Secretly he was flattered. No tribute more flattering than from one's own fellows, he thought. They appointed Pierce his deputy. That again pleased Florence : while some of them might have had a better military training, there was nobody he could trust more than Ferriter. A Ferriter never left a thing half done.

Next came the other commands. There were four companies A, B, C and D of approximately one hundred and fifty men each. The first was Corca Dhuibhne and then, North, East and South Kerry. To these commands they voted Captains Walter Hussey, Garrett Fitzmaurice, Walter Mac Elligott and Daniel O'Donoghue, respectively.

But perhaps one may wish to hear and see this council of war as it deliberated at this grave moment. Let us leave the flaccid Englishry, then, trembling for their lives and scampering like rats to shelter, and let us come up the hill of Ballard and thence onwards down the dale, only soon to rise again, ever rising till we reach the snug little Glen of Scotia, folded so primly, so neatly, so picturesquely indeed, round the opening in the mountains that leads down to Castlemaine. Though the dreariness of December hangs in the air yet, here autumn lingers on far into winter. Here there is peace, peace far from men and their erring ways. Here one can be alone with the great mystery of creation and look down on the little town and the puny men that live and struggle there as if they lived in another hemisphere.

But on this December day in 1641 the glen has not its usual calm. Here and there among the bushes sentries are posted, but the reader walks on and on till at length he comes to the last house, almost near the summit, where he can gaze across at the rippling peaks of the Reeks. In this little grey house, or rather large hut, from which the smoke trickles so softly into the grey sky, let us pause and listen to the patriot army now in deliberation.

CHAPTER XXI

" WELL, GENTLEMEN," Florence says as he seats himself, " we've heard many suggestions from you during the past few days. This morning we were happy to admit Captains Ferriter and Hussey to our ranks—officers whom I'm sure would like to hear your proposals ; now what have you got to say ? "

" I suggest we enter the town immediately and take as many prisoners as we can," said O'Donoghue.

" We want no prisoners," interrupted Fitzmaurice, " where could we put them ? "

" What do you think, Captain Ferriter ? " asked Florence.

" I suggest, on the contrary," said Pierce, " that we allow all the English to enter both castles, and then lay siege to them ; the swollen numbers will hasten surrender."

" Excellent, Captain Ferriter," said Florence, " I thoroughly agree : how would you set about it ? "

" I'd first attack the districts near the town."

" What kind of attack ? " asked O'Donoghue.

" Drive away the cattle and burn their houses, like those of Huddleston and More at Ballybeggan."

" What about Ballybeggan Castle ? " asked O'Sullivan Mor.

" Ballybeggan Castle is no use to us," answered Pierce, " it's too far away ; but we could make a feint at attacking it and terrify Exham from sending help to the town."

" Splendid, Captain Ferriter," said Florence, " no wonder Lord Kerry was anxious to obtain your services."

" I suggest that we also burn Denny's Manor at Carrignafeely and drive away his cattle," said Richard.

" I agree, Captain Hussey," said Florence. " Next there's the matter of Captain Dermot O'Dingle, who's somewhere in the north of the county ; would you agree he should join us ? ”

“ No, Major MacCarthy,” said Pierce, “ I'd prefer he'd wait on the outskirts of the town and join us when we require him.”

“ Where do you think he should wait,” enquired O'Donoghue.

“ Somewhere near Killeen,” answered Pierce.

“ Do you all agree ? ” enquired Florence.

There was no dissent.

“ Very well ! I'll send him word. Now there's another matter. As you know, our very good friend, Mr. Henry Lawrence, began to visit us some few years back. We all appreciate what a sincere friend he's been ; but when we're on the eve of great changes I feel he'd be safer in England.”

All eyes turned to Henry.

“ You know, gentlemen,” he said, “ that I'd far prefer to be with you.”

“ Thank you, Mr. Lawrence ; if it's your wish you may stay.”

There was a murmur of approval.

“ I've been talking of a plan with Mr. Lawrence, who has a *carte blanche* with the English,” continued Florence. “ Now, suppose he visits the Great Castle in the King's name and tries to get all the information he can and afterwards goes to the Short Castle.”

“ Provided I'm able to cover my tracks,” said Henry, “ I think it rather a good move, and the fact of my being an Englishman, I suppose, will impress them.”

“ True,” exclaimed O'Donoghue.

“ If I might make another suggestion,” said Mac Elligott. Florence nodded.

“ I think we should change the course of the river.”

“ And deprive the garrison of water, Captain Mac Elligott ? ’

“ Yes ! ”

“ Haven't they wells ? ” asked O'Sullivan Mor.

“ No ! ” said Pierce, “ of that I'm certain ; I remember Sir Edward telling me once that the water inside was unfit for drinking ; but do you approve cutting off the water ? ”

"If possible, Captain Ferriter," answered Florence.

"But that isn't war," said Pierce.

"What's your opinion, gentlemen?" asked Florence.

"We can't afford mercy," said Mac Elligott.

"Agreed!" replied the others.

"Your plea for mercy goes by the board, Captain Ferriter."

Mercy would be Ferriter's undoing, thought Florence: that and poetry were his chief failings. A clean fight, yes, but surely no mercy.

"Has anybody anything else to say?" queried Florence.

"Yes Major," said Mac Gillycuddy, "to my knowledge they've stored five hundred quarters of corn in the town: we should burn it."

There was a murmur of assent.

"A good idea," said Browne, "but who'll go within range of the guns?"

"We'll decide all that in good time, Captain," replied Florence.

He was in a flippant mood, but one that suited admirably the occasion, thought Pierce. The cold logic of Florence divorced from the white heat of patriotic fervour, saw instantly to the root of the matter. His wide experience, too, of men and battles made him admirable to carry through this campaign. Gone was his preoccupation with himself: gone also was most of his cynicism. He was born for war as some men are born for poetry; and others for statecraft. But Pierce realised that once the war had begun he would give no quarter: that when he smelt blood he was sure to kill. What would happen to the women and children inside those hideous walls? Father Thaddeus might help matters—if he could be found. His stern eye might assuage somewhat the blood-lust of the men when revenge would be their cry.

Why do I consider my adversaries so much? Pierce mused. Did Denny or Crosby think of all they robbed or raped? Did the first Browne or Herbert, or for that matter, the early Ferriters? Is it ties of blood and friendship that make me so scrupulous? But I've made my choice and there's no going back. Here's where I want to be and it's war to the end : they in the castle are my enemies too—Manuel Gabriel, Walter Ware, Nathaniel Harrison and the rest of them—one's friends turned to enemies, one's thoughts bent to kill.

"Now, gentlemen, if you've finished, I'll say a few concluding words," said Florence.

Nobody spoke.

"Very well : each will go to his district immediately and return as soon as he can with his men. Remember, I want discipline first of all. We must show these planters we're no rebels, as they call us, but soldiers fighting a just war. We want justice, not revenge. These are anxious days ; there's no need surely to tell you that. If I've been flippant, pray overlook it. We differ in small matters, but all agree upon one thing, to drive Denny and his crew from Desmond. So, let there be a spirit of sacrifice amongst us. With that, and hard work, we shall win. Then we'll be at least masters in our own land."

Brave words, thought Pierce. Brave words, indeed, Master Florence. There's so much of the Celt in you, the volatile Celt, dismal, cynical in adversity ; but like a peacock in success.

CHAPTER XXII

THUS, FLORENCE, ON the strength of Henry Lawrence's nationality, sent him down to the town ; and then ordered him to go to Castlemaine and see how the Irish garrison there was getting on. He might also have an opportunity of calling at Castle Drum, where he might learn the whereabouts of Father Thaddeus, or even cross the mountain to Camp where he might hear some news. Accordingly, Florence asked Pierce, whose name might count for more among the English, to write the following :

"I have employed this gentleman, Mr. Henry Lawrence upon some special occasions, for the furthering and advancing of Catholicism, to go to Tralee, and from thence to Castle

Drum or Camp, wherefore, I pray the Irish and English not to molest or hinder him in body or goods.

Given under my hand, this 8th day of February, 1641.

PIERCE FERRITER."

Florence decided that, according to plan, he would first lead a small force to attack the English still remaining in or near the town. He chose his time well. Towards the end of January, while the English were at their prayers in the Great Castle, he sent twenty men under Walter Mac Elligott, to Lohercannon to drive off the cattle of Peter White, the Provost. It was a very large herd, about three hundred in all, and the bellowing and confusion got to the ears of the sentry on the battlements. Harris immediately sent thirty horse and foot to meet the attackers. Florence, though outnumbered, gave battle. Three of the English were killed but two of Irish were taken prisoner, one of whom Harris hanged that night. The other was poor Tomás Rua who had arrived the night before from nowhere and had somehow got himself mixed up in the fracas ; but the English spared him so that he might play for them.

The next day, Florence with sixty men, entered the town. They halted to the north side of the Great Castle. The guns of the Short Castle opened fire and two of his men were shot, and also a woman, a servant to one of the merchants, was shot in the leg. Florence retreated towards Lohercannon, making an attempt to burn White's house and again driving off his cattle. As darkness was coming on, he ordered large bonfires to be lit so that the English might think their houses were in flames. The patriots also took three Englishmen prisoners, Hugh Dashwood, John Jones and John Hale. Florence and his men then marched to Clahane, where they found two old sackers, which they brought back to headquarters with them.

A few days later, with a larger force still, Florence, with Richard Hussey and young Maurice Mac Elligott, a brother to Walter, marched towards Ballybeggan Castle, held by Richard Exham, an Englishman. They drew one of the sackers with them by the aid of twelve oxen ; but this was but a stratagem. They marched southwards, instead, to the house of Henry Huddleston, which they burnt. They did the same to the houses and haggards of Hore, who lived nearby, and here in Hore's garden they built a Sow.

This Sow was a long, wooden vehicle with boards at three sides and drawn on four wheels. There were doors that opened inwards and loop holes to shoot through. There was room for ten or twelve men, who placing the open end against a fortress wall, would hack away with picks and crows till a breach was made.

From thence they went to Denny's house at Carrignafeely, where they remained for some days, for it was a district of many planters. While they were there, Exham sallied out and burnt the Sow. With a little trouble they could have brought it with them; but Florence didn't think the Englishman would have so much pluck. However, it would be easy to make another.

During the whole period of the Siege of Tralee, a small party of English held Ballybeggan Castle. The patriots, not considering it worth the trouble, made no effort to force a surrender, concluding, and rightly so, that if Tralee came to terms Ballybeggan would quickly follow.

From the Great Castle, Harris marched to Killeen where he missed Captain Dermot O'Dingle by only half an hour. Dingle's real name was Moriarty. However, two of his men who had remained behind were taken and one of them, a sergeant, was hanged; but Harris spared the other, a harper, to play for the English.

That infuriated the patriots further. Hanging, indeed! Those English never seemed to learn sense. Florence found it hard to control them for a few days and the only way he could placate them was by sending on the following day a company along each side of the Lee. They began at Ballard and went eastwards till they met at Ballycarty. They had strict orders to molest nobody; but merely to attack the houses of the planters and drive away their cattle, thus forcing them to flee to the town.

In all, four hundred refugees were taken in by Harris. Already there were two hundred in the Great Castle and a hundred in the smaller one, with provisions for two years ; but the provisions could now last for only about seven months.

A day or two after, White went to his house at Lohercannon to see if his cattle were still there ; but another raiding party, commanded by Captain Fitzmaurice, cut off his retreat and he was forced to take shelter with Lord Kerry at Inishmore, near Listowel.

By this time, the English in the county had become frantic with fear and many of them fled to St. Leger, begging protection. Others tried to go to England. Even Lord Kerry, giving up all hope of carrying on the war, went with his lady to Cork, hoping to cross to that country. He subsequently went ; but his wife was made of sterner stuff. She wrote to Pierce from Cork :

" Lady Kerry to Pierce Ferriter.

" Directed : For my very loving friend, Pierce Ferriter at Ferriter's Towne in Kerry.

" These :

" Honest Pierce, and I hope in God I shall never have reason to call you otherwise, this very day is one come out of Kerry unto mee that by chance fell into the company of Florence Mac Carthy and the rest of that rebellious crew, the very day that they robbed Haly, who tells me that you promised (as he heard Florence say), to be with them the week following, and to bring a piece of ordinance with you from the Dingel and join with them to take the castle of Traly, but I hope in God it is far from your thoughts, for you that have ever been observed to stand upon your reputation in smaller matters, I trust will not now be tainted with so fowle and offensive a crime to God and man, nor give your adversaries that cause of rejoicing and just way for them to avenge themselves upon you, nor us that are your friends that cause of discontent which would make us curse the day that ever we saw you.

But I cannot believe any such thing of you and, therefore, will not take much pains to persuade you, knowing that you

want not wit and understanding enough to conceive and ap-
prehend the danger and punishment justly due to such offenders ;
and, therefore, doubt not of God's mercy in giving you grace
to avoid them, which none can more earnestly wish and pray
for than

> " Your loving friend,
> " HONOR KERRY.

" Cork ye last day of June, 1641.

" Here I am settled and do intend to stay until the times
grow quieter, which I hope in God will be ere long ; for here
is news come of a mighty armie a preparing in England for
to come over."

She gave it to an old serving-man, Jack Francis, with whom
she also entrusted another letter for Sir Edward. But it was a
long time before Pierce got his letter, for Jack, hearing at
Castle Island that the Irish had surrounded both Tralee castles
and that Captain Ferriter was one of the high command on the
" rebel " side, entrusted his missives to a tavern keeper and
beat a hasty retreat to his mistress.

CHAPTER XXIII

DURING THE FALL of the year 1641, and all during that
winter, rainstorms deluged the land, not alone in the Three
Kingdoms but throughout western Europe. The patriots thus
practised their " hit and run " tactics in conditions none too
favourable, especially when their headquarters lay on the bare
mountain. But now that would change ; for the great attack
on the town was coming and if they succeeded in establishing
themselves there, they at least would have comfortable quarters.
So, one January morning, when low, leaden clouds crawled
drearily across the sky almost six hundred men, led by Major
Florence Mac Carthy marched from the Glen of Scotia for the
final onslaught.

At their head were a dozen pipers piping the marching song of Brian Boru. Banners, blue, white, red, green, some with the Desmond saltire, waved in the breeze. They were well armed, for besides muskets, blunderbuses and pistols, they had pikes and Spanish rapiers. At the rear were the horses who pulled a dozen or so quick-firing four-pounders, and behind them again was " Roaring Meg," drawn by two horses, that famous piece of ordnance about which Lady Kerry thwarted Pierce in vain.

The flabby Englishry may now well shiver for the day of reckoning has at last come. But Denny has gone ; Denny the fox. What a pity, thought Florence. Yes, the Dennys always saved their own skins. But no matter ; his day will yet come. There are more—more hucksters running in terror from Dunquin to the Island of Kerry and from Scattery to Skellig. When they first came to Desmond they trembled when they heard the banshee of the Geraldines wailing for her dead. Yes, the traders of Tralee and the gombeen men of Dingle turned yellow with fear when they heard the lonely cry sweep from Loch Gur in County Limerick to Slieve Mish and thence westward to Brandon, that piercing weary wail dying down to a whimper over the four fortresses of the Ferriters, Dun Caoin, Dun an Oir, Dun Urla and Dun Meidhreach.

At that time, " the traders of Tralee gathered up their golden store and prepared to flee," wrote Ferriter. That was when they heard the Geraldine banshee keening for Maurice Fitzgerald. And the English merchants of Dingle, too, trembled for their miserable lives ; but there is no need to fear said Ferriter with his stinging satire, no need to fear at all because surely it isn't for such as you that a banshee must wail. But surely all that belonged to the past and now a brighter era was opening. No doubt about that indeed as six hundred firm feet sweep down Ballard to the rhythm of the pipes. When they came to the Abbey a salvo from the Great Castle, re-echoing through the empty street, greeted them. Mac Carthy halted and gave orders.

Small bands armed with sledges ran to batter down the doors of the black-and-white timbered houses of the merchants and also the gaol gate, as all the while the heavy firing continued from both Castles. In a short while they had forced open the gaol and five or six of the houses, with scarcely any casualties. Florence ordered Lawrence Thurslston, the gaoler, with his wife and sister and Edward Hale, his workman, to be locked into the dungeons for the time being.

The firing, however, from the Castles soon died down and Florence, calling his men together, placed them at their various posts. To Companies A and B, under Captains Hussey and Fitzmaurice, he assigned the Great Castle, giving them the Gaol, on the outskirts of the Square, as their headquarters ; and to Companies C and D, under Captains Mac Elligott and O'Donoghue, the Short Castle, quartering them in the large new house of Daniel Grey, the merchant, in Moyderwell.

After a hurried meeting of the council, they decided that the gaoler and Hale be hanged at the Market Cross in reprisal for the two patriots hanged a few days before by the enemy. The women, however, were allowed to go free.

Laurence Thurlston the gaoler, his wife, and sister, and one Edward Hale, who was left to guard the prison but the night before, were all stripped naked by the Irish, and put into the dungeon, where they were kept all that day and the next night. The men in the other houses escaped to the short castle by the back-doors, and were lifted up by the ropes to the battlements. The gaoler and Hale were hanged next morning at the market-cross and left naked in the street. The women escaped quite naked, and ran three miles to a place where they were sheltered.

Before they executed the gaol-keeper, they brought him home to his house, to shew them where he had hid his money. They compelled him to sit down and drink his own beer with them, until he was exceedingly drunk ; then they lashed him, making him skip and dance about, until he could neither breathe nor stand ; whereupon, being a very corpulent man, he fell down, and then they dragged him to execution.

Next, a few dozen men began to change the course of the river, which till now, as one remembers, ran as a moat round the Great Castle and thence through the grounds. They dug a channel so that it went directly down the town. The English feverishly sought wells inside the walls ; they found a few but the water was totally unsuitable for use. " As black as ink " says the old chronicle.

The next morning there was a parley, the patriots promising each man of the besieged a safe conduct to any garrison in Munster, and to allow the women and children free. There was little ambiguity, however, in the Governor's reply : " he wouldn't surrender it to any rebel in Ireland." But they called a truce to bury the dead.

Again the next day Florence sent another message to Harris advising him to surrender. He reminded him that all the other garrisons had laid down arms ; and though it was the patriots' plan to take their goods, yet they had strict instructions not to harm the English. Sir Thomas, thanking him for his civility, replied that " he would rather make the castle his tomb than surrender it to the rebels."

Nothing for it then but the instrument called the Sow. When word went round that evening that the Commander wanted a dozen men to make a breach, almost twice that number offered themselves ; for they were anxious to see the siege ended and get back to their work. Florence picked three from each company with Finian O'Shea as their officer. Pierce watched the preparations with interest.

" As you know, men," Finian said, " on this may depend the ending of the siege. Major Mac Carthy has given me authority to make whatever plans I please, and I propose to attack the Short Castle to-night after dark. We'll first try to make a breach in the brew house nearby ; this we'll set on fire so that the smoke may somewhat ward off attack as we pierce the west wall. Is that clear ? "

" Yes, sir ! "

" Very well : you'll meet here at dusk. Till then you're free. And a final word ; tell nobody your business."

That evening Florence and Pierce with Captains Richard Hussey, Walter Mac Elligott and their companies, waited in the woods along the Lee. It was a pitch-black night and everything favoured the attack, and after about an hour, thick smoke and sparks arose from the brewery. Florence, telling the others to remain behind, crept forward with Pierce.   They treaded carefully along the path through the trees and soon they could hear the tapping from the Sow. They still crept forward but it was now getting dangerous. A shot rang out. They stood quite still. The tapping became louder, or perhaps it was further tapping for it seemed to come from the battlements ? One could never tell what these devils would do. Pierce saw figures on the battlements ; unmistakably there was tapping on top. They had come to the open space about thirty yards from the castle and they daren't go any further.

The smoke and sparks turned to flame and they could see the figures a little clearer now. They had crowbars ; and Pierce immediately saw their plan : they were loosening a block of masonry to send it crashing down on the Sow and Finian and his men could neither see nor hear them. Florence, too, understood for he glanced at Pierce and then both stared again at the feverish figures, who, though the smoke blew straight at them, kept doggedly to their task.

" Captain Ferriter, stay here and watch ; and I'll bring up a few dozen men."

Pierce had not long to wait. Shortly, from the trees, a score of muskets blazed out. A cry came from the battlements, the tapping ceased, but in a few moments continued. The muskets blazed out again but this time the defenders took care to keep out of sight. The block rocked from side to side : soon it would be free. It gave a last heave backwards, and with a cheer from the besieged, went crashing down.

There was a thud, then screams and nothing more.

They never recovered the bodies. The large blue flag with the white cross flew at half mast next day. The loss of Finian was a bitter pill ; one of the gayest of the gay, now his charred bones and those of his men could not be given even a proper burial. But the pipers played the coronach at the Market Cross while the army stood round to attention. Surely no rebels these lines of men, row upon row, standing stiffly in salute to the dead. It was the great lamentation the pipers played, the *ceol mor* ; but it was years now since Tralee of the Sasanach had heard that great lament—not since the days of the old Earl. For to give them their due the Desmonds had kept up all the externals of Gaelic life; they kept the O'Dalys as their brehons; they practised fosterage or the giving of their children to be reared amongst the Gaelic clans; they continually spoke the Gaelic language—indeed their use of English resembled the French of Stratford Atte Bowe; and when great moments of triumph or of sorrow came, it was the pipes that expressed for them their deepest and most profound thoughts.

How these same pipes roused the blood, thought Pierce. They seemed to have the anguish and suffering caused by all the slaughter and havoc in Banba during those dreadful years— the havoc and slaughter in those her four green fields, her beautiful green fields; but one seemingly more beautiful than the others, for her hold on it was less firm—her lovely Ulster. Full of greasy planters it was, foreign devils from nowhere for whom the patriots showed more mercy in the rebellion than they ever showed when masters.

The men didn't want revenge, not even for Finian. They were sorry for the suffering of the planter women and children. They only wanted to come to grips with their old enemy, a fair man to man fight. They were good, clean lads who had always wanted to strike a blow for the green. Even in their teens they itched for the day when they could strike an iron blow and fight the old fight again.

Next day there was a requiem in St. John's, now again returned to the Catholics. The beautiful chant once more encircled the walls, the sombre tones of the "dies irae" with its gracious rhythm, the cry of a naked soul before its dread judge.

God be with you, Finian, for all your idealism and beautiful thoughts. So you never lived to see Eoin Roe sail over the seas to victory at Benburb, but it is spirits such as yours which have tilled the soil for Eoin Roe and the others, and made Banba glad to gaze upon the beauty, that "terrible beauty," that was to flourish in her four green fields several times in the sad centuries that were to follow.

CHAPTER XXIV

ONE NIGHT WHEN the moon threw silvery beams over the little town, Pierce stood behind the bars of one of the top windows of the gaol and gazed at the blackened battlements where now and then figures darted furtively across. Down to the left the river, with its clusters of thatched cabins and timbered houses, flowed peaceably by. How he wished the dirty business over. Spring was now in the air, and the land would surely miss these broad strapping fellows.

He thought of his own straggling estate. After Sybil's death he didn't mind anything much ; but these late years made a farmer of him as well as a sailor. What should he have done but for the land ? Nothing like hard work to make a man forget— the drudgery of cutting through banks of turf, or guiding the plough through the heavy earth. How short it seemed— incredibly short—since his bride and he gazed over the silver seas to a land of beautiful things——.

It was on such a night as this, too, that he stood with Sybil in the moonlight by the Corrib and whispered soft things to her ; and then she put her face shyly against his and was silent for a long while. The gods give great gifts surely but as quickly they snatch them away. They gave great love to Abelard and Heloïse but it had a tragic ending ; they gave great love to Anthony and Cleopatra but it wrecked empires ; they gave great love to Sybil and himself, but it brought Sybil to a horrible death and made his own life a sombre and a dreary thing.

No ; he mustn't let his mind wander like this ; he must keep his thoughts on the crops. Nothing like the crops for keeping a man busy. Also, the training of the men, in compliance with Florence's wish, helped to keep him from brooding too much.

His thoughts turned to Lord Kerry. Poor Lord Kerry ! And what thanks does he get for his loyalty to the Crown ? None ! In England he is, no doubt, suspected of being an Irish rebel. It was always the way with the King's men in Ireland : English to the Irish and Irish to the English. The more he thought about it, the more sure he was he had done the right thing in coming in with the patriots. It hadn't been very hard so far but his experience of life warned him there might be storms ahead ; for the Irish couldn't win all the time. What of the mighty army, Lady Kerry said was " a-preparing for to come over " ?

A thin, harsh scream rent the air ; it was like the cry of a woman and it came from the Castle. Some poor creature going demented as likely as not. God ! Would the siege ever end ? The screams were repeated ; and there was a pitiable sobbing and then silence.

He looked again at the moon. How beautiful it was ; see how it turned the stream to silver, and how it lighted the little town with a ghostly glow. How beautiful the three Stacks Hills yonder, like the beauty of chastity ; the cold ivory of chastity.

He thought of his boyhood days ; how different was the old town then with its air of contentment, and the bustle of the market days, and the good cheer in the taverns ; to listen to the mercers ply their trade, and the haberdashers with their nimble tongues, and to watch the weavers, the spinners and the tanners. And afterwards to walk up Clahane towards Glen Scotia ; it surely was a restful change from Latin verbs to run along the mossy banks amid the clusters of fern and furze ; and to sit by the stream and listen to the piping of the blackbird on a yet leafless thorn as she busied herself with her nest.

The sentry accosting somebody brought him back to reality. There were voices and then steps on the stairs.

" A visitor to see you, Captain," the subaltern said.

" Name ? "

" Moriarty ! "

" I'm coming."

Father Thaddeus Moriarty of the Order of St. Dominic stood in the mess-room, wearing now without let or hindrance the habit of his order. His fine dark face had changed little and his blue eyes still held their merry twinkle ; but his hair was slightly more grey.

" You scarcely expected to see me, Pierce."

" Well, not for some time, Father. So you got my message : we want you here badly. You'll stay, of course ? "

" Yes, if you want me."

" I'm very glad of that. I'm afraid your quarters aren't very good, but you'll share with the officers."

" Anything will do, Pierce, thank you. How quiet the old town has got."

" Yes, like a grave, isn't it ? There's a fine view of the castle from the top window here : would you like to see it ? "

" Yes, if you don't mind."

Both of them climbed the narrow stone stairway and then, keeping well in the shade, gazed across at the grim pile.

" Beautiful, isn't it ? "

" Yes ; has there been any pillage, Pierce ? "

" None ! "

" I suppose our old friends Harrison and Gabriel are with the rest."

" Yes, the herd instinct gripped them all."

" But a cultured fellow like Harrison in that filthy dungeon —a man that loves books and reads Master Shakespeare."

" War is war, Father Thaddeus."

" But still—"

" Yes, I agree. Do you think it's a pleasure for us to listen to the screams of the women as disease and hunger gnaw at their sanity ? Why didn't Walter Ware and the rest of our friends stay where they were ? We shouldn't have harmed them."

" How were they to know that, Pierce ? Who was to tell them you were with the patriots ? How were they to think about anything, poor creatures, as they ran with their few chattels to the shelter of those walls ? You must remember the terrible reports from the north ; that the Irish there strip their victims naked and turn them out to the winter frost. It's hard to blame them for not staying."

" I suppose so, Father."

" I wonder what they do all day ? "

" Curse Denny, I suppose."

The priest smiled.

"By the way, here is a letter Lady Kerry sent me."

"Beginning ' Honest Pierce ' ? "

"Exactly : she never forgets it."

"She doesn't like your joining the Irish, I presume."

"Joining the Irish ! Little did she think she'd live to see me among that vile crew, she says. Poor Lady Kerry : she had such faith in human nature. Let's get back to the light where you can read it."

Returning to the mess-room, he handed Lady Kerry's letter to his friend.

"No, Pierce," he said as he returned it, "she won't be pleased with you when her suspicions are confirmed. This rising seems to have finished Lady Kerry and her set."

"Inevitable : I've wanted them for years to strike against Denny and his likes. Now it's too late."

"True : they might as well be rebels for all the thanks they get."

"Would you care to meet the others and see the defences ? "

"Nothing I'd like better."

They went over the bridge to the Island of Geese. Just as they reached the other side, a sentry sprang out from behind a pillar.

"Halt ! Who goes there ? "

"A friend Micil : don't you know me ? "

"Pardon, Captain."

"Excellent, Micil : that's what we want. Anything stirring ?"

"Not a mouse, Captain—except that screaming."

"Yes, yes ! dreadful. Well, good night, Micil."

"Good night, Captain."

They went on.

"You see, Father, our men can be relied on : they're keen young fellows."

They crossed the Market Square to The Golden Key.

"Florence and the others are quartered here in Walter Ware's. You'd better be careful : stray bullets often come this way. Would you like to get a closer view of the castle before we enter the inn ? "

" Yes ! "

They walked down by the shelter of the wall. Across the river, the huge, gloomy pile seemed like a house of the dead.

" You've discussed terms, of course ? "

" Yes, twice."

" What were they ? "

" A safe conduct to Cork with their baggage."

" And what did they say ? "

" Harris said he wouldn't surrender it to any rebel in Ireland."

" Denny wouldn't have held out like that."

" Not on your life : neither would anybody else ; but Harris, for all his faults, has character."

" Evidently : so much the worse for him."

" But come, let's return and meet the others."

Pierce was glad they hadn't again discussed his marriage. The last time it was Father Thaddeus, the realist, who championed romance against romantic turned sour. It had been unsatisfactory, each talking at cross purposes. At least so it seemed to him. Only a very sensitive soul broods as long as you have, his friend said. Hearts aren't as brittle as all that ; everybody naturally thinks there's nothing comparable to his own misfortune ; besides, you keep going round in circles ; one moment blaming fate, the next yourself.

" No, Pierce, what you want is another wife," he concluded.

" Another wife, Father ! but surely—"

" Yes, I mean it, Pierce."

Impossible ; for his heart lay forever in the stoney silence of Dun Urlan. If he could help it, there would be no further talk of wives or marriages.

CHAPTER XXV

FLORENCE AND RICHARD were in the inn as they entered ; and there was a hearty handshake, and they spoke for some time of the old days. Then, after supper and a general introduction to the officers, Pierce and his friend had a long talk alone. The conversation turned inevitably to their old companion, O'Daly.

They spoke of that evening when O'Daly sailed with the cargo of wool from Barrow. He reached Louvain safely, though the little ship was followed for a while off Southampton by a man-of-war; but they shook it off and eventually reached the Lowlands. He was happy in that Louvain, where Bonaventura O'Hussey; Nuala and Maighreid, the sisters of Red Hugh; Domhnall O Domhnaill and Aodh Mac Cathbarr O Domhnaill all slept their last sleep.

At that time there were but five of the fathers there. They had got a disused chapel and a small house beside it, but funds were scarce and besides, boys were constantly coming from Ireland. The Franciscans, especially Father Ward, were good friends; but it was a struggle.

One day, however, Isabella, governor of Belgium came to visit him. She asked him where he came from and enquired much about his younger days. She was deeply interested in his story of the Abbey at Tralee and said it was her wish that the bell would ring out from the steeple once again. She had often heard of Kerry; for indeed how could the Royal House of Spain forget the sinking in the Blasket Sound of the Santa Maria de la Rosa, with the King's son on board?

Then he showed his distinguished guest through the little building. She could not but see how inadequate it was. She asked him if he would care for a bigger house, telling him there was a vacant one near the chapel of Saint George. She would not hear of a refusal and a few days later, when he undid the royal seals and found that not only had the fathers got a house; but also a pension of one thousand, two hundred golden crowns a year.

In no time, the place was a hive of activity and all Louvain got to know the fine figure of the Kerryman striding through the streets in his familiar black and white. Everybody seemed to want to consult him about one thing or another. Isabella telling her nephew, Philip IV, about him, he naturally wished to see him. So to Spain he went. That was, of course, when

Spain and Portugal were united and before the present war broke out.

The King graciously received him and on no circumstances would permit his return to the Lowlands. He noticed his rare skill in dialectic; his quickness to grasp point at issue; his command of languages together with his natural ability as an Irishman.

He spent some time visiting Lugo, Burgos and the other places in northern Spain, where both he and Father Thaddeus spent so many happy years. Finally, he settled at Lisbon because he saw there was more to be done there. Many years before that a brief was given for the founding of a college for Irish boys coming abroad to join the Order; but the plan had made no headway. So Father Dan said he would make a beginning. With the King behind him it should not be too difficult. He got a small house and soon boys began to flock from Ireland. But the great trouble was money; money; money. There never seemed to be enough.

A few years later, the Countess de Atalaya offered him her country house at Belem, near Lisbon, as a convent for Irish nuns, also of the Order of Saint Dominic. He gladly accepted it and at that very time Father Thaddeus was trying to arrange for some young ladies to travel out there.

"Imagine a boy from Kerry rising to such eminence."

"Tralee might well be proud of him, Pierce. In years to come you'll see a monument to his greatness in the finest street; and men will vie with each other to do him honour."

"True, Father, provided we drive out the Dennys."

"I agree; but I've more to tell you. It's whispered that he's now employed by King Philip on a secret mission to King Charles of England."

"I wonder if we could get the King's consent to restore the old Abbey."

And then he told him that King or no King, they were going back, and that he had heard Major Mac Carthy had given orders that it be put in a fit state for worship; and how even more wonderful, King Charles himself had given permission to return to the Abbey. It happened thus. There was a banquet at Whitehall for the new Ambassador from the Court of King Philip. The lights from the crystal candelabra shone in the glass and silver on the long table, at whose head were seated King Charles and his Queen, Henrietta Maria. Down on one side were the representatives of the Lords and Commons and on the other the diplomatic corps. The King looked pleased. He liked functions like this and besides he was trying to cultivate good relations with His Most Catholic Majesty. " Gentlemen, to the Envoy from our brother of Spain," the King said, getting on his feet. They all rose, with the exception of the Envoy himself, Daniel O'Daly in his friar's garb. He was doubly proud —proud for the honour being done his master, but prouder perhaps that diplomatic immunity allowed him wear his white wool in the very teeth of heretical opposition. When they were again seated, he rose to propose the toast of King Charles. In a short speech, he paid all the usual compliments but towards the end his sentiments ran away with him and he broadly hinted that relations between both countries would be far more cordial if only England would relax somewhat the penal restrictions in Ireland. " Where there is a measure of toleration in Ireland," he said, " it depends on the whim of an official. In my own native town of Tralee for instance, Your Majesty, our priory is still used by stray cattle. My brethren live in a rented cabin ; and sometimes even that meagre shelter is denied them by Your Majesty's squire in those parts, Sir Edward Denny."

" How wonderful."

" Yes, Pierce, and how wonderful for us, his old school-fellows. You know, I suppose, that Portugal now wants to break away from Spain. I admire her courage in singeing His Majesty of Spain's beard. It must have been a hard choice for our friend, but he ultimately threw in his lot with Portugal. Thus, all his hopes are now bound up with that brave little kingdom. And what happened ? The Court was just as quick to see the merits of this outstanding friar as was that of King Philip. He moves in the most intimate circles. No important step is taken unless Father Dominic O'Daly be first taken into the royal confidence. He has become confessor to Lucia, the

Queen. And the extraordinary part of it is that he has refused all honours, ecclesiastical or civic. They wanted to make him Archbishop of Goa ; then Bishop of Braga ; but he would have none of it. ' I came abroad,' he would say, ' to help my poor Ireland ; not to reap honours for myself or crown myself with splendour.' That is the Daniel O'Daly we knew, Pierce ! "

" Yes, I can still see Dan in my mind's eye, the day I upset the apples in the Market and we ran down the river with Paul Jones at our heels," said Pierce.

" And then he took us from shop to shop ; first to Nathaniel Harrison's. Poor Nathaniel ! I hope God is good to him over there. And next to Manuel Gabriel's. Did Manuel ever discover the philosopher's stone, I wonder ? "

" He has plenty of leisure now for it."

" Yes, poor soul ! Man's inhumanity to man. Why can't we live at peace ? Why must we have these rebellions and wars ? I know what you'll say, Pierce. Our rights and liberties and all that. But, truly, wouldn't you far prefer old Nathaniel's company with his folio of Master William Shakespeare spread on his knees, than many of our so-called friends and allies."

" That's the difficulty. Of course I would. Something within me made me turn my back on Lady Kerry and her set ; but there's no denying that many of our brother Gaels lack much of the accomplishments of civilized existence."

" And what will it be if we don't rout the robbers this time ? "

" Well, I suppose as the poet said the other day : Rest and peace to Ireland's bones."

" Yes, rest and peace, Pierce. That reminds me of that laybrother I met lately, the poor brother Michael O'Clery. He doesn't seem to think we stand any hope of maintaining our separate existence. He says that once the Parliament have the Royalists out of the way, and it seems very like it now, that it will send over such an army as was never before seen in this land. And God help us then."

" You mean we'll lose everything ? "

" Well, this poor brother Michael O'Clery is feverishly collecting every piece of parchment he can lay his hands on and sending it over to Father Ward in Louvain."

This, too, was another beautiful story, as moving in its own way as the career of Father Dominic O'Daly. In many ways Father Ward was different from the usual ; he had vision. He was about to compile a series of lives of the Irish saints and his search for manuscripts brought him over much of Belgium, France, Italy and Germany. In Paris he met a young man, Patrick Fleming, an excellent student who felt inclined towards the religious state ; so much so, that he joined the Franciscans at Louvain.

When he had finished his studies and been ordained priest, Father Ward, who was going to Rome, chose him as his companion. In Paris, he told him his ambition to preserve for posterity some little of Ireland's past. The younger priest was a ready listener and thereupon they pledged each other to give every minute they could spare to finish this work. Continuing their journey, they searched for manuscripts and made known their plan wherever they stayed. On their return to Louvain, letters and bundles of parchment poured from everywhere in Europe—from Clairvaux, Obrier, Lyons, Bobbio, Rome itself.

But there was one drawback ; there was nobody in Ireland to collect the old records ; nobody sufficiently free from the daily round, or endowed with the necessary sustenance. It was the great problem ; who would tramp the lonely roads of Ireland searching, searching, always searching for manuscripts ? Such a one would be no ordinary man : he would need grit, as well as the finesse of a scholar and that rare gift of selecting the gold from the dross.

But one fine morning an extraordinary thing happened. At the door of the Franciscans in Louvain, a traveller knocked and asked to be taken as a laybrother, if the good fathers would have him. His name was Tadhg O'Clery and he had already a brother, a priest, among the friars. "Father," he said, as he sat in the waiting-room, "it would be the crown of my life's ambition if you would take me as a laybrother. I've walked Europe for twenty years, from Leyden to Montpellier and from Montpellier to Rome. I know some little thing about manuscripts."

" About what ? " asked Father Ward.

" I have worked in most of the libraries of Europe, Father if that is any qualification to become a laybrother."

Father Ward instantly saw he had found whom he wanted. The Order accepted the traveller ; and after his profession, the poor brother Michael O'Clery came to Ireland to continue his tramping. Often spies dogged his steps but he somehow kept on. From time to time he sent the fruit of his labours back to Father Ward.

The booming of a cannon brought both of them back to reality ; Pierce started as if wakened from a dream. For in truth it was a dream ; one of the most beautiful dreams in the world ; a sandalled friar tramping the bogs for scraps of writing ; guarding them as he would his life ; seeking a trusty sailor to bear them away to the Lowlands. After that it would be silence. Rest and peace to Ireland's bones !

Pierce was silent as he gazed at the embers. He had often heard of the peace and beauty of the Lowlands. Delightful Bruges with gondolas skimming past on its quiet canals bearing great ladies in silks and satins—the glorious churches with their priceless paintings—Bruxelles with its wonderful Hotel de Ville which told of the Middle Ages and the guilds—the friendly roofs of Louvain.

CHAPTER XXVI

THE CANNON BOOMED again ; the besieged were getting restless. An orderly hurriedly entered and saluted.

" Well, Sergeant ? "

" There's been shooting, Captain, near the river."

" Who disobeyed orders in going into the open ? "

" Captain Mac Gillycuddy and some men who arrived last night from Killarney."

Pierce turned to his friend.

" Excuse me, Father, but I must investigate this."

" Certainly, Captain ! "

A half dozen bodies lay strewn by the river bank directly in front of the Castle drawbridge. It would be death to anybody to remove them till the moon had waned, and that would be in an hour or so. He returned to the inn and begged to be excused by his friend.

Midnight had struck in the belfry of St. John's when Pierce and a half dozen men crept over the cobbles. The moon had gone but yet they took no hazards for they walked in single file close to the wall. As they came near the river they could dimly make out the corpses. Not a very difficult operation that ; each man was to rush out at a given signal, take a body and return. They stood in the shade for a few minutes ; all was as still as the grave.

" Go, men," their captain whispered.

He himself was the first to leap forward ; the others, with hunched shoulders, crept behind. They were as silent as the dead they were about to bring back behind their lines. This must be the corpse of Major Mac Gillycuddy thought Pierce catching the gleam of a jewelled sword-hilt. He caught the body under the arm pits and was about to drag it backwards when there was a flash from above and, oh God, the pain that shot through his left arm ! He could scarcely keep from crying aloud, but he had the presence of mind to fall flat on his face and lay still. There was further firing and he heard one of the men fall with a groan. He tried to look about him ; the place seemed strewn with figures, the dead and the quick mixed anyhow. He felt the sleeve of his jerkin grow moist, and the pain, that paralysing pain, seemed to shoot through him from his feet to the crown of his head. He tried to crawl on his belly. He moved a few inches. Then a few inches more. Some of the others were doing the same. Again shots rang out. Damn their blasted souls. Blast them down to hell. Dear kind God forgive me ; stop this frightful pain. Help me to get back to the shelter of the lane. A few more yards, God !

He had dragged himself forward about two feet by now. He knew there were people waiting in the lane. And then a rope coiled about him. He grasped it with his right hand. Then they began to pull. The left sleeve of his jerkin was now

quite wet ; but in a few more minutes they would see to that.
The pain, too, the red hot blinding pain, might perhaps not
last so very long. It couldn't last for ever. Maybe Eoin Ó
Callanain, the surgeon, will do something for me. There were
more shots. A bullet struck the cobbles a foot in front of his
head. Firing at the rescuers they were. But surely, God, the
scum of the Kingdom can't win all the time. We have them
cornered at last ; 'tis only a question of time ; only a question
of time, God. They're eating the rats, they're eating the cats ;
and there I go bumping, bumping over the cobbles, bumping
over the cobbles. But that pain, God ! And I hear others
being dragged, too. Good fellows all. Was there ever an
Irish soldier that wasn't ? For the green. This is the first real
pain I ever suffered for the green. If you want my life, God, I
give it to you. If you want my life for the green. And it won't
be long. It won't be long, for they're eating the rats ; they're
eating the cats. The traders of Tralee are eating the cats. A
pity they haven't the gombeen men of Dingle with them.
No, gombeen men ! 'tisn't for you she wails. No, gombeen
men, 'tisn't for you she sobs. She never even knew of your
existence.

And now they are all about me. They're lifting me up.
It's much better than the jumping and the bumping ; the
bumping and the jumping. And my dead hand. Where am I ?
What's happening ? For the rats and the cats, the cats and the
rats——.

*   *   *

Spring with its magic had broken upon the land before he
was able to go abroad again. He had suffered much but Eoin
O Callanain, the doctor, knew a little more about medicine
than a mere acquaintance with pills, powders and plasters.
Having skilfully extracted the ball from his elbow, he cauterised
the wound and tied ligaments in the forearm. It was a careful
piece of work. Then he slowly nursed his patient back to health.

He had lost much blood and many whom he met in his short
walks during those soft April days scarcely recognised in the
wan, pale features the once dashing Cavalier. It had even been

rumoured that he was dead; a report to which his friends quickly gave the lie.

One morning, a merchant on his way from Cork brought him a roll of parchment from another of his school friends, the priest Domhnall Mac Taidhg an Gharain. Quickly he untied the red silk ribbon. It was a poem, a beautiful poem, and his eyes danced with delight. Good old Domhnall!

"We praise the God of the elements that his beautiful white limbs were unhurt: indeed his escape without injury lifts a mist from the hills. We were struck dumb on hearing how his sensitive shapely hand, so tempered in the school of poetry, was hit by this stray bullet. It was, no doubt, a stern hand in combat—the hand of Fionn with the Fianna—but it was a generous hand, too, a hand that never refused anything to a poet. It was a hand desired of maidens. Yes, the young maidens sing his praises, as well as the scholar and the fighting man."

He showed it to Eoin, who was almost as pleased as himself. For Eoin had proved one of the truest and finest of friends. In those first days when Pierce had lost so much blood that it was feared he would not live, the surgeon waited by his bedside as if he had been his own son, and slowly nursed him back to health. He saw with gladdening eye the colour drain into the cheeks again and the lustre come back into the eyes. And when his patient could sit in the inn parlour he sat with him, too, and tell him of his early years in London town where he learned the art of the chirurgeon at Saint Bartholomew's great hospital in Smithfield behind the cattle market. He would tell him of the public anatomy at the Barber Surgeons' Hall and how he heard Dr. William Harvey say in a lecture that the blood goes round from the arteries to the veins in a perpetual circle. But of course, many considered this far fetched.

They were merry fellows, merry like all the students of the art of Galen and Hippocrates. Many a tavern they knew —was there ever a student of physic who didn't? Up and down Fleet Street and the Strand they used to roam, calling at The Sun, The Dog, The Triple Tun, and then over the river to the Globe Tavern. Sometimes, too, they stopped at the Mermaid in Friday Street, where old Ben Jonson used to quaff

the hours away. And right good sack they kept too. They
used to meet poets ; the place was full of them. Dreamy
fellows all, but when filled with sack they would talk to anybody.
There was a Henry Vaughan from Wales who would drink
till the cows came home and long after. Then he would start
reciting Anacreontic verses—those lines about filling the cup
and drinking oneself into a frenzy. There was also a poet
called Suckling, Sir John Suckling, a court poet and his friends ;
and another named Lovelace ; all Cavalier poets. And a great
pompous fellow called John Milton. But he didn't carouse :
far from it. No ; Master Milton had a mission in life ; he was
to be a high priest of poetry.

"That's what I like, Eoin ; I can never reconcile myself
to poets carousing in taverns ; it isn't done."

"No, not here, perhaps, but it is in England. This John
Milton fellow was, as I said, an exception. You should just
see him walking down the Strand. A fine-looking man, I'll
admit ; but by the way he cocked his head in the air, you'd
imagine we were all inferior to him. No fine fashions for him.
No, just a plain white starched collar and a suit of black. You
see he is one of those Puritans."

Then Eoin went on to tell him of his fears that the Puritans
would rule England soon ; how he had seen the mob rushing
through the streets the night Strafford, or Black Tom, lost
his head. "His head's off ! His head's off !" they kept shouting.
In one way it was hard to blame them, for the antics of the
Cavaliers would make a sinner in disgust turn saint ; but like
all reformers the Puritans go too far. They loathed little Laud,
the Archbishop, and had lately put him behind iron bars.
"Hocus-Pocus" and "Little Willy" they called him. They
jeered in public at the poor bishops of the Establishment and
pelted rotten eggs at them in their carriages. More and more
they defy the King. Some time before that, His Majesty ordered
five members of the Commons to be arrested for high treason.
The Parliament made no move in the matter. Thereupon the
King himself walked into the House but the five members had
disappeared before he came. The rest of the House calmly
awaited the entrance of His Majesty. In he strode and, glaring

round, demanded the five members to appear. But the whole assembly preserved a stony silence. Finally, baffled, he had nothing to do but take his leave.

Then King Charles stood absolutely alone. The Queen sailed with her jewels from Dover to buy munitions of war. The power of the Parliament grew and grew, till they wanted to appoint and dismiss the royal ministers and name the guardians for the royal children. " If I granted your demands," the King said, " I should be no more than the mere phantom of a King."

His great problems were arms and money. One day he demanded entrance to Hull, the magazine of the north, but they denied him. So the royal party withdrew from Westminster and joined their Sovereign at York. The Parliament, too, was preparing and any day, England would fight England.

Many such talks he had with Eoin till Spring had fully broken upon the land. Whitethorn on every hedge ; a golden riot of furze ; the blue of the mountain beyond. He would walk along the tiny winding roads lined with ash and hazel ; past the sycamore and beach which had just burst into green ; watch the meadows white with daisies. Each day he became stronger.

CHAPTER XXVII

THEN CAME SUMMER when the woodbine trailed along the hedges ; and the meadows turned to gold. He was now almost his old self. It was pleasant to see the cows pacing lazily homeward at milking-time. Myriads of red apples gleamed in White's, the Provost's orchards at Lohercannon and in Denny's empty acres at Carrignafeely ; and at night, as the dew fell, the scent of new-mown hay filled the air.

Still the siege went on. Then one day word came that Eoin Roe had landed at Lough Swilly on the last day of July. General Eoin Roe O'Neill—the very magic of his name put the men on fire—and the wine ran freely that night.

Eoin Roe had seen much since as a little boy he romped

upon the decks of the vessel that brought his uncles across the seas to exile. Such was the exuberance of the men that the hucksters, peeping over the parapets, feared for their lives. They thought there was a general attack preparing. Pierce sat with his fellow officers in The Golden Key. Even Florence was convivial and he chose to forget many of his former ideas about the great general. Pierce, with little demonstration sat back and sipped his wine. He listened to the songs and joined in the fun and felt that events had vindicated him, for years ago when he wrote those lines to his Eoin Roe, then far away in Flanders :

> If poesy have any truth at all,
> And if a Lion of the Gael
> Shall rule the lovely land of Fail ;
> O, yellow mast !
> O, roaring sail !
> Carry this letter o'er the sea !
> Carry the leadership from me
> To great O'Neill.

he was accused of undue partisanship towards an Ulsterman, one almost a foreigner. Why should Munstermen have an O'Neill to rule over them ? Why indeed ?

Your generosity exceeded all bounds, O Pierce Ferriter : wrote Donnchadh Maol Ó Suilleabhain. It was always the way : they could never get beyond their petty provincialism. That was the great fault of the native race, their jealousies.

"Well, Captain Ferriter, you've been vindicated and I congratulate you," Florence said.

The others raised their glasses towards him and all together as one man repeated his lines.

"Thank you, gentlemen," he said, when they finished.

Yes, it was a pleasant night ! And to crown all, old Diarmuid happened to be near and he came and played for them.

At times of introspection Pierce often wondered if he had the courage necessary to play the man ; it was easy to talk and prate and make speeches—aye Florence, talk is cheap ;

it was so easy to tell other people what to do and it was simple enough even to write patriotic verses and deliver eulogistic harangues; but the thing most important was to feel within you that you wanted to follow in the wake of so many gone before, whether they died for their religion or because they wished to strike a blow for the old land. Then, knowing that, one had but to act on it. Pierce knew he had strength to strike that blow; that he had all the ability necessary, the intellectual qualities, integrity, strength of purpose, but of one virtue he was doubtful and that was perseverance. Could he go through to the bitter end? That was the question he put to himself time and again: it is a question which every soldier must ultimately face as it is also one of the dominating principles of leadership. Could he persevere? The way was dark he knew and dreary and lonesome and there was but one ending—death, a cruel, savage death for times were then savage and cruel. With all the glamour of army life and military success, he knew somehow he was doomed. Yes, the blue and white and yellow might float in the breeze, and the planters might starve inside Denny's walls, yet the thought always kept running through his mind that his span of life would be short.

But he had to go through with it to the end, whenever that end would be. His finer nature, that better part of him, well knew the need for sacrifice—even death—to bring life again to the little Black Rose. The music had stopped; no, he must try and think of more cheerful things—things like wine and song; no, no women; no, never again.

Diarmuid was preparing to depart. "Please Diarmuid," the company chorused, "one tune more and then you may go." "I agree," said Diarmuid, "if somebody sings." That was the difficulty; who would sing? A few names were mentioned and finally the choice fell on Pierce. "Very well, I'll stand in the breach," he said, as he got to his feet. He wondered what he would give them; all his favourite songs raced through his mind. Yes, why not, "Cailin og a stuair me," again? He hadn't sung it since that day in Killarney long ago when they were on their honeymoon. Yes, three short days it was, one at Tralee, one at Killarney, and the third the return. He hadn't dared sing it since her death—but tonight was a night of nights ; in any case nobody knew the associations it had for him, and so what would be for them a beautiful song would be for him infinitely more than that, a re-creation of some of the most beautiful moments he had ever known.

He walked over and bent towards Diarmuid and told him what he would sing. Diarmuid left his hands wander through the strings for a moment or two and struck up that exquisitely tender air that had so captivated Sybil's heart.

And then he began to sing. He was wandering again with Sybil on that lovely day when she asked him to go to the waterfall at Torc with her. They saw the waves and tresses of foam lightly skip from ledge to ledge and they were reminded somehow of a dryad or some wraith-like priestess at the sacrificial rites amidst the groves. Everywhere at their feet was the mountain heather and the universal arbutus and the gleaming yellow of the furze, while here and there the ivy intertwined itself amidst the holly bushes ; there were ferns on mossy banks, while the scarlet berries of the mountain-ash contrasted bizarrely with the copper of the beech and the dark green of the firs. Yes, Sybil was beautiful that day, God how beautiful. The morning was slightly foggy but as they ascended the pathway above the waterfall the sun came out and soon Torc Mountain began to show itself through the mist. He held her hand as they walked over the rough stones and now and again he would stop to let her see more clearly the foliage of all possible tints, from red and orange to every shade of green, and to point out on Torc opposite the hundreds of small firs. Then along the ascending pathway they continued, this time with his arm around her lovely slim body. Further onwards the pearly whiteness of Muckross Lake showed itself through the morning's haze. And then as they sat on the seat in front of the cascade, he kissed her.

Afterwards he remembered her wondering why Nature gave so much of herself to Killarney.

"Just for the same reason, my love, that Nature gave so much of herself to you," he answered.

"And what reason is that, Sir Knight ? " she asked again.

"That you might stand apart from all other women, as Killarney stands apart from all other places, so that men would worship you both for your beauty," he answered.

She gave a delightful little laugh and stroked his cheek ; they were silent for a while and then she said :

"Pierce, will you sing for me ? "

"My love, of course I'll sing for you ; what would you like ? "

"You know well what I like, Master Ferriter."

"Very well, my darling ; of course, I'll sing it for you."

And then he sang that very song through which Diarmuid was delicately intertwining his threads of golden melody, and to which the company listened as if music had but then come down from Mount Olympus to stay with men forever as the choicest gift of the gods.

And then she asked an unusual question.

"Tell me, Pierce," she said, "would you die for the green ? "

"What an extraordinary question, darling ! " he answered, "why do you ask ? "

"Because so few women have done so ; because it seems to be the prerogative of men to have all the deeds to their credit, perverse as well as brave. It's rather a doubtful compliment the bard pays us when he says we never pillaged or plundered : we seem never to have done anything."

"Except rule the world, my darling."

"You really think we do, Pierce ? "

"Of course you do, and you know it."

"I often wonder ; sometimes I'm inclined to think it's a man's world, because it's men who do the real things, the fighting and so on."

"But Florence always says that real things are dreams when dreams are as realities."

"What did he mean by that ? "

"He meant that the real world of the spirit is hidden from materialists, in other words, real things are hidden from them, they are dreams to them, because the world of the materialist is based upon the physical which soon passes away."

"I see ; but to return to my original question, do you admire those who strike a blow ? Or do you think that going out for the green is a shibboleth, a mere remnant of," and here she thought for a word, " of an antiquated conception of motherland, a screen for pride and self-glory," she continued, and added quickly, " not that I think so, of course."

Then he told her how he had often thought over that very question in all its different phases and had made a few generalizations : Irishmen were somewhat different in their psychological make up to other nationalities, he said. When a young Spaniard or a Frenchman comes of age and begins to think, like all young men, that they are going to change the world and they begin to fashion strange new philosophies for themselves, it is religion which they doubt and even cast aside : with the Irishman it is different ; he never for a moment doubts his religion but he does doubt his patriotism ; he queries the veracity of that exalted picture of Ireland, the beautiful, sorrowing queen which he cherished so much as a boy ; he becomes cynical ; he commences to mock, like Florence. And just as in other countries some of the doubters never again return to the fold of religion, so here a few are lost to the cause of the Green.

"And we can ill spare even one," he said, turning to her with a smile.

And now as he sang the sweet words, Walter Ware's Tavern, old Diarmuid, and the faces looking up at him vanished and he was once more ascending that little pathway of bracken, azalea and hart's-tongue, and listening to the roar of Torc down below them.

He was greeted with tremendous applause ; for truly he had sung it well. They made him sing another, and this time it was the song about " fair Una " that he chose. That, too, brought back the misty Corrib and the whisper of the sedges in the moonlight.

After that old Diarmuid retired and their revels came to an end, but not before they had again toasted the royal Pope, His Most Catholic Majesty, King Louis, and finally their darling Eoin Roe.

CHAPTER XXVIII

SOON AFTER, General Preston arrived at Wexford, Cardinal Richelieu promised a thousand crowns. Surely the days of the Sasanach were numbered !

*   *   *

While the enthusiasm still ran high, Florence called for volunteers to attack the Great Castle with the Sow, and the men eagerly responded. He picked twelve as before with O'Sullivan Mor as their leader. One August night they stole across the river, and placing the Sow near the main gate, began to dig ; but scarcely had they begun, when the garrison heard them. They threw down blazing brands and, at length, one fell directly on the Sow. Then many more. Soon it was alight and the men had no choice but to run for it ; but the muskets on the battlements were aimed straight at the door ; for each man as he put his head out, had his brains blown away.

Then the hucksters continued to throw over brands till nothing remained below but one half-burnt corpse. On this a cat came and fed every day for several weeks.

It was at this time, towards the end of August, that Father Thaddeus, summoning a few friars ministering in the county, went back to the Abbey. Denny had left the roof but little else. Craftsmen roughly fashioned new stalls and other furniture, and temporarily filled the mullions with plain glass. The silversmith Charles Sughrue wrought, at the desire of the officers, a set of holy vessels which they gave to Father Thaddeus, the new Prior, to celebrate the home coming.

Swing back doors, higher yet ; reach higher immemorial gates, and let some of those who have joined the Great Majority return for a short while and hear the old walls ring with the chants as they did for four centuries. Come back from the Great Beyond and see the glory that is come once again to Desmond ! Ye ghosts of the Geraldines leave your cold tombs and take your place with the other spirits filing through. Where are you Gerald the Rhymer, and John of Callan, and poor wavering Garrett who lost his head in Gleann na nGeinte ?

Pierce sat thinking, thinking of the ghosts. Yes, there was Garrett now coming up the aisle. I can see you have your head on nicely again, Garrett. Had you to go to the Tower for it ? Did you bring it back underneath your arm or put it on here ? Is it firm, do you think ? Oh, and there you are Elinor, who used to wear Eliza's cast off gowns. Did you see her at all in your travels ? What kind of a gown is she wearing now ? And James Fitzmaurice, how do you do ? Well, too bad, James you didn't succeed with that rebellion. Did you make it up with the Burkes yet ? Come on lords and ladies, plenty of room, plenty of room. You make such little noise ! Do you hear the guns outside ? That's noise enough for anything. They must guess we're having a big day. And here comes John of Callan with, trotting by his side, Tomas an Apa. Did you make friends with the Mac Carthys yet, John ? And would you ever think in your day that old Harry would start a new church and level all these priories ? You mind the fine carving that used to be in the stalls, John. Well, the Dennys broke it up to make horse boxes. and you remember when the sun used to shine through the lancet windows, how the blue and purple and crimson would colour the friars' robes with variegated hues and make you think Father Prior had a purple patch on his bald pate. That was when you were a child, John, four centuries ago, and you used to wonder what the chants meant.

Yes, to direct our feet in the way of peace. Peace ! Peace ! If only we could bring peace to Ireland, John. Peace to England, too. The ending of the German wars. See there in front is Father Thaddeus Moriarty in cloth of gold, praying for peace. And do you hear the choir chant the words ? I don't know if ghosts can hear, or even see. But if you look about, for nobody will notice ghosts, you may see all our men, a real Irish army at last ; not a *corps de garde* like you used to have, John, or you Garrett, but an army well ordered, well trained. Old Irish and Old English have come together at last—and even some of the new English. What a pity you aren't with us, Garrett ! We might teach you some character. Do you remember the day you were waiting on the hillside watching the fight between the natives and the new English? You were waiting, Garrett, to congratulate whoever won. That was no way to bring peace to Desmond, that peace Father Thaddeus and we are praying for now. At least Father Thaddeus and the others. I don't seem able to pray to-day. I never can on grand days like this. The splendour takes hold of me and I sit and gape. See Florence over there with bowed head. I mean Major MacCarthy, our Commander, Garrett. Well, he looks devout and so does my friend Richard. That reminds me, I must say a prayer for Finian. Poor Finian, still beneath the Sow. See O'Donoghue striking his breast. He certainly means what he says. But I'd better keep my eyes on my book.

The doom written against Denny, with pride we his servants execute. And we also carry two-edged swords, ready to take vengeance upon the psalm-singers and robbers. Not vengeance for vengeance sake, but a lasting vengeance: to drive them forever from Desmond, back to their alleys in Bristol, in London, in Glasgow, the scum of two Kingdoms.

What is that you ask me, Gerald the Rhymer? You have an eye for poetry. Well, those are our soldiers with the great yellow and blue flag with the words: " For Christ and His Truths. " And the flag behind is green with a red band and a white cross and underneath the words : " Vivat Rex Carolus." They are marching up the aisle and when the solemn moment comes they will present arms and dip their flags in salute. Yes, it's a change from the spacious days of great Eliza and our James. Though Charlie is no great shakes, even if we have him emblazoned on our flag.

Pierce smiled as he looked up at Father Thaddeus. How solemn he looks in his cloth of gold, with his assistants bobbing round him. It is merely for that the good Queen would have your bowels out, Father. Wouldn't it be easier to take off your head and be finished with it.

Now who have we? Sir Walter Raleigh ! Ah, Sir Walter, how do you do? Surely you recognise the old place. You remember when Ned Denny had his horses here. A pleasant fellow, Ned. Maybe he's with you. No ! He couldn't get out. What a pity. He'd enjoy it, no doubt. You remember they said he was a courtier in the chamber and a soldier in the field.

As an honest ghost, Sir Walter, is that true now? Didn't he falter the smallest bit as he ran his sword through the men at Dun an Oir? And surely his tongue yielded to flattery when he coaxed the old Earl's six thousand acres from Eliza? But it was worth it, Sir Walter. Where would he get the like in England? Hard to come by a priory anywhere these days. He was just in time; took the bull by the horns, so to speak. But his grandson, the second Sir Edward, put up a poor show. Made a dash for it, he did, the sly fellow. That slyness is in the family. But he'll never see his six thousand acres again. Not if we can help it.

But who's that behind you, Sir Walter? Why bless my soul it's Sir Edmund Spenser. How is the Faerie Queene, Sir Edmund? She's not troubling you, you say. What is it then? Blood! Where? I can't see any blood. You mean you can't wipe it out. Nonsense, gentle Edmund; it's only your imagination. Your hands got like that from fowling or deer-stalking. Besides look behind you at my Lord Grey. See how high he holds his head. He was ever like that. Did you meet Fiach Mac Hugh O'Byrne since, my Lord Grey? Or perhaps that last encounter in Glenmalure was sufficient. You'd have revenge, would you my Lord Grey, when you came to Dun an Oir. I thought you were above that. I woundn't mind sneaking Spenser doing such a thing. Poet and all that he is, I never thought much of him. And Sir Walter? Well he always was a bigot. But you, a soldier! Denny you say. You're trying to put the blame on Denny. Really, my Lord Grey!

Are you happy here, my pretty ghosts? See the soft lights of the tapers; wouldn't they make even Ned Denny pray? But poor ghosts, I forgot your praying days are now over. You can but gaze upon, gaze back from the tomb with longing eyes upon these soft lights and swinging censer; and hear the organ steal through the chancel. You rattle your mouldy bones, poor ghosts, and you sigh. You look around at our army in the freshness of its manhood and you think of your own days on earth. But what a difference ! You pillaged and plundered ; ravin'd and raped. These young lads only want what is their own. They have seen the fair meadows of Iughuine laid waste.

Yes, laid waste by you, spirits, in the days of your pride and lust. Truly it was grief to us to see the Spouse of Criomthainn, Con and Eoghan make her bed with beggars, with beggars like you ; beggars for all your ruffs and cuffs and fine array. No wonder sorrow brooded on the plain of Art.

But not any longer, ghosts. Didn't you hear they're eating the rats, they're eating the cats, they're eating the rats in Traly ? Never again shall they lord it over the rightful rulers of Clar Ri Eibhear. For who could treat with them ? Who come to terms with robbers ? They used to sport with those seeking terms as does the cruel cat with its prey. But the cat has now no prey ; he has become lean, very lean, He hasn't water even to drink. There are sores on his body, putrid sores. That's what comes of the rout of the royal rulers of Clar Fodla and the extinction of the House of God. But vengeance is not ours ; we want only justice. For that we pray. For that Father Thaddeus and his ministers in golden robes pray. For that the patriot army in the trenches round Tralee pray— pray that they may reap the fruit of their evil deeds.

No doubt about that now, with Eoin Roe in command. Just when he was needed he came. And from the University of Salamanca. If anybody can do it, Eoin can. For Ireland and my poor Ulster. My poor Ulster ! 'Twas what he dreamt of as a boy, as a boy on his way to Spain. That was why he joined the Spanish army, an army which still boasts the best soldiers in Europe. At first Sergeant of Halberdiers in the Royal Foot Guards ; then to the Lowlands where he fought with, and later commanded, the tercios. Next a Colonel of Foot. Eugenius Rufinius O'Neill ! Or Eoin Roe O'Neill. Was that better ? Or plain Eoin Roe ? Not that a name mattered much. 'Twas the generations before him that mattered. How many generations go to the making of a Prince ? A real Prince ? None other shall we have to rule over us. I'm

glad I sent him those lines.   How they keep ringing in my
ears :

> If Poesy have any truth at all,
> And if a Lion of the Gael
> Shall rule the lovely land of Fail !

Yes, good lines.   Ferriter you're getting good.   Surely
not lines to be ashamed of.   I like "Lion of the Gael."
I wonder if they'll agree to have him King.   I don't see why
they shouldn't.   Or will they begin another "Contention of
the Bards" ?   Is Munster better than Ulster ?   Or the other
way round ?   Are the O'Neills above the O'Briens ?   And
to think that twenty years ago sane men, ollamhs in the Bardic
Schools, nearly came to blows on that question.   Like the
cat and the fox who both killed the plump swine, they
agreed the one who could claim seniority should have the fat.
But during the argument a wolf came up and swept everything
away.   So was it with the wranglings between Leith Chuinn
and Leith Mhogha.

Of course we'll have Eoin Roe rule over us.   Fie on you,
Donnchadh Maol Ó Suilleabhain, and your provincialism.
Here Captain set your ship and carry this letter to the great
Lion of the Gael.   Tell him, tell him we want him and will
bend the knee to none other.   Tell him we trust neither the
old nor the new English ;   that the old proud race, and none
other have the rightful title to this fair land.

> O, yellow mast, O roaring sail
> Carry this letter o'er the sea,
> Carry the leadership from me
> To great O'Neill.

But come ghosts, poor ghosts.   That's the final Amen.
Do you hear the victory in their voices ?   Come along ;   you
can't stay here.   Yes, Gerald the Rhymer, make the others come
on.   Don't forget your head, Garrett.   Oh, I forgot ;   it's on
again.   No, it's Sir Walter Raleigh I meant.   Sir Walter, mind
the step, and don't let your head fall.   Tell Eliza and James

when you go back that they should have some other way of
getting rid of unwanted subjects. It must be awkward to
have to carry your head under your arm. No, Sir Walter,
that's not the road ; that's the road to Dingle. Whatever do
you want to Dingle for ? This is the way back to Hampton
Court or whatever place you haunt. Goodbye, goodbye,
all of you. Yes, come again anytime you like. 'Twas so
pleasant. Don't forget to remember me to Eliza, Sir Walter !

CHAPTER XXIX

AUTUMN LIT the valley with flame and clothed the mountain
with many hues ; and then October winds sighed round the
Castle walls.

"Surely they won't keep us another winter," said Pierce
one day to Florence.

"It's difficult to say, Captain ; there's a rumour that Denny's
sending a ship to raise the siege."

If Florence but knew it, there was plenty of foundation
for this rumour. An adventurer named Alexander Lord
Forbes was at this time off the southern coast and the President
of Munster tried to get him to go to the relief of either Tralee
or Sligo, where help from the sea would make every difference
to the beleagured garrisons. But Forbes spent a few days
harrassing the Arran Islands and arriving at last at Ballingarry,
the fortress on the coast near Ballyheigue, he heard that Tralee
had fallen.

"But the garrison doesn't know about this help, Major,"
said Pierce.

"Again it's difficult to say ; it's extraordinary how news
travels."

"Spies ? "

"We can't rule them out, Captain Ferriter."

It was winter. The scream of the gull and the call of the
plover came over the misty waters of the Bay. Surely Tralee

Bay was the bay of birds—countless birds circling and ever-circling, swooping and ever-swooping—the sky alive with them. Near the shore the swans were a vivid white against the dull green. In January there was a fortnight's frost; the men in their comfortable quarters could scarcely bear the cold; and in the Castle there was little fuel.

On a grey, freezing morning they raised the white flag; quickly they opened the main gate and two men marched out. Florence and Pierce went to meet them.

"Sir Thomas Harris, I presume," said Florence to the taller.

"Sir Thomas Harris died a month ago; to whom have I the honour of speaking?"

"Mac Carthy, and this is Captain Ferriter."

He saluted.

"I'm Richard Jackson, Sir Edward Denny's chief steward, and this is Captain Fell."

Florence and Pierce saluted.

"You've won gentlemen," Jackson said, "due to greater odds. Your terms?"

"The same terms I offered Sir Thomas Harris ten months ago: I shall give each man a suit of clothes and allow him to join any garrison he wishes in Desmond."

"What about the women and children?"

"No conditions whatever; they may go wherever and however they wish."

"How shall we march out?"

"In the usual way, with pennants flying and drums beating; you shall have an armed escort for ten miles."

"What of our possessions?"

"What do you mean—possessions?"

"I mean money and trinkets and such like."

"They fall to the victors."

"But Major Mac Carthy—"

"Master Jackson, I've said what I've said. It's my last word: take it or leave it."

"Is there no alternative then but to accept, gentlemen," said Jackson.

"No alternative," was the reply.

Florence ordered Captain Richard Hussey with his company to enter the Castle and receive the surrendered arms. There was little rejoicing, for who could rejoice over so many broken men and pitiable women? They handed up their arms, listlessly, and then stood sullenly by.

"You may form into marching order, gentlemen, and go your way," said Florence.

Pierce called him aside.

"I wonder if we should let these poor wretches go away with nothing," he said.

"Why not, Captain Ferriter?"

"Well, it's the middle of winter and they surely should be allowed some of their belongings."

"They should consider themselves lucky to be allowed go as they are."

"I've been talking to the rest of our men about it."

"And what did you say to them, Captain Ferriter."

"I offered to give up all my own share of the booty if they'd restore one-third of theirs."

"And what do they think of your humane intentions?"

"Some of them are willing enough; but the final word rests with you."

"Fiddlesticks, Captain Ferriter, fiddlesticks. They're lucky to be left go as they are."

He looked once more at the miserable rabble.

"Gentlemen, you may form your column," he called sharply.

The glow of health was gone from the once plump cheeks of the Reverend Devereux Spratt. He looked incongruous in a suit too big for him. He rubbed his hands in misery and shuffled towards Pierce; every step seemed to pain him.

"Please, Captain Ferriter," he said, "will you help me to get to Ballybeggan?"

"Why Ballybeggan, Mr. Spratt?"

"Because all my friends are there; at least they were there the last time, the last—"

He sunk his head and said no more.

"Very well, Mr. Spratt; I shall do my best."

Some more of his old time friends, pale as ghosts, approached.

There was Nathanial Harrison with an ulcer on his neck. And poor Walter Ware, broken, miserable. Somebody said Manuel Gabriel had died, and nobody seemed to have any tidings of Tomás Rua.

" Friends," he said, " I shall help you as far as I can. Here's some money ; go and buy yourselves food."

An hour before noon he set out for Ballybeggan with the Reverend Devereux Spratt. Their progress was slow as the clergyman could scarcely sit on a horse ; but nevertheless he was able to keep conversation going. He told his escort much of the inner workings of the siege. He said that Harris should never have taken in the four hundred extra refugees ; that there was almost a mutiny when the men learned what had happened ; they had had a stormy meeting the day he admitted them and made him promise on oath that for the future he would make no important decision without the consent of the majority of the garrison.

" He always was obstinate you know, Captain Ferriter ; but yet he was a brave Englishman and none died that night with greater glory."

He also told him of the murmurings of the men against Denny—Denny who had left them in the lurch.

" But Captain Ferriter, all the Dennys were like that ; they always saved their own skins."

And so on ; he said that poor old Tomás Rua had died very early in the siege, but it was in describing the pitiable scenes of hunger and the search for water that made Pierce catch his breath, and even sometimes bow his head with grief.

He said that after seven months the victuals gave out; then it was the rats and the cats. But he was forgetting : there was another thing. In the grounds was an Elizabethan Knott Garden. Exquisite it was with its beds of every shape and size, filled with carnations, cowslips, roses, violets and primroses. There, too, were lilies of all kinds, Madonna lilies and the flower-de-luce.

" But they dug them all up, Captain Ferriter ; they dug them all up to make broth ; and then after that they began eating the cats ; hard to get a cat anywhere in the end. That brought on a plague of rats, but they also soon quickly disappeared. We somehow got used to it, Master Ferriter."

All during the siege of Tralee, Colonel David Crosby was entrenched at Ballingarry with a garrison of two hundred. The place was practically impregnable, for when the drawbridge was up, it would have taken a great deal to induce the garrison to surrender, especially as Lord Inchiquin, with the assistance of Forbes, supplied them with provisions from the Clare coast.

It was to this fortress that most of the men and women from the Castles of Tralee marched on that winter's day. They were accompanied the whole way by a guard at the front and rear, and placed by Florence under the commands respectively of Captains Mac Elligott and Mac Gillycuddy. St. Leger later on commended Crosby to the notice of parliament because he " hath defended at his own proper charges two hundred troops, within his own fort at Ballingarry, and relieved two hundred refugees from Traly."

Later on Crosby came to terms with the Confederates and was allowed enter the castle at Ballybeggan. Devereux Spratt left Ballybeggan again ; he tells us that after preaching to the Protestants there he went to Ballingarry, where he fell sick. He soon returned to Ballybeggan, however, and from thence went to Cork, where he got a pass to England from Inchiquin.

III
CRAFTY COUNCILLORS
The Poet Watching

AFTER THAT most of the officers and men, including Florence, went to join the forces of Lord Muskerry and General Barry who held the centre of Munster. Pierce and Richard wanted to go, but Florence disuaded them. "We must leave someone to watch the west," he said. "Far better to bring your men back to Corca Dhuibhne, Captain Ferriter, and see how events work out." The patriots also left a small garrison under Mac Elligott at Tralee to guard against the return of odd planters; and to prevent Murrough of the Burnings, Earl of Inchiquin, now on the prowl around Desmond, coming thither.

Eoin O Callanain and a few score of the men, seeking adventure on a wider scale, tramped their way to the North to join the army of Eoin Roe. A lesser number went to Kilkenny to enlist with the Leinster men under General Preston. With them went Father Thaddeus who was a delegate to a chapter in the Black Abbey. O'Donoghue and Browne, also by orders of Florence, returned to Killarney to watch and wait, but keeping their men in training. Henry Lawrence felt his duty to the King obliged him to go back to England.

Thus Pierce came back to Castle Sybil and to the quiet of the hills. Robert was glad to see him ; he had kept the place going as best he could but with all the men away at the wars there were few to do anything on the land. However that could be quickly righted ; it was only February and before many weeks the ploughshare was well polished by the clean red sod. Pierce was very unlike the young man who had returned years before to his father full of academic theories. He knew how to handle the men ; how to get from them honest labour and loyalty. But still he had the vein of poetry in him and sometimes at night when Robert lit the lights and put fresh rushes on the floor, he would scratch away with his quill, fashioning and re-fashioning a poem.

For the times were pregnant with hopes, with ideas, with dreams. The patriots' cause was in the ascendant and it seemed as if victory might finally be theirs. They bound themselves by oath never to lay down arms till the Catholic religion, in all its splendour, was restored.

" Ye faire citie " of Kilkenny presented a brilliant facade, and even began to take on the airs of a capital. High street and John Street were full of colourful uniforms, and down by the Tholsel any day one could hear Italian, French and Spanish ; emissaries from His Majesty constantly came and went as well as couriers from the courts of King Louis XIV, Anne of Austria, and the city states of Italy. And over all waved the great blue flag with the white cross with the words : For Religion, Covenant, King and Kingdom. In Rome, Father Luke Wadding urged His Holiness, Pope Urban VIII, to grace the Confederation with a nuncio.

These reports reached Corca Dhuibhne by several means ; generally by the galleons and fishing boats putting into Smerwick during stormy weather ; sometimes through a Dingle merchant ; and less often by a direct despatch from Florence whose summing-up of a particular situation was generally concise and lucid.

Murrough of the Burnings and Lord Broghill were mainly on the southern coast, he said. Ormond, setting out from Dublin with a large force tried to cut a passage into Munster to join them ; but the brave people of New Ross drove him back. Murrough then laid siege to Kilmallock but the Confederates under Lord Castlehaven marched against him and cut to pieces a portion of his forces near Fermoy. The patriots then prepared to march further afield but soon ceased operations as Kilkenny announced it was negotiating a truce with the wily Ormond.

Then Father Scarampi, the envoy or pro-nuncio, arrived from His Holiness, bringing muskets, pikes and swords from the forges of Milan, and thirty thousand crowns which the friar, Luke Wadding, had collected. By this time the truce had been signed but Father Scarampi was quick to see how little in common the Catholic lords of the Pale had with the native race, that the oath of association was the " only essential tie " between them. They were loyal to the King first and to Ireland after. They could not, or would not, understand the intransigeance of the proud Gaels whom the centuries had well taught to be wary of England. There was jealousy and suspicion on all sides ; for this planter stock had for countless generations hated " the savage old Irish " ; and the native race, who knew themselves for the real Irish, returned hate for hate. In vain for my Lord Trimbleston, my Lord Slane or my Lord Fingall to echo pious platitudes in the chamber ; the real Irish led by Eoin Roe, knew the lords of the pale were full of trickery ; that those who ultimately signed the truce were the creatures of Ormond ; and that Ormond's one object was to sow the seeds of jealousy and dissenison among them.

The truce, Florence said, was of no benefit whatever to the old race. It was sought for only by a desperate King in desperate straits. When it was duly signed many of the Leinster regiments crossed the sea to Chester " to deliver His Majesty out of his troubles." Another one of the terms was that help be sent to Scotland ; so in due course two thousand five hundred men landed on the Scottish coast to assist Montrose.

There was also a letter from Henry Lawrence. He was now an officer in the King's own regiment at Oxford. The tide had begun to turn against His Majesty, he said. At first the Parliament thought one battle would decide the issue, for the King had little arms or money but His Majesty, nothing daunted, raised the Royal Standard. He met the forces of the Parliament at Edgehill and the result was a draw. He then fell back on Oxford, which received him royally. This gave him a grip on the midland counties while the Parliament held London and the east. Then Cornwall rose and joined the Royalists ; and Bristol surrendered to Prince Rupert. It seemed as if Charles would win the day and the citizens of London even considered asking for terms.

But it was at this point precisely the King's star began to wane ; for the truce with Kilkenny threw the Scots into the arms of the Parliament. Irish papists, forsooth ! No, Your Majesty ; anything but that. Even his own officers flung down their swords ; and the Commons, with raised hands, swore death to popery.

Then the Parliament set to in earnest ; it raised three powerful armies, a force of fifty thousand men all told. One was put to watch the King at Oxford ; one in the west and another in the east. It was said that one of the officers in the eastern division named Oliver Cromwell had made a considerable name for himself. Sir Thomas Fairfax was in Yorkshire. In January, 1644, the Scottish army crossed the border and the Royalists marched from York to meet them. This gave Fairfax the chance to hurl himself upon the Irish troops recently arrived at Chester and cut them to pieces.

Then the Parliament gathered its troops round Oxford. The King, having got help from Wales, decided to make a stand ; and the two armies faced each other at Marston Moor one day in July. It was a complete rout for the Royalists and the end of their cause in the north. " God made them stubble to our swords," wrote Cromwell, whose brigade particularly distinguished itself.

But in the south Charles was doing well. He drove the Parliamentarians back to London and hemmed in another army in Cornwall. The Confederates duly landed their forces on the coast of Argyle ; Montrose called the clans to arms and spread terror from the Tweed to Aberdeen.

Eoin O Callanain in a message from the north said that

Munroe and his Covenanters held Carrickfergus and the surrounding country. Kilkenny, alarmed by their growing force, determined to march against them. To the bitter disappointment of Eoin Roe, they appointed Lord Castlehaven commander-in-chief. Immense preparations were made but Castlehaven was a poor soldier; the enemy harassed him so much that finally his army was reduced to half and the Confederates lost thirty thousand pounds.

It was at this point that Cromwell assumed real power. Born soldier that he was, he saw the great weakness of the Parliament's forces was that they could not drive home a victory. This was not due to lack of military skill but simply that they faltered before the great veneration and antiquity which surrounded the throne and the King's royal person. In a lesser way it was their deference to the chivalry of the Cavalier. "They are afraid to conquer," said Cromwell, and as a counter measure he began to work up his men to a frenzy of religious enthusiasm. At one battle they charged singing psalms.

Many of the old officers were retired and Sir Thomas Fairfax appointed the new commander-in-chief—though Cromwell was the force behind him. All the officers were young and not a few of them had been raised from the ranks.

In July of that year Pope Urban died and Belling, secretary to the Confederation was sent to Rome to congratulate Pope Innocent X on his accession and to implore His Holiness to send a nuncio. Belling besides being a fine linguist had " a winsome tongue " and much was hoped from him.

The patriots next determined to destroy Murrough of the Burnings and sent Castlehaven with a large force into Munster for this purpose. He wasted all the country to the very walls of Cork where Murrough had retreated. He returned to Kilkenny however leaving Broghill in possession of Youghal —a serious blunder.

Then the King sent the Earl of Glamorgan to discuss new terms. In return for ten thousand men he agreed to give them free and public exercise of their religion, and to allow them keep the churches they held since '41 and all the other ancient churches except those then in the possession of the Protestants. The clauses were not to have effect till the arrival of the nuncio.

Henry Lawrence again wrote from England and said the King's cause went from bad to worse. In June of that year— '45—he met the Parliamentarian forces at Naseby but was no match for an army that had been completely re-organised. Five thousand of his troops surrendered and two thousand followed their royal master in his flight along the Welsh marches. In Scotland the story was no better for Montrose had been disastrously defeated.

All this to Pierce was of vital interest. If only the King would be straight; but he never could. Always making promises he knew he could never keep; procrastinating; always seeking a loophole. Promising one thing to the Confederates and the very opposite to the Scots; embroiling whole kingdoms if that suited his own plans.

Not that old Ironside Cromwell could be trusted either, thought Pierce. A crafty devil Henry Lawrence called him. A plump, plainly-dressed fellow he was. They said he wielded immense power; that though General Fairfax was the commander-in-chief, it was Cromwell who held the sceptre.

As time went by there were signs that at last the routine of life was returning. The threat of famine had been averted and the men seemed to have regained the *savoir-faire* of King Jamie's days. Richard sometimes rode over from Castle Gregory and they would sit by the great log fire or stroll along by the stormy headland discussing the fortunes of this war of the three kingdoms. Often too a poet would come along, sometimes from as far away as Ulster, to ask the advice of Pierce about some matter of metre or rhyme. He would get lodgings for as long as he wished to stay; often two might come; or even three. Despite the grumblings of Robert they too were fed and housed. For hours Pierce would sit and talk with them, suggesting another word here, or alternate rhyme there. But during the past year their numbers exceeded all bounds; though it was a tribute to himself it was a tribute which might be expressed with less trouble to the recipient, as Robert broadly hinted.

But Pierce did not leave his own pen become idle during these busy interludes. Old Nicholas Pierce of Clanmaurice sent him a gift of a harp. Not since before his marriage had he played, though often during the dreariness of the siege he felt tempted to do so. When Sybil died, he felt that though he might listen to music, yet he could not find it in his heart to awaken the strings ever again to golden song. But somehow the beautiful instrument, as beautiful almost as a woman, tempted him. He sat down and began to adjust the wooden pegs ; then his fingers rippled over the strings. He first played in the Cruaidhchleasach or bold, heroic marching time ; but soon he turned to the Cuigrath or dirge time. That was the mode he thought which best suited his temperament ; and the harp responded as if it were a living thing. It seemed to whisper its approval and even strive to respond more and more to his wish. On and on he played ; the minutes passed ; an hour passed. It was like meeting an old friend, or like a draught of good red wine to a parched palate ; it was like gliding dreamily over golden waves and gazing at a sky of untroubled blue, listening to the lark, to the magic of his voice, for ever.

And softly, before he scarce knew, he was playing *Caleno o Casture me.* Yes, beautiful women—beautiful like crystal— how they grace the earth with their faery tread—no wars or ravaging of churches for them—no, peace was their world— peace and beautiful things—gracious things.

God, she was lovely that night, that night of his marriage, when Tom Trant gave an impromptu celebration for him at The Rose. She was dressed in pale blue, a flowing dress tight at the waist that spread out as it were in ripples around her and reached to the ground. Her eyes sparkled with all the brightness and beauty of youth and on her head she wore a little blue band of the same colour. He scarcely knew what he did when she looked at him ; and when she said she would like to dance he thought he was in the midst of a beautiful dream and at any moment he would waken and hear the wind howl through the draughty corridors of the castle. She was everything that a woman ever was ; and not alone had he his own eyes to see but the eyes of all The Rose as well ; heads

bent with furtive whisperings : " who was the damsel ? "
Surely someone of the English breeding from the Pale ; or
was she a Spanish senorita ? No, she was too fair ; it must be
English, or perhaps Irish-English ; those beautiful blue eyes
and golden hair could scarcely come from a Latin clime—.
And thus they went on. But he had better read what old Nicholas
said.

" My dear Pierce," the letter ran, " I'm sending you as a
gift the dearest object to me of all I possess. I'm now very near
the grave and I feel that somebody like yourself who puts a
value on real things should have this lovely instrument. As I
often told you as a boy, four craftsmen had the making of it :
Mac Sithdhuill planned the frame ; Cathal did the woodwork ;
Beannghlan and Parthalon Mor Mac Cathail the gold orna-
mentation. The pin board was got at Magh nAoi in Ros-
common ; the front pillar in Lios Seantraoi ; and the beautiful
slender waist at Eas Eagonn at the mouth of the Erne. Its
like, I can assure you is rare in these troubled times.

What the future will bring, who can tell ?

Pray for me,

Nicholas."

Pierce felt he must send nothing less than a poem in return ;
such a gesture from the old man surely merited the very best
that was in him. " No lord or chieftain," he wrote, " ever
possessed such a gift ; no King of Ireland ever had the like of
this instrument of the golden strings and soul-stirring strains,
as beautiful as a woman. Neither Laoghaire nor Niall nor
Brian nor Corc Caisil ever had such a treasure."
But Pierce had other things to do as well as poetry and
music. The men scattered throughout the four parishes had
to be brought together sometimes for parade drill ; their
muskets to be kept trim and powder ready ; the spinning in
the cottages to be speeded up and the weavers encouraged to
turn out more cloth ; for the uniforms of his own company
had become threadbare and besides, Florence had sent word

from Blarney, where Lord Muskerry had his headquarters that O'Donoghue, O'Sullivan Mor and the rest of them wanted more jerkins, trewes and hose. But above all the work on the land had to go on or else starvation faced them all. It was work for which Pierce did not feel himself fitted but, however, he did his best. At any rate there was none of the monotony of that year at Tralee. The weather was bright and vigorous and everybody hoped the young year would bring them none of the wind and rain of '41 and '42.

CHAPTER XXXI

IT WAS OCTOBER and one evening as Pierce was at supper, Robert announced Richard who had ridden over in haste.

"Have you heard the news, Pierce?" he said as he burst in upon him breathless.

"What news?"

"The Pope's nuncio has arrived at Kenmare."

"Kenmare! Why Kenmare?"

"Oh, I don't know; perhaps anywhere more southern would be too dangerous. But, at any rate, His Excellency's here at last. I hear the ship, the *San Pietro*, was chased by an English squadron for a great part of the way and only barely succeeded in getting here."

"Hm! I wonder what'll be His Excellency's first move?"

"I hear he's already on his way to Limerick."

"Then Kilkenny, I suppose; if anybody can settle the differences between both factions, it's he."

"I don't envy His Excellency; how did Father Thaddeus get on there?"

"He didn't stay long," replied Pierce. "He was a delegate at a provincial chapter and made only a short stay. The Confederate flag flew everywhere, he said, and coins were struck and taxes levied. It's within the past few months that the breach has widened; and now let's hope that with the nuncio's efforts 'twill close again. He's sufficiently aloof, Richard, from our affairs not to be so much influenced by the crown ; at least not so much as our fawning Anglo-Irish. But we'll see."

John Baptist Rinuccini, Bishop of Fermo, was accompanied by a small retinue. Everywhere he was joyously acclaimed. The bells rang, cannon roared and bonfires blazed from Brandon to Beann Eadair. People knelt in the street as he passed and tears of joy streamed down their cheeks. When last had there been a nuncio ? Nobody could tell. Men debated the question in taverns but could come to no certain conclusion. To think that after all these years of the barest toleration for, and more often active persecution against all they held dear, a new dawn had come at last, a dawn that would surely brighten into a glorious noon. Welcome Rinuccini ! " Cead mile failte," they shouted. Ring out bells your silver tones ; ring, ring to him, the blessed envoy of our Lord the Pope ; sing to him ye children and drop petals before his path ; bow down to him, ye people for the winter's past and the rain is gone ; the spring is come again and the flowers appear.

His first lodging was in a shepherd's hut in which animals also took shelter. To keep out of Murrough's way he went through the hilly country of Macroom and thence to Kilmallock and Limerick. He was met everywhere by foot soldiers and mounted troopers ; and at the great gate of Macroom Castle the Lady Helena, wife to Lord Muskerry received him. From thence onward he was accompanied among others by Dr. O'Connell who rushed across the mountains from Kerry to be the first bishop to greet him ; and by Boetius Mac Egan, Bishop of Ross. The friars gave him a right royal welcome at Kilmallock and arriving in Limerick, he found the whole city waiting at the gates to meet him. Then by slow stages he reached Kilkenny.

Again the city stood to receive him. Regiments of infantry lined the streets and the bells of St. Canice's and the Black Abbey rang out clear and loud as, wearing his pontificial robes, he rode through the streets. Onwards to St. Canice's he went, where amid the splendour of that brilliant congregation of clergy, lords and commons, a *Te Deum* was intoned.

But for all that the Anglo-Irish did not like him. No

Rinuccini, we don't want you, they said in their hearts. You see through our plans too readily. You know how we despise these tribes from the hills who of late have begun to strut about our beautiful city, built by us, Normans, for ourselves. Their Kilkenny! their Leinster! No Rinuccini! Back to their bogs they'll go as soon as King Charles is out of trouble. Do you think that but for His Majesty's difficulties we'd tolerate them for one hour? We're English by birth and breeding, Your Excellency; English too by language, custom and inclination and English we wish to stay.

In a very short time the nuncio saw indeed how matters stood and made no secret of his adherence to the cause of Eoin Roe and the real Irish. He saw the lords of the Pale were interested only in their "temporalities" and would be satisfied with the barest toleration for their Faith; they understood nothing of the "splendour of religion" of which he so often spoke and which he desired to see once more throughout the land.

There was little indeed of the "splendour of religion" in the terms of Glamorgan's treaty which Ormond's friends forced on the Council some time after. The King was to have his troops, no doubt about that—ten thousand of them; and in return the Catholics were exempted from the oath of Supremacy, the plantation was revoked in some parts of the country, with a few more minor concessions.

Away in Corca Dhuibhne Pierce was becoming restless. Having once tasted war he felt entirely cut off from the world in his remote peninsula. Why did Florence wish him to return to Duibhne? To dig? Just merely to dig? And at night-time puzzle his brains about Eoin Roe and Kilkenny. Whatever about Kilkenny, the valiant Lion of the Gael would surely do something soon. Perhaps he was biding his time; maybe he didn't yet consider his army in sufficient shape. Trust him not to do anything rash; 'twasn't for nothing the Spanish called Eugenius Rufinius O'Neill a most competent and illustrious officer.

Pierce heard again from Eoin O Callanain who was still in Ulster plying his trade in the army of Eoin Roe. It was easy work so far he said ; nothing but a pill or a plaster or perhaps an accidental pike thrust. But big things were coming ; for O'Neill had done wonders with the men. Before that they had been wandering round Ulster in ill-disciplined bands, robbing, fighting, drinking, wenching. Now all that was gone ; nobody knew how he did it. Something in his eye, O Callanain said, some fire which held the men and made them turn to any task. Grumbling there was and plenty during those four long years ; why should this aristocrat from Spain come and break our backs ? But break their backs he did with his iron will ; break their backs with discipline and toil—but for his " poor Ulster "—and Ireland.

The following year, '46, was a year of many happenings. In the Spring, King Charles with the remnant of his troops made a last stand at Stow but was finally and utterly defeated. He himself escaped but in the following May, after weeks wandering about like a beggar, he placed his royal person at the mercy of the Scots.

But the very next month an event occurred in Ulster which caused Pierce, Florence and the others to forget Charlie, the Scots, and old Ironside for many months to come. Eoin had crushed and ground into the dust thousands of the foreign scum at Benburb just over the borders of Tyrone. He wanted to prevent a meeting between the forces of Munroe and Stewart in the north and Coote and Inchiquin in the south ; so taking up his position at Benburb, with characteristic coolness, he bided his time. His army had rested all that warm day in the shade. Then Munroe, with his men all hot and tired, rode up. He crossed the Blackwater, a foolish move as he then had no retreat, and gave battle immediately. It was an overwhelming victory for the Irish ; losing as they did only forty men, with less than two hundred and fifty wounded. Munroe lost between three and four thousand of his forces.

The nation, the real nation, went wild with joy. As on the nuncio's arrival, the bells again rang out their silver notes and most of the cathedrals and churches, now since Glamorgan's treaty returned to their rightful owners, were thronged for the thanksgiving. The captured English colours were brought

to Limerick and there in solemn procession brought to the
Cathedral of St. Mary.

All through the land during those happy summer months
men began to hope anew. Nothing now was impossible;
above all the dreaded Puritan menace was no more. Abroad,
the victory, coming as it did when England and royalty lay
under the heel of hucksters and tradesmen, was considered
momentous. In Rome itself, Pope Innocent heard a solemn
Te Deum in the church of Sancta Maria Maggiore.

For Pierce, the rejoicing was temporarily checked by a
rumour of the death of Eoin O Callanain; killed by a sword
thrust from one of the fleeing planters, they said. Pierce
could ill spare another friend; he had looked forward so
much to Eoin's return. However, the mourning was short
lived; for, two days afterwards, a messenger arrived with a
hastily scribbled note from Eoin himself. He was wounded at
Benburb, he said, but it was not as serious as was first thought;
he was rapidly on the mend and would soon be back with
General Eoin Roe's army. Pierce wrote a poem to congratulate
him on his recovery.

Pierce, finding the source of his grief vanished, felt he must
celebrate the victory on a grand scale : he would have a banquet.
He thought over his guests; there would be Richard, of
course, and O'Donoghoe and Browne; and Walter Mac
Elligott. Whom else? But he could think that out on his
way to Tralee; perhaps he might even go to Killarney and
spend a few days with O'Donoghue in his castle at Ross.

He had heard there was a week's feasting in Dingle, so he
was not surprised to find The Rose fairly full on that bright
June day. The town was festooned with flags and banners;
and fiddlers, pipers and ballad-singers plied a busy trade. He
was soon away again and stopped only at Aunascaul and Camp,
the usual halts.

At Aunascaul he had a long talk with Mistress Curtain all
agog with excitement at the rapid turn things were taking.
She had heard she said that since O'Neill's victory the old
English in the Confederacy had begun to attack the Nuncio
more and more fiercely; they accused him of trying to with-

draw the people from their allegiance to the Crown ; of plotting to bring in a foreign government ; of tyrannical conduct and of trying to undermine the Constitution. He had to send his confessor, Giuseppe Arcamoni to Rome to clear his good name. Finally the Confederates went so far as to order him out of Ireland to make his defence before the Pope in person.

Pierce had been to Tralee several times since the siege ended and each time noticed that though the town resumed a little more of its former busy hum yet it never was quite the same as in the old days. It was a year since he had been there last and was all the more struck by this difference between its former trade and traffic and its present comparative solitariness. Many of the friendly shopkeepers and innkeepers such as Nathaniel Harrison and Walter Ware were of course allowed to return and open their doors anew ; but the large, solitary timbered houses of the merchants stood barred and bolted. Florence ordered the doors battered down at the beginning of the siege to be repaired, and the buildings themselves to be put under lock and key. Mac Elligott who had his quarters in the Castle, was now Provost as well as Military Governor. He would allow only the old natives, whether Gael or otherwise, to return and would permit no tampering with the property of the former merchants, at least until the issue of the present conflict be decided.

He called to the Priory to see Father Thaddeus who told him that Dr. O'Connell, the Bishop, had lately founded a seminary in the town, and had gathered some fine theologians to teach there.

Pierce also spent a few happy hours with Walter Ware and Nathaniel Harrison—for what else are old friends for ? Of the two, Nathaniel had aged more. Being a scholar, he was more sensitive than the tavern keeper, used as the latter was to noise and bustle. With his dreamy eyes and long beautiful hands, Nathaniel seemed to Pierce like something unsubstantial, something that might have come from between the pages of his vellum tomes. He sat with his back to the diamond leaded panes as Pierce came in and he gave a little start as the shadow fell across the floor.

" Master Pierce, I didn't hear you. I was just thinking and thinking ; you see one can't do much these days but think."

They spoke about the old times of comparative peace and quiet when the Lord Deputy, Strafford, tried to bring prosperity to the land. True the King had never granted his Graces, or only half granted them ; but wasn't anything better than what followed Master Pierce ?

" No, Pierce, I've seen too much in that horrible dungeon of a castle ever to be the same again."

True, he wouldn't ever be the same again : he was a broken man. But Walter Ware had a little of his cheerfulness left.

" Why yes, Pierce, trade isn't bad at all, not bad at all. You'd be surprised all that come and go."

Pierce could see he was trying to persuade himself that all would shortly be the same again. Both of his old friends seemed somehow incapable of adapting themsleves to the changed times. Perhaps it was their nationality ; for Englishmen are notoriously stubborn that way. Eoin Roe's victory swept them off their feet into a new world they didn't understand. Pierce tried to puzzle it out that night as he undressed in his room at The Golden Key.

The town was very quiet ; none of the boisterous merrymaking of Dingle or even of Aunascaul. Was it because it was still half empty ? Or was it something deeper in the town, something that could never enthuse over anything ? Was it that mixture of Gael and planter which left it characterless, neither Irish, nor English ? The shadow of the cursed Dennys seemed still to hang over it.

Next morning he rode away to Ross. He galloped out by Ballyseedy, climbed the shoulder of the mountain and saw the road, straight as a die, in front of him. It was a pleasant morning and the larks sang high in the blue. He soon came to Aghadoe and to the sylvan magic of Loch Lein, and swerving down to the left arrived at Ross.

O'Donoghoe was glad to see him. He said his men duly reported for drill several times a month ; also he had a small force quartered in the castle itself in case Murrough came along. But little fear of that ; for Ross was ever thought to

be impregnable—at least until ships should sail up Loch Lein :
Till on Loch Lein strange ships shall sail : the old rhyme said.
What was the likelihood of ships getting there ?

Pierce was pleased he had come. He loved to listen to the
lapping of the lake and the soughing of the wind amidst the
reeds. The bold turrets of Ross peeping amidst the trees made
it seem like a castle on a faery lake at the end of the world ;
and he would walk through the shady dells where the thrush
sang at dawn, and the primrose peeped forth to fairyland.
No, not even old Ironside himself dare penetrate the walls of
Ross.

His host, O'Donoghoe, sent to the castle at Killaha for his
relative, Geoffrey, who had lately been making a name for
himself with his poetry. He came with alacrity for he had
long wanted to meet the renowned Ferriter. There came with
him a friend of his Daibhi O Bruadair from Cork who was then
on a visit to Killaha. O Bruadair who was also a poet, was
learned in the Irish tongue and well versed in history and
genealogy.

"I've never in my life seen so much beauty gathered into
one place," O Bruadair said. " Master Geoffrey, no wonder
you are all poets in these parts of Desmond."

What Pierce noticed most as one evening they skimmed along
the lake were the ever-changing hues of the waters, now blue,
now gold, and then a steel-grey beneath a dappled sky ; again
shimmering like pearls and now glinting and flashing that light
which is the secret of Killarney's charm. Innisfallen lay slumbering in the stillness as they glided past and rounded the Ross
peninsula towards Muckross. The Castle with its bold turrets
rose serenely majestical from the edge of the lake. Over in
the quiet of the woods was the old friary of Irrelagh sometimes
called Muckross, again in its glory. There again the chanting
of the office rang through the chancel and nave. But the
brethren were not always at prayer ; sometimes they ascended
the tower to view Loch Lein of the everchanging colours,
the dark shadows and the dancing sunbeams. Torc and Toomies
might be clothed in a gossamer-like mist that failed to hide
here and there the deep blue patches ; and as the sun set, streaks

of gold might be cast over the grass, yews and grave-stones lying about the walls of the friary and clouds of fantastic shape drift across the opal sky.

The days passed all too quickly; but before he returned Pierce made his friends promise to ride westward in a week's time for the banquet. He took his leave and in a short time reached Dingle. Tom Trant, oily as ever, bade a very good day to Master Pierce. Yes, to be sure, he would send out six hogsheads of Xeres the first thing in the morning. And did Master Pierce want any usquebaugh? Why yes, he would send a dozen quarts. And what about ale?

When he got home, there was a poem from Eoin O Callanain in return for Pierce's ode of congratulation on his recovery. "Keep, O God, my friend in Thy safe keeping," Eoin said. "Protect him from hate and spite; for he is a friend that quenches in me pride and enmity."

Pierce had never known his mother; for she died when he was a year old; but Eoin in his younger days in Corca Dhuibhne was fascinated by the charm of that gracious lady. No wonder old Eamon became grumpy and difficult when early in the century, on that wild January night, she passed away, leaving her tiny babe to the fate which fortune had in store for it. For if Pierce and his guests but knew it, that night was to be the last time the merry laugh would ring round the walls of Castle Sybil. Don't you hear death in the air, gentlemen, even as you lift your glasses? Don't you hear the banshee wail, sweeping westwards from grey Loch Gur, rising to a horrble scream over Slieve Mish, Brandon and Dunquin? For you are all doomed—doomed. Even as you sip your Xeres, our darling Eoin Roe lies dead, his white limbs, his lime-white limbs, cold in death. Drink awhile and be merry; these hours are the only happiness you'll ever have here again. Have you heard that the Nuncio, weighed down with cares, has taken his leave? See him drag his weary steps to the quay at Waterford. And that soldier, Oliver Cromwell, who so distinguished himself in the war against the King, has arrived with his army at Ringsend. For a few short hours the sun shines and you, so naïve, think it will last for ever. But it won't. See Rinuccini sail away in the San Pietro from the troubled land. To the very end they thwarted him and even when he excommunicated those who kept to the truce with Murrough, some of the bishops and clergy rebelled. Happy for you, John Baptist Rinuccini that you've shaken from you for ever the dust of this sorely vexed nation. And perhaps it's well for you, too, Eoin Roe that you lie in the cold earth in the friary in Cavan town. But what of those of us that are left? What have we against the diabolical cunning of this Cromwell?

CHAPTER XXXII.

SOMETIME AFTER THE banquet, a bright day in May, Walter Mac Elligott rode over from Tralee. Pierce saw there was something the matter. He asked no questions during supper but afterwards as they strolled to the end of the headland and watched the waves play among the rocks, he asked :

" What news, Walter ? "

" Not so well Pierce, there are ugly rumours going around."

" For instance the one about Eoin Roe ? "

" Yes, about Eoin Roe," he said in surprise, " how did you know ? "

" So it must be true then ; I heard it a week ago from a ship which came into Smerwick but I was afraid to believe it. How did he die—poisoned ? "

" Yes, that's what they say."

" Our last hope gone."

" But there's more."

" How do you mean ? "

" They say General Cromwell's arrived in Dublin."

" Yes, I've heard that too; we must to arms again, Walter, nothing for it but the sword ; these planters understand little else."

Refugees began to pour into Desmond. Pierce soon had the whole story of Eoin Roe's death from an old soldier who came tramping back over the hills to his native Ferriter.

" I remember well when he first came, sir," he said, " we were wandering about Ulster with nothing to do—bands of us here, bands of us there, drinking, gambling and quarrelling. We had no leader to drill us into shape. But one night when we were near Enniskillen, a horseman flying past shouted that Eoin Roe had returned. We doubted it at first but more and more travellers along the way had the same tale.

Yes, it was true right enough ; next day we heard he had landed at Aghboe. I shall never forget the first time I saw him ; he wasn't too tall, not much above five feet, but he had the bearing of a prince. He was one you'd look twice at. He could be very distant and was particular to whom he spoke —but then he was a prince, wasn't he, sir ? "

But prince or no prince, he disciplined them and drilled them into an army. Night after night the smiths hammered at the pikes, supplies were put by, men from everywhere came pouring in. There was little he didn't know about warfare ; in the service of Spain they knew him as an illustrious officer. And now back on the hills of his own Ulster he put every ounce of energy into his task ; the hucksters who held the lovely lands of Ulster spurred him even to greater heights.

It took four years, hard years no doubt, but yet the happiest of their lives. For they were all one ; not a grumble was heard even on the longest march under a blazing sun ; not one deserter in the bitter cold nights as they sang and toasted the King of Spain around the blazing camp fires. For they were young then and loved the discipline, the work, and above all the companionship. There was lightning in their blood and many a night they pledged hand and heart to rid their fair Ulster of the planter stock.

Sometimes General Eoin Roe would talk to them. Not of course sit around the camp, but he would call the men before him and address them from his white charger—for he was always on the move. It's not very difficult to imagine the aristocratic face, the dreamy eyes, the aquiline nose and thin lips, and the beautiful sensitive hands—surely the hands of an artist. He had all the hauteur and breeding of an aristocrat.

Sitting on his horse, with plumed hat and looking fixedly at them, he would say :

" You have made good progress men, and I'm proud of you. But men there's much more yet to be done ; those Puritans from England have the cunning of foxes and no tie is sacred to them. Only discipline, training and eternal vigilance will win us the day. Let us turn to it again with even a greater zest, a greater will. Keep your Spanish broadswords well sharpened for the time now is near when we must give battle. Remember that Sancta Maria is your watchword, and what better watchword could you have ? "

" Yes, he was like that, sir, going from company to company, travelling from the Glens of Antrim to the Highlands of Donegal, building up a corps of officers whom he could trust— Colonel Henry O'Neill, Major Myles O'Reilly, Lieutenant Colonel Brian O'Neill, Captain Owen O'Doherty, Captain Bryan Mac Mahon, and the rest of them.

" Then came Benburb. We knew Munroe was in Carrickfergus and Stewart in Derry. O'Neill wanted at all costs to prevent a juncture between their armies and those of Coote and Inchiquin in the South. It was here both his coolness and daring were seen. We marched from Loch Sheelin northwards every man of us with step light and our standards of green, blue, yellow, white waving in the breeze, and Eoin Roe's own pipers piping the ancient marching song of the O'Neills. On we came company after company, vanguard, battle and rear. I can still hear the beat of the drum and the tunes we hummed on that march. We never stopped till we came to Benburb, where we rested for the remainder of that day.

" Then Munroe with his men all hot and tired rode up. They crossed the Blackwater—a foolish thing of them. When Munroe saw O'Neill's army drawn up waiting, he decided to give battle just then. Hurriedly assembling his army, he discharged some of his Saker guns. But of course we stood firm. Then he advanced his right flank. Thereupon O'Neill sent forward his left flank. There was a tussle but the foreigners were driven back. Munroe then foolishly repeated this procedure. Again the British were driven back. O'Neill, seeing the enemy was in no condition to withstand a continuous assault, decided to give battle.

"He trotted down the lines on his white charger, with there before him the flower of royal Ulster. Never did I see him looking more of a prince. The eyes were steel cold that looked at us through the narrowed lids. There was a ring in his voice as he spoke :

"'You see your old enemy before you men ; no need for me to go over again how they have torn our province to pieces ; no need for me to tell you again how they robbed us of the six fairest counties of Ulster. But by God their day has come ; the Red Hand of Ulster is itching to strike a blow. Let your manhood be seen in your push of pike and give not fire till you're within pike length. Your word is Sancta Maria. In the Name of the Father and of the Son and of the Holy Ghost— ADVANCE.'

"With a cry on the lips of every man we went across to meet them. I had a match lock musket but I would have been better off without it. I used my pike instead : it was a day for pikes. Yes, we obeyed our leader well enough. They fought every inch of the way but they couldn't stand up to us ; for they had had a long day's march. They were falling back more and more. Then it became a rout ; and then a massacre. You might ask me why hadn't we mercy. But who could have mercy thinking of how they carved up our lands years ago when the Earls had flown away to Spain. Who could have any pity, I ask you ? All night long we butchered them. We avenged in that fight many a poor old withered frame who died by the roadside. How could I forget when my own father lay dying, how he asked me to raise him up so that he could see for the last time his beautiful green fields of which they had robbed him ? And then people talk of mercy and pity and forgiveness. Yes, more than three thousand of them, we killed—three thousand to one hundred and sixty on our side."

"And what did O'Neill do then ?" enquired Pierce.

"Well sir, after a few minor successes he marched southwards till he came to Kilkenny. The Confederation, as you know, was in full swing. He saw at once the trickery of the new Irish.

They were really English at heart and hated him and all he stood for. So he decided to return to Ulster and wait. Thus all the fruit of Benburb was thrown away.

"Then Cromwell landed at Ringsend. Eoin Roe marched from Derry to meet him and paused at Cloch Uachtair on his way. There he fell sick and died.

"The men took it badly. I remember the night well; we were encamped about the lake. One of the officers came up with a grave face.

"'I'm sorry men,' he said, 'but I've bad news.'

We thought it might have something to do with Cromwell; that he was a few miles away or something like that. We waited for the officer to continue.

"'General Eoin Roe is dead,' he said.

"Dead," we repeated.

"'Yes, he has just died.'"

"One of us blurted out, 'Eoin Roe dead. You mean General Eoin Roe has died? But that's impossible! General Eoin Roe couldn't leave us like this: whom else have we?'"

"That's not the point; he's dead."

"'But how? But why? Where? What?'"

"Yes, he was dead; our darling was dead! They say he was poisoned, but I don't believe that. I think it more likely he took a chill; he never would rest and care for himself; it was all for his poor Ulster as he called it—his poor Ulster and Ireland.

"And that funeral, that lonely midnight funeral to Cavan town. We put him in the same grave as the Bishop O'Reilly beneath the shadow of the old Franciscan tower. Six of us were there and we had no lights for we didn't yet want the news of his death to get about. The service didn't take long. Soon his beautiful white limbs were covered and then we left him alone.

"Some of the men drank and drank; others pretended the situation wasn't so grave and they tried to be more cheerful than they felt. But we knew in our hearts it was the end— the end of everything. Our General had gone to join his fathers; but we were left to face Cromwell."

" And what did you do then ? "

" The army flitted gradually away. Most of them went to fight the Ironsides ; our regiment marched towards Dublin but hearing Cromwell was on his way to Drogheda, we proceeded towards it. But he got there before us ; only for that I wouldn't be alive to tell the tale to-day. Then we wandered southwards, our ranks thinning more and more. Now and again we met a few stray men who had escaped from one or other of the beleaguered towns. I remember one night in a tavern in Cashel town, we met a poor wretch who had escaped somehow from Wexford. He told his story so simply, so unaffectedly, that I felt as if I'd been in the Bullring while the slaughter went on. Blood, blood everywhere ; blood running along the gutters ; blood making more ghastly the frozen horror in the faces of the dead. Yes, that was Cromwell, sir ; he did things well."

" But how did you escape the order to cross the Shannon ? "

" Easy enough to escape that ; if you met an official you could always pretend you'd lost your way ; but we met many heading for Connaught. We remained for a while near the bridge at Portumna, and now and again a whole family, or, perhaps, a group of ten or twenty, with their few acres of summer corn, their cows, garrons and sheep, would come trooping westwards. Sir, I shall never forget that sight.

" We sighed a sigh of relief when Cromwell at length sailed away, but Ireton, I believe, is almost as bad. He tried to take Limerick but Lord Muskerry, hoping to raise the siege, attacked him at Knocknaclashy and was routed. I heard, sir, that Major Florence Mac Carthy was killed in this battle."

" Major Mac Carthy dead ! "

" So they say ; Major Mac Carthy that was at Tralee ; and I hear, sir, that General Ludlow is coming over the mountains to Ross."

For a moment or two he could not bring himself to believe that Florence was dead. After the succession of disasters, this final blow had the contrary effect on him that one might suppose : the news seemed to rebound off him as the news of a far away disaster might rebound off a schoolboy ; in reality his mind had become so hardened by events since Cromwell's coming that he never expected but the worst. For the moment he continued talking : so Ludlow was coming over the mountains to Ross.

" We'll give him a royal welcome," he replied, " but, tell me did you hear of or see the physician, Eoin O Callanain while up north ? "

" Well, sir, I heard tell of him all right ; he was attached to Colonel Brian O'Neill's troops and when the break up came, he left, I think for Drogheda. Whether he got there before Cromwell or not, I cannot say."

It took him some time to get used to the news of Florence's death ; to realise that he upon whom he depended more than anybody else in the world, had also passed away. The old, familiar ways were breaking up ; the things he loved and laughed with were fading away, slowly fading. To-day it was Florence ; to-morrow it was somebody else ; the next day a whole garrison gone down before Cromwell. Each one's passing brought death nearer, always nearer. No need to ask for whom the bell tolls ; it tolls for thee.

CHAPTER XXXIII

THE WALLS OF ROSS echoed to the ring of steel : youths rubbed shoulders with the old-timers who had fought at Tralee. Florence was the only missing one.

" We've lost a fine soldier, Captain Ferriter," said Muskerry.

" I agree, sir."

" Major Mac Carthy always fought a good fight : that day in the storm and rain, and with horse head to horse head, we hacked at the enemy till we could hack no more ; fortunate we were to get away with so many men."

" I don't think he was ever happy : he seemed to spread gloom wherever he went."

" True ! Whatever happiness he had, he found it in war ; but we shall miss him here in the next few months."

"Do you expect it to be as long as that, Lord Muskerry ? "

"Well, the place is, as you know, supposed to be impregnable ; I should think it's the one place in Ireland where we can successfully outmanoeuvre Cromwell."

"Do you believe in the old rhyme"

"I don't ; and neither do you, or anybody else, Captain Ferriter."

"You're right, probably."

"How about yourself : I regret you'll not remain here."

"Not remain here ! you surely——"

"Now please, Captain, don't take it like that ; let me explain : you'll be far more useful to us along by the Laune ; our numbers here are far too big ; you'd only be one among many. But I'm giving you a mission of great trust ; you'll be an important link in our communication system—our only link, perhaps. You'll send all information that comes your way to us at the quickest possible speed."

"Moves of the enemy and so forth ? "

"Yes, and probable moves as far as you can judge. I've some men in the Gap of Dunloe who will row across with food daily ; you'll give your despatches to them. You understand ? "

"Perfectly ! "

"Remember, Captain Ferriter, this is a mission of special trust. I've more men posted at various strategic points in Desmond, but yours is the most important of all ; for the Laune is, as you know, the only outlet to the sea. It's simple enough to calculate the enemy's probable tactics elsewhere ; but on the Laune anything might happen. It's the one route by which we could be attacked."

"I understand ; how many men shall I have ? "

"About half a hundred should be sufficient, I think."

When some further details had been arranged, Muskerry returned to his other duties and Pierce spent an interesting night meeting many old friends. Next morning he left early ; everybody was surprised to see him go ; for he had kept silent about his mission. It was hard to part from the camaraderie of the Castle and set about the unknown.

He rode along by the right bank of the river, a little in front of his men. Soon the river widened considerably, and here he paused for a few moments to watch a heron in mid-stream sieze its prey ; the birds warbled for the joy of living ; the crows cawed with glee. And Ireland was fighting her last fight.

They turned westwards. In front he could see the Slieve Mish and Corca Dhuibhne range almost back to Brandon ; on his left were the eternal Reeks, beauty and poetry and worlds of fantasy in their rippling peaks. Now and again between the trees sparkled the lovely Laune, gliding softly, gracefully to the sea. To the right a line of white cloud fringed the horizon.

He paused to view the turrets of Ballymalis, outlined against the Reeks. Empty too ! Was there nobody left to strike a blow, nobody or no place except Ross-i-Donohoe ? There was no doubt Kerrymen had grit : all else gone down before Cromwell. The defenders fought heroically at Limerick, Drogheda, Wexford, and most valiantly of all at Clonmel, but at that time there was fight still left in the country ; now there was none. Here, in this remote corner were a handful of Kerrymen defying the whole Commonwealth. True, old Noll had returned home ; but Ludlow was bad enough it seemed. He had come round by the southern coast to Cork and thence to Ross. It was hard to imagine a war there ; one felt as if wakened from a dream. Only elfin bells in sylvan shades could tell of the beauty of Loch Lein—the islands—the fierce beauty of the mountains—the Reeks, those Reeks which would make a poet of any man—the bright sunlight—the gleaming furze— the browsing cattle. The rest of the country was a shambles —to Kerry or to Hell.

Lord Muskerry had given him a list of the houses where he could billet his men. These were at Beaufort Bridge, Bally-malis and Killorglin on the right bank ; and at Knockane and Meanus on the left ; but he would first reconnoitre the whole valley before deciding what to do.

While still at Ballymalis he looked at his map for a few minutes to study better his terrain. Yes, that should be sufficient, sixty men on the right bank, twenty on the left ; and the remaining ten perhaps somewhere near the mouth of the Laune, either on the Killorglin or Kilcolman side. He himself would stay as near as he could, in the territory from Killalee to the Gap ; but he would first bring the men to Killorglin and thence despatch them to their posts.

They were waiting for him a little distance behind, so he remounted and set off. The Reeks again caught his eye ; they were like a magnet. But they were now different ; that was always the way ; never the same for two minutes together. The Dingle mountains were seldom thus, except at the close of day. Perhaps it was the faery peaks of the Reeks that did that ; they wove a golden spell. Like Loch Lein, they spoke of elfin grots and tinkling bells and a world of lovely things far, far removed from thoughts of war.

The little party was soon nearing Killorglin. Acres of bog stretched all about. The Reeks seeming at length weary of their lofty heights descended abruptly to a serrated line of hills which formed the backbone of Iveragh. When they came to the town, Pierce went to a tavern where he ordered a cup of wine for his men. The landlord, bowing and pleasant, was glad to show Pierce and his five non-commissioned officers to a private parlour. It was there that Pierce allocated to them their tasks, gave final instructions, and warning them to send him every tittle of information, rode back to Killalee. Here, in a cabin near the ruin of the old church, he spent the night.

In a day or two General Ludlow had moved into Kerry and laid siege to Ross. It was like all sieges, protracted, dull and with desultory firing. Sometimes the white flag would go up on either side for a parley ; then the troops would relapse into a sullen waiting. Sometimes at night-time Pierce would come as near the enemy's rear as he dared. These Roundheads were orderly enough and under strict discipline ; it was only when they were near " the kill " that one saw the blood lust in their eyes. A few hundred of them had squatted in the direct pre-cincts of the Castle ; the remainder were in the town, where they were easily available in any need.

In the beginning he himself had nothing whatever to report and neither did the men send him any word. No doubt, if anything unusual were happening they would inform their leader ; but nothing did happen.

It was a blazing hot summer that Summer of 1652 and he wished he could be riding the billows at Béal Bán. But war was war. One day he rode down to the Gap where O'Donoghue was in charge and where he had five or six men quartered at the head, middle and exit to the ravine. The people supplied them with sheep and cattle, which when slaughtered, were brought over to Tomies, thence down to the lake and across to the garrison. With such supplies Muskerry could hold out indefinitely.

He met O'Donoghue coming down the glen. Times were indeed changed since they sang with such gusto over the battle of Benburb.

"Ludlow asked for a parley again yesterday," said O'Donoghue after the usual greetings.

"Why?"

"Wants to finish up and get away, I suppose. He must be sick of it, too."

"Probably ; but what were his terms?"

"Generous : he lets everybody go free except those charged with murder."

"And who is to define murder?"

"Don't ask me."

"Muskerry turned it down, I suppose?"

"Yes."

"Anything stirring up the glen, O'Donoghue?"

"Not a thing : three duck passed over as I crossed the bridge ; I wished I could have had a shot."

"Don't you think you'll have enough shooting before Ludlow goes."

"Perhaps, Master Pierce!"

"By the way, where's Geoffrey?"

"I've no news of either him or O'Bruadair ; probably gone on one of their mysterious missions."

"I was reading a poem of Geoffrey's the other day ; very good, I thought."

"What was it about?"

" Oh, just the Cromwellians pretending to be gentlemen."

" They'll find it rather difficult ; are you writing any poetry yourself these days ? "

" Nothing very much ; but a few good lines have flashed across my mind over there in Killalee during the quiet of the night. O'Donoghue, I'm afraid we're finished, we're finished at last. In the loneliness of that cabin I felt it's no use going on. I was never one to accept defeat easily ; but isn't all Ireland now smoking ashes ? Even if we hold out for a year here, or two years, where will it get us ? Doesn't the Commonwealth rule the roost and old Noll its golden calf ? "

" Ha, Ha ! I like that, a calf ! Cromwell a calf ; that's good, Ferriter."

" But jesting aside, isn't it true ? It fills me with dread at day-time and at night brings me to the depths of despair ; it leaves me without the strength of a woman in travail, spiritless and without sensation."

" You're taking it too seriously ; nobody can take Ross."

" Ross doesn't matter one way or another ; it's the tidings that come from the rest of Ireland that afflict me, tidings without hope, the beginning of our total ruin. See the destruction of the men of Fodla, no longer defiant, they the flower of the flock, robbed of their lands held by right of charter and equity. The extent of our loss neither you nor I are able to reckon ; the days of hospitality are coming to an end ; we have no priests in the land of Fodla, no nor Mass nor ritual. What will the young do with nobody to fight for them, nobody but the God of Glory as they are conscripted and beaten over the seas ? If we had Tuathal the Ready with us now, or Feidhlim who would rout the robbers, or Conn victorious in battles, the foreigners wouldn't oppress us thus. Where is Art who loved valour ? Or the son of Conn, hard in battle, the terror of the clann Oilill Oluim ? It's well for the foreigner these mighty ones are gone. Woe, woe to Banba ! But for the death of Eoin Roe, the raging unbearable Gaill would not thus rob us of our lands ; we would have power, prestige and prowess, right and might would be ours, our husbandry would prosper, if the hand of God were with us."

" The hand of God is not with us, Pierce ! "

" No, I'm certain it's not. It's not the savagery of Cromwell nor the fierceness of the troop from Dover, nor all the mighty power of our enemy that afflicts us, but the vengeance of God on the green meadows of Eireann."

" The vengeance of God ! But why, Pierce ? "

" Chieftain against chieftain ; clan against clan. The sins of the elder, the perversity of the younger, knowing Christ but deaf to his precepts, the rape of maidens, the breaking of marriage vows, gluttony, greed, robbery and swearing. Hatred everywhere and insult to the clergy, the plundering of churches, deceit and violence, the weak left to their fate, the ruin of all by these vengeful erring ones."

" I don't ever remember any insult to the clergy."

" Many and many a time ; did you ever hear of the slaying by Fitzgerald of the abbot of O'Dorney, standing at the door of his own abbey ? Or the burning of Innisfallen by O'Donoghue ? At that time in Eirinn, God was forsaken for wealth ; kindred and family forsaken too ; fleeing from danger but trampling on the weak, the perversion of judgment, justice abandoned."

" But surely the country wasn't always like that ? "

" I'm not saying it was, O'Donoghue, but sometimes it was hard to get them to agree. When Brian ruled in Tara there was peace in the land. But now he and his nobles have gone— Brian who was once our King—neither have we powerful and valiant Murchadh, our strength at Clontarf. When these our nobles had power, joined by Clan Carty and other illustrious ones, little did the foreigner think of banishment across the sea or banishment in the land of Fodla. Now the howling wolves are in the place of the lions, with their flaccid pleasures, their luxury, their chambering ; gluttonous they are, talkative, selfish, rude, chattering and inhospitable. I am truly grieved to see the spouse of Criomhthainn, Conn and Eoin make her bed with beggars, with never a thought by them of her vows."

" All perfectly true, Pierce ; but we still have a hope left."

" None, except in this tiny corner. See this land bursting with produce in the grasp of the new invader ; what can we do but beseech the power of the Only Son of the Virgin that right might yet be done. Oh, it frightens me like death the plight of my people, those mild and cultured ones, where they once gave commands, they are now ordered to come and go ; with sometimes a respite or a small favour, a favour which only lasts ' till further order.' "

" Yes, till further order ; that's true enough."

" To my grief it's a disease from which there's no escape ; if I call them cutthroat robbers I speak true ; the rout of the rightful rulers of Clar Fodla and the extinction of the Church of God. From dawn till noon an eclipse clouded the sun's fair face ; there are signs in the heavens that our days are numbered."

" I didn't think you were an astrologer or a stargazer."

" No, seriously O'Donoghue, it's a foreboding, a very strong foreboding that the end is near. Look at all our friends ! None of mine have now sufficient to give me even sixpence. Where is Father Thaddeus ? Does he even know his abbey is in ruins, really in ruins this time ? The other night the robbers pursued Bishop O'Connell as far as the Laune, who while wading through the river, had his crozier swept from him by the current. What state is Tralee in ? Or Killarney with Noll's fat swine wallowing by lovely Loch Lein ? A torture to me it is the truth of these things, this bloody invasion of the foreigner ; but I know well the reason, it's for our sins that God permits it."

Yes, for our sins that God permits it, he thought to himself, as he rode away. Back in Killalee, he found there were still no despatches. He decided to ride on to Killorglin and see how events were. Soon he was passing Pallis, the castle of the Mac Carthy Mor ; it would one day have been Florence's. Poor Florence ! Life seems different without you ; I always had confidence when you were by ; your smile, your cynical smile made me cease day-dreaming and come down to earth. Now I'm forever day-dreaming ; seeing portents in the sky and thinking my days are numbered. I wonder if they are ? I'd like to know what O'Donoghue thought of my outburst ? but I couldn't help it at the time ; I was just in that mood ;

probably, 'Cailín óg a stuair mé,' was in my thoughts,
I'm full of moods these days. Florence always knew what
to do in a war ; if only he were here now, what a difference it
would make. He'd know how to handle the men : I don't !
I know they respect me ; but I'm always afraid they'll find
out how little I really know about warfare. I wonder why
Muskerry picked me for this mission ? "Remember, Captain
Ferriter, this is a mission of special trust." Perhaps 'tis because
I know the country fairly well. But I feel I've now nobody
to rely on ; I muddled through at Tralee because Florence was
there. Poor Florence ! Captain Ferriter don't be an ass, he
used to say. Captain Ferriter, incompetent though you may
be, please don't let the men see it. But I knew he didn't mean
that ; he never said it to anybody else even though sometimes
they made worse mistakes than me. Even the night Browne
and O'Donoghue disobeyed orders at Tralee by walking out
under the noses of the enemy, he never said a word. He felt
Browne beneath his contempt. But it was always Captain
Ferriter, don't do this, and Captain Ferriter, don't do that.
If he were here now he'd say, " Captain Ferriter, no despatches ?
Are you really serious about your military career, Captain, or
perhaps you'd prefer to return to your parchment and
quill ? "

It was zeal that made him a cynic : he knew we were capable
of far greater things, and when neither we nor the country
came up to his expectations he turned sour and found fault
with everything. " Why have we always the poor mouth ? "
he used to say, " aren't our soldiers the best in Europe and if
we'd only unite nothing would stop us ? Why do we always
think the stranger superior ? "

How well he commanded the siege at Tralee ! Few of us
noticed it at the time but now I see it all ; it must have been a
considerable mental strain ; but he was able for it—he delighted
in it. Pretended he was no patriot ; that it was solely for
military reasons he acted ; but all the while his one desire was
to see the country as great and as prosperous, as free and as
faithful to old traditions, as any in Europe. But it isn't, it's
only a wilderness, a windswept weary wilderness without law

or peace, order or security. Hard to blame you, Florence, for turning sour !

He called on his man, Fitzgerald, at Killorglin but as he was not there, he continued onwards to the Laune estuary. There were thick woods all about and it was rarely he caught a glimpse of the sea ; but whenever he did, he thought he saw a vessel lying at anchor. He went on for another mile and then took the sharp turn to the left which would bring him to the delta. On his way down he saw his man, Fitzgerald, galloping towards him, who when he came abreast, blurted out :

"Sir, there's a vessel yonder unloading."

"Unloading what ? "

"Timber."

"Why didn't you tell me sooner ? "

"She only arrived an hour ago and Rice sent me word to go down and investigate ; I was on my way back to inform you."

"Very well ; let's go down and see."

Down they went. After a few hundred yards they tethered their horses out of sight of the road, and went carefully forward. It was no easy matter tearing through the briars or dragging their sodden boots from bog-hole to bog-hole ; but in the end they came upon the ship. She was a fine vessel of about fifty tons with the flag of the Commonwealth fluttering gaily from her mast. She was anchored in the middle of the estuary with dozens of little boats bobbing all about her ; those going towards the shore were loaded with beams already cut and fashioned for some purpose ; then on to waiting carts ; and the horses would lurch forward with their loads. God in heaven, what did it mean ? Not for firewood ! What then ? What were all those loads of beams for, load after load, now on their way up the Laune ? And chisels, hammers and saws ? Infantry, plenty of infantry were there to guard them on their way. And it all happened in little more than an hour. What devilish plan lay behind it ? Did they take the old rhyme seriously ? They surely weren't going to build boats to sail on the lake ?

Some instinct told him it was true. And the garrison,

immediately they saw ships swim upon the waters would capitulate. No doubt about that ! They believed in that rhyme as firmly as the people of Loch Gur that Gerald the Earl rode over the grey lake on a white steed with silver shoes once in seven years. These lines were implicit in their beginning the siege at all ; for who would dare resist the Cromwellians at this stage ? It would spare valuable lives, many had said, to disperse before the invaders came ; but no, Ross-i-Donohue would never be taken, could never be taken, until—.

Still, all's fair in love and war, I suppose. But who would have thought of it ? They will probably make a great display on the lake, keeping at a safe distance, of course. That, coupled with intense fire from Ludlow will strike terror into most of these raw young lads. Kerrymen surely had grit but not all the grit or doggedness could fight superstition.

I must ride back immediately and try and get word to Ross. By what route ? Better to ride into Milltown and then take the direct road from there to Killarney. Luckily I can turn westwards to Killalee before reaching the town.

Bidding his man remain where he was—for they were still unloading—he untethered his horse and waited for a chance to slip past. This was not difficult as the loads were fewer now. It took him very little time to reach Milltown and then turning sharply west, reach the main Killarney-Killorglin road by way of Listry and Faha ; then on to the Gap.

He found O'Donoghue at his headquarters, a small house at the entrance to the Gap.

" Something extraordinary is happening O'Donoghue," he said.

" What ? "

" Loads of timber are coming up the Laune."

" That explains this message then," he replied, handing to Pierce a slip of paper ; it read :

" News has reached us that something is afoot at Kinsale. They are building ships. Watch Dingle Bay and the Laune.
Greetings,
Muskerry."

" That's probably where your timber comes from," said O'Donoghue.

" No doubt."

" What do you think we'd better do ? "

" I'm just wondering ; I'd like to know when the news left Kinsale."

" It must have taken days."

There was a knock ; a man entered and saluted.

" They're building boats at the bend of the river behind Dunloe Castle, Captain," he said.

" How many men have we here at the moment, Sergeant ? "

" Three, sir ; the rest are bringing sheep from the Black Valley."

" We'd better try and do something," he said turning to Pierce, " let's go across to Tomies and bring the men with us."

The little party went down the Gap and then quickly crossed over to the hill-country. The sun shone in a sky of deep blue and a soft breeze blew down from Tomies. Soon the lake and its islands came into view ; little flecks of foam reminded Pierce of the white horses on Smerwick. A cannon boomed out. Another !

Down to the left they could see hundreds of men hammering away. A gunboat, with white sails was already completed and lay at anchor a few yards from the shore. Then a second one, also with white sails, followed. Men were now pouring into smaller vessels, and reaching the gunboats, clamber aboard. It was the speed of the operation that mystified Pierce. They must have had nothing to do but nail the boards together, everything being fashioned beforehand. What devil planned it ? Most surely somebody with a brain.

Now the two gunboats were filled and were moving forward, breasting their sails to the breeze ; then the smaller vessels followed, full to the brim. Slowly they rounded the island and disappeared.

I wonder how they'll take it, Pierce mused. A soldier like Muskerry will laugh at the ruse ; but what about the rank and file ? If they refuse to go on with it there's nothing

more to be done. Nothing harder to fight than superstition ;
they'll feel the fates are against them and surrender at once.

There was nothing to do but wait. An old blind piper
stumbled towards them and sat on the grass a few yards
away.

" Please Peter, what about some music ? " said O'Donoghue.

" If you wish, gentlemen," he said, arranging his pipes.

At first he played a martial air, grand and sweeping, but
then a bright little melody rippled out over the holly and the
furze. It made one think of Ross peeping amidst the branches,
Ross with its solemn dignity, its mystery, its magic. Ross
like a faery castle where the whitethorn bloomed the earliest
and the thrush sang her sweetest ; Ross of the glassy waves
and grey stones ; Ross of the sedgy lake and winding paths ;
Ross with its bold battlements ringed round by the massive
mountains. Ross, with its young red blood, the one last hope
of Desmond.

Pierce saw there was nothing they could do so he decided
to return to Killalee and leave the others make whatever
plans they pleased. He at least must see to his own men.
What a day for war, he thought, as he walked quickly downwards ! Now and again through the trees he could glimpse
the flotilla gliding onwards to Ross. The sun still shone in a
cloudless blue and the birds made a sweet chorus : it was
difficult to persuade oneself that Hell had at last come to Kerry.

On reaching Killalee he found his man, Sullivan, from
Ballymalis waiting for him. He told him to approach the
town as near as he could and try and find out what was
happening. He then rode cautiously along the Laune to see
if the last of the cargo had arrived. All was quiet. He reached
Killorglin and told Fitzgerald and Rice to stay at their posts.
One never knew how they would be wanted. Then he
returned to Killalee.

His messenger from Killarney had arrived before him. He
reported tremendous firing from the besiegers. During the
hours that followed dozens began to pass westwards on their
way from the town. During the night they increased and
towards dawn there was a regular stream of refugees. All

night the roar of the firing reverberated from hill to hill and crag to crag. No garrison, they said, could stand it.

But yet they stood it, every man a hero in that fateful hour. Word had long since got about the town of the ships on the lake ; and it was thought the besieged would surely lose heart. Towards mid-day reports came in that Ross had fallen. The refugees, each with a few chattels and a cow or a donkey, continued to pass. Then Sullivan, who had gone again to Killarney, returned. Yes, it was true. Ross had fallen ! Rest and peace indeed to Ireland's bones : Pacata Hibernia.

CHAPTER XXXIV

THE TERMS WERE moderate. Ludlow seemed in a hurry to finish and he again offered freedom to all except those convicted of murder. It took a fortnight to agree upon the precise meaning of the term. Muskerry was allowed to go to France and the others dispersed quietly. Pierce returned with his men to Castle Sybil.

Robert, now grey and growing feeble, was glad to see him back.

"Many times I've welcomed you, Master Pierce, but none where circumstances were so tragic."

"No, I suppose not, Robert."

"It's the end of all, I suppose."

"Yes, the end of all."

"And what about yourself, Master ? Are you staying here ? "

"No, Robert ; there's a warrant for my arrest as I didn't formally surrender at Ross ; I'd reason to believe they'd have kept me. You see we came straight here from the Gap. No, you can carry on ; I'll keep around the district and if needs be I can cross to the Island."

"True, Master Pierce ; but if the soldiers come, how am I to deal with them ? "

"Yes, I suppose we must be prepared for that. Let me

see. Obviously the men couldn't defend the place for ten minutes. Have you ever thought of digging trenches ? "

" Trenches ? "

" Yes, trenches ; we could cover them with bracken and staves ; I've often thought about it."

" Quite a good plan, Master."

" How many men have we ? "

" Eight."

" Sufficient ; do you see the opening in the cliff ? Suppose we dig further inland, say for about six yards, and then cover it with sods ; it would lie directly on the pathway here."

" True."

" Call the men, then, while I look about for other likely places to dig."

That evening, and for a week afterwards, they laboured. So thoroughly was the work done that it would be impossible for a stranger to know that beneath the inoffensive looking bogland there were six large holes, all under the main pathway. At the worst, they would give a small garrison a certain breathing space.

A breathing space indeed ! Little they thought that these half dozen trenches would annihilate more of the enemy than the sieges of Tralee and Ross combined, an annihilation so complete that centuries afterwards in the folk-tales old men would still tell of the massacre of the Dun.

When the enemy would come in sight, Pierce's plan was to advance with his men as far as Baile Uachtarach, and with a feint at defence, retreat to the trenches. Here they were to face forward and run as fast as they could across the pathways that traversed the maze of trenches. The enemy thinking panic had seized them would pursue as quickly but would soon realise his error.

After a week's waiting the enemy did appear and everything happened precisely to plan. But it was the " rout " which Pierce and the men enjoyed. They had had several days practice in running fleet as deer over the intricate system of pathways, practice so thorough that each man knew exactly the path he was to take. The Cromwellians with a roar pursued them like wild beasts jumping on their prey ; but it was a rude awakening ; for in less than two minutes there were but ten of them on firm ground ; the rest were wallowing—as many as thirty of them together—in the deep pits.

There was no restraining the men. They jumped on them, sword in hand, and made shorter work of them than even Lord Grey did at Dun an Oir. The enemy were so dazed by their fall that they put up but a poor defence ; besides, they had mostly lost their swords and muskets and could but use their fists against the gleaming blade of a Spanish broadsword raised to strike or a musket fired at point blank.

Not a soul was left to tell the tale. Pierce knew however that their comrades at Ross would revenge every man of them, so he decided to dismiss the company and let each soldier fend for himself, for it was certain trenches would not suffice next time. He himself, he had determined, would take to the hills and if the scent there were running hot, he would cross to the Island.

He felt the wrench at parting from Robert far more than he did at leaving the Castle. " Master Pierce," he said catching both his master's hands in his, as the tears streamed down his poor old cheeks, " Goodbye and God be good to you. I never thought ' twould come to this ; I thought somehow that like your father, we'd hold on, yes, hold on till a better day came and the King, as bad as he was, would again rule his Three Kingdoms ; but that I'm afraid is but a wan hope."

" Well, goodbye Robert."

" Goodbye Master Pierce ; but before you go will you grant me one request."

" Anything that's in my power to do, Robert."

It was one of the most unusual, most extraordinary requests that one ever heard, no less than that Pierce should grant to his steward the right to bear the name of Ferriter.

He looked in amazement at Robert scarce believing his ears.

" You surely can't mean that you wish to take my surname," he said, after a pause.

" Yes, Master Pierce ; you see for the first time in five hundred years Dunurlin is without a Ferriter. When you return, and

I hope the day is not far distant, you will of course resume the chieftaincy, but I thought perhaps, perhaps in the meantime, that, that———"

The old man was surely going crazy, mused Pierce ; what benefit could it possibly be to him—surely no benefit but the contrary. However time was precious and he did not wish to hurt Robert's feelings by a blank refusal.

" Very well, Robert," he said, " you may bear my name till I return."

But he never returned ; and Robert till the day of his death proudly insisted to his neighbours that his master had given him the right to bear his surname. In the beginning they thought it a very strange procedure indeed ; but as time went on the two names became associated and they would speak of " Robert Ferriter " in a semi-jocose way. After his death, however, Robert's relations continued to use the surname.

Pierce prepared to stay for one last night but word came from The Rose that the Roundheads were in Dingle ; so taking a a cloak and hat he wandered over past Baile Uachtarach to Ard na Caithne. The night was warm and he didn't much mind. He sat for a few hours in a hut near Binn Dhiarmada ; and just as dawn brought the magic of a new day, went down towards Béal Bán. The glory of the sky over Brandon made him forget for a while his danger.

A peculiar purplish tinge came over the steel-grey clouds, followed by long streaks of palest blue that stealthily turned a little brighter. The scream of a snipe arrested his thoughts ; but in a moment his glance was again on graceful Duibhne that seemed to become darker in the rays slowly rising from caverns of gold, purple and sapphire. The grey sea seemed strange in this new world ; there was something raw, something almost cruel about it.

Then he slowly made his way over to the side of Marthain where William, the weaver, lived. William was glad of his company and Pierce helped him with the carding of the wool and the mixing of the dyes. He changed into an old garment and looked as if he had spent all his life at the loom.

Next day they sighted a figure with a staff coming with

difficulty towards the hut. When he came to the door he
rapped on it loud and long. Pierce at length opened it.

"I am Rathai Mac Sionna," he said, "from the furthermost
limits of Eireann, and I've come to throw a rann with Pierce,
son of Eamon, the redoubted and redoubtable bard. Will you
please show me the way to this castle."

"Pierce, the son of Eamon, is not at home now," answered
Pierce, "but if it's somebody to compete at verse with you,
you want, anybody here is just as good."

"That's a hard saying," said Rathai, "you mean to tell me
you could sustain a verse duel with me?"

"I do," said Pierce, "although you see in me but a weaver;
come inside."

Rathai entered and sat on the form by the fire.

"Yes, Pierce the son of Eamon isn't a bad rhymer," he said,
"but of course nothing compared to the poets of Ulster. Take
these lines of his, for instance :

> She was most fair, most excellent,
> So very grand to see ; "

he said, quoting one of Pierce's early poems. But before he
got further, Pierce continued :

> " *But ah ! her heart to me was cold,*
> *Would stone cold ever be.*"

He pretended not to be surprised, and continued :

> " She left me for the gleam of gold
> —For never much had I—

Again Pierce interrupted :

> " *This love by her was easily borne,*
> *Scarce worth a passing sigh.*"

Bravely Rathai went on :

> " If once again she comes to me,
> And says she'll be my love,"

Again Pierce finished it for him :

> " *My eye shall be to her as steel,*
> *I'll call the gods above.*"

Bravely Rathai tackled the last verse :

> " I shall speak in ringing words,
> With venom, too, implied."

Again Pierce prevented him from finishing :

> " *But what if she no more returns*
> *To hurt me with her pride ?* "

Pierce looked at the stranger with a mischievous smile. William purred with delight at this unexpected pleasure ; Rathai alone seemed downcast. " If the weavers here have such technique " he seemed to say, " what of the redoubted and redoubtable Ferriter ? "

There was no doubt that he was astonished, dumbfounded almost, by this extreme versatility of a mere weaver. Immediately the poem was finished, forthwith taking his staff, he made for the door and quickly went his way.

" That'll silence the old braggart for a while," Pierce said smiling to William.

The news came that the Roundheads were coming his way and he decided to walk down to Dunquin by the short way at Graig. He had no sooner arrived, however, than a sharp breeze sprang up from the south-west. The tide was coming ; that meant it would be against them on the way to the Island. The wind became stronger and the sea even more restless.

" It would be a tough pull," said John the boatman.

John threw his wise old eyes across to the Great Blasket resting so calmly amidst the Atlantic swell, and then looked southwards again to where the surge of the tide came up the Sound—that same Sound where lurked the treacherous *seanduine* which shivered the timbers of the Santa Maria de la Rosa.

" But Chieftain, you must cross over ; we've got to take

you," John continued, even though he knew the tide would be still against them on their return in the evening.

They did take him even though their arms ached and their palms became raw. Still, it was a wonderful crossing; it seemed to have all the adventure of youth : like riding to Dingle on the old grey mare when he was a boy. They passed near Beginnish ; the huge, jagged cliffs stood like giant hags above the foaming, boiling waters. John had a fishing-line and left it trail along after the boat ; once he felt it give a tug and hauling it aboard he landed a huge eighteen pounder pollock.

Then there was the arrival on the quay where all the islanders gathered to meet them ; the soft, warm words of welcome with a slight obeisance to their Chieftain ; the march to the "King's" house where there was a royal feast of delicious meats, sweet breads, lobsters, cray-fish, washed down by the choicest of Spanish claret and flagons of Bordeaux rouge. Everything as wonderful—externally—as in the old days ; for these good islanders could scarcely yet realise that the black cloud now looming on the horizon would soon blacken out all the world that Ireland had hitherto known.

The rhythmic beat of the ocean round the tiny kingdom lulled him to a sense of comparative ease ; he thought of old Seamus, the seanchai, now long in his grave, and of his stories of the Armada and the Spanish main. The islanders, though grieving at his misfortune, were nevertheless proud to have their lord amongst them ; they vied with each other in serving him and of carrying out his merest whim.

"Ah, Master Pierce," said an old man, Tomás Bán, "little did we think that our Chieftain would come among us in such circumstances ; but bide your time, Master, bide your time. Even if they do come, you'll always be safe in the cave yonder."

"Why does everybody speak about that cave, Tomás ? "

"Because, Master, it's a steep climb down the cliff-side and then the pursuers can only enter one by one ; so you'll have ample time to deal with each one."

Then he went bounding across the island with old Micil to find the cave—that cave almost beyond the reach of man. They went along by the winding north-westerly pathway and thence across the bare bog till at length they saw it, jutting out very far down in the cliff-face. But how was it possible to get there ?

They could not descend direct but walked on for about a hundred yards and then began to climb down obliquely. Micil still led the way, and Pierce made a feeble protest once or twice, saying he would be able to reach it himself, knowing as he did that his guide was an old man.

" No, you'd never be able, Chieftain ; and even if you did get near the entrance, it would be just as difficult to crawl in."

True indeed, as he found, when after a most difficult and precarious climb, he at last reached the narrow opening barely big enough for a man to crawl through. By this time Micil was calling him from inside, and scarce daring to look at the sea, he climbed down a few more feet, turned forward and with extreme difficulty crawled in over the mud and stones. Inside it got gradually bigger till a man could stand at its further end. The floor was wet from a horrible drip which came through all parts of the roof from the boggy, heather-covered soil above ; drip, drip, it continued till it drove one almost to distraction. Through the narrow entrance came the shivering northern breeze ; and below almost perpendicularly down, was the angry lash of the sea. However, he returned again to the village that evening with Micil, and from that onwards, availed of the proffered hospitality of the " King." He was to use the cave only in case of a raid on the island.

One day he was seated listening to the " King " tell one of his tales of the Fianna, while his daughter Maire, the " Princess," busied herself about the house. Suddenly the door opened and six Roundheads came in. The " King " who had his back to the door kept on talking, thinking it was only some of the neighbours, but noticing the strange look that came over Pierce, turned about and with an expression of dumb stupefaction stared at the six glum figures with their plain black jerkins, white starched collars and black round hats, who stood there in silence and stared at both of them in turn.

The " King " was the first to speak ; he asked them to sit down, which they did. Then one of them, evidently their officer from the tone of his voice, began to speak and asked Pierce to corroborate the fact that he was the Chieftain Ferriter, which Pierce did. He told him there was no use trying to escape ; that he had more men posted down on the quay to guard the boats, and even if he did try to get away they would take good care he got a bullet in the back.

Pierce was thinking furiously ; so was Maire, in whose fertile brain a plot was hatching. She asked them if they would have a cup of wine, with perhaps a light repast. They willingly agreed, having been at sea a long time, for they had rowed from Dingle a good way out, and then so as to minimise their chances of being detected, approached the island from the western end. Feeling sure of their quarry, they placed their muskets, with their bores turned up, along by the wall near the door, approached the fire and took the chairs which the host offered them. Maire was preparing the meal in the little room off the kitchen, and in a very short time announced it was ready. She saw to it there was plenty of wine as the whole company, including Pierce and the " King," sat about the table. Pierce noticed by the gleam in her eyes she was up to something. And so she was. She had been putting only water into Pierce's cup, for it was pewter cups they used, and when the soldiers were at their fourth cup, with a slight nod she beckoned Pierce to the door. He was up in a flash and away. In a second or two the officer saw how matters stood and rushing towards the muskets, grabbed one and levelling it at the retreating figure, fired. But nothing happened for Maire had taken care to pour plenty of water down the bore of each. In a moment he saw he had been tricked and calling to the others to follow him, ran post-haste after his quarry. But Pierce had had a good start and he felt sure he would reach the cave, which he did ultimately. His pursurers, however, followed him every yard of the way, and as he was coming down that last few difficult feet near the entrance, he took one glance about and saw a few heads a good distance above among the heather. Then he crawled in and waited.

In about an hour he could hear somebody with heavy breathing slowly and laboriously approaching ; then a hand appeared at the entrance and next, a pair of eyes full of hatred looked out at him from a hot, perspiring face. It was the officer and he commenced to wriggle his way in ; but Pierce realising that desperate means require a desperate remedy, gave him a push and he toppled backwards into the sea. He smiled grimly to himself as he watched the body hit the water and watched the ripples for a while after.

He had not long to wait for the next one, and he also tried to crawl in, oblivious of what had happened his predecessor, as the incline from the cave was particularly steep and an observer overhead would see nothing. But Pierce used the same remedy with him and watched again the ripples on the water. He was getting used to it; one could get used to anything, Florence used to say.

The third, obviously thinking the first two had the Chieftain well trussed up by this time, commenced to crawl in at his leisure ; he was even humming a tune—but it was a tune he finished in eternity. The next was even more blasé for he felt sure the prisoner was now safely bound ; and when he saw a hand stretching out towards him he felt grateful indeed for the kind gesture in helping him over the last few feet ; but it was the hand that dealt him his death-blow, for in a few seconds he too had sunk beneath the brine. There was a wait of half an hour before the fifth came on and he bore a quizzical expression as he peered in through the entrance ; obviously, the inexplicable silence mystified him. Pierce had pity in his heart for the poor wretch as he rolled downwards, bounding and rebounding against the sward. And then the sixth, a huge burly fellow, came panting to the opening ; he too thought the hand that came out was to help him forward, and Pierce wondered afterwards if his victim realised at the time that he was being sent to his doom, for it needed but the barest push to send a man sliding down that steep slope, sliding down, down—oh God, down to the seals and the sharks, down to the treacherous sound that sank the Santa Maria de la Rosa and many a brave battleship besides.

But this was no time for introspection or misguided pity; rather a time for the utmost thought and deliberation. There were still Roundheads on the island; the officer said he left men guarding the boats; what would they do? Search for the fugitive, no doubt.

This they did for a fortnight afterwards; searched high and low like fiends for their quarry, but all to no purpose; for, as one can readily understand, they never knew the cave was there, and there was nobody among those faithful islanders to betray the least hint of its existence. Day after day with bayonets fixed they scoured every accessible yard of the island, prodding stacks of hay and ricks of turf, searching under the thatch and clearing the cupboards in the cabins, never thinking that an insignificant looking rock a mile or two away contained the fugitive's hiding-place; never thinking that each evening after dark one of the islandmen stole down to their Chieftain with food and drink, and told him how the chase was going.

But the days were long and miserable in that insufferable, dreary den; at night-time he would come out and lie on the heather but during the day he had to re-enter his foul prison and sit and listen to the drip till night again gave him welcome release. " Oh, Almighty God ! " he would mutter, " you alone know what I'm suffering here; but it's my cross, Lord, my cross for Ireland. What a change from the time in my father's day when the Dun would be all lights and the coaches would rumble over the cobbles and five and twenty of us would sit down to dinner—and even we thought that number small.

" Oh, Almighty God, pity me as I am," he wrote, for he would sometimes scribble a few verses as the thought struck him, " pity me here in this cold prison cell with scarcely the light of day; from the rock above the drip is ever in my ear, and below is the roar of the ocean."

Yes, it was indeed different from that night at the Rose when he danced with Sybil; how gracefully she tripped in the minuet and how her golden hair shone in the flashing lights from the crystal candelabra which Tom Trant only lit for special guests. She was beautiful with a beauty scarcely mortal ; one felt that her feet scarcely touched the oaken floor as she circled round and round. But memories of past joys are such poor things when thrown against the misery and pain of the present—a sorrow's crown of sorrow is remembering happier things.

Then the soldiers suspecting what was happening sent for extra men to Ross, about thirty in all, and billeted two in every house on the island, so that there could be little possibility of food being smuggled out from anywhere. But the "King" had a plan to circumvent this. He sent a note to Pierce telling him to leave his hiding-place that night and go to the extreme western end of the island where a canoe was waiting to take him back once more to the mainland. Everything went well, it was a pitch-dark night, and arriving at Dunquin he made his way to William the weaver's. There he remained for several weeks till the Cromwellians grew tired of waiting and returned to Ross, reporting their mission a failure.

Later on came a message from Ludlow :

" Captain Ferriter would be given a safe conduct and a free pardon if he reported at Killarney."

" Better go," he thought.

He crossed back to Dunquin, got a horse from Micheál at the inn, and rode to Dingle. After a glass of wine at The Rose, he went to Aunascaul and thence through Inch to Milltown. There, while changing horses, he learned that the Roundheads had taken Father Thaddeus. The news made him all the more determined to report to Ludlow, for, perhaps, he could do something for his friend.

Ludlow had a thin, pale face with a high forehead and wore a short, black beard. He was extremely affable.

" Hm, Captain Ferriter, so you got my message ; you had confidence enough in us to return."

" I trust, General, that a soldier's word will always be taken at its worth."

" True, true, Captain Ferriter ; but as to your future, I

want you to sign a formal declaration of surrender and then you'll have a safe conduct home."

"I suppose it's inevitable that I follow the others."

"I suppose so, Captain Ferriter; I think, after all, the terms were pretty generous: we've kept only a dozen or so."

"Hm, and Father Moriarty."

"That's a different question. A soldier is one thing; a popish priest another. Let me quote the Lord Protector's words on the matter: 'I meddle not with any man's conscience, but if by liberty of conscience you mean a liberty to exercise the Mass, I judge it best to use plain dealing, and to let you know, where the Parliament of England have power, that will not be allowed of.' And might I remind you, Captain Ferriter, the priest Moriarty was caught in that very act."

"Hard words, General."

"That's a matter of opinion, Captain."

"But surely you yourself don't agree with them?"

"I am a mere servant of the Commonwealth: I both express and interpret its laws. The priest Moriarty was caught in the act of his popish practices and for me that is sufficient: he must pay the penalty."

"What is the penalty, General?"

"Death by hanging."

"That's final, then?"

"Final, Captain Ferriter. You are now free to go."

IV
SHADES OF DEATH
The Poet Dreaming

PIERCE RODE OUT beneath the twin towers of Ross, and wondered if anything could still be done. As he cantered on towards Faha and Listry, his thoughts were still busy. At Milltown he got his original horse and with little delay rode towards Castlemaine. He was almost at the bridge when he heard horses behind. In a few seconds a half dozen Roundheads rode up to him.

"Captain Ferriter?"

"Yes."

"We've orders for your immediate arrest."

"But General Ludlow gave me a safe conduct."

"General Ludlow's changed his mind: you'll accompany us to Ross."

He scarcely knew what to think; what an extraordinary *volte face*. Had Father Thaddeus escaped or had the Irish broken some clause? His train of thought was interrupted by the commander, a pleasant fellow enough.

"I'll tell you, Captain Ferriter, I'll make you a proposition: you're a poet, aren't you?"

"Yes."

199

" Well, do you see that seagull yonder standing on one leg ? "

" Yes."

" If you make twenty-one verses about that seagull all ending in the same rhyme, and before she puts down the other foot, we'll let you free."

What an extraordinary proposition ? It was like a thing hucksters would say. To them a poet was a mere rhymer. No wonder O Bruadair called them bondmen and ill-bred whelps.

Even suppose I descend to their level and encourage them in their buffoonery, he thought, how could one any more take them at their word ? How could one trust these tradesmen from London without pedigree or pride, without lore or learning ? What had he, of a long line of proud Norman blood, in common with Goody Hook and Father Salem, Gammer Hook and Goodman Cabbage ? With their fat, stupid faces ; filthy ways ; hatred of books ; with their shouting, wrangling and lying, they were not even fit to wait upon his servant, Robert. Truly, these were no times for a man to be learned in Latin and the arts ; in music, geography and the lore of the seanchai ; to be refined and gentle in the hall though fierce in the fray. No doubt these tradespeople go to the greatest pains to walk in the footsteps of those they had supplanted : they want a jerkin like the Viscount ; and my lady wants a tiny boot like the Countess ; but that is but the merest foppery ; for the craft of the bard means nothing to them and the sweet tinkling of the harp is like the corncrake in their ears. They've never heard that every hour, every minute in Heaven is taken up with music ; that the devils flee before its magic strains. A pity indeed the man without music. But our new masters prefer their cattle and swine ; their curds and whey ; the bellowing of the bull.

Something new indeed to Ireland was Clan Thomas.

" Gentlemen," he said, " I've little time or inclination for merriment : will you please execute your duty."

So they returned to Ross. He was quickly taken to Ludlow.

" Captain Ferriter, I think that after all, you'd be safer here with us than roaming round your mountains."

He turned to the guard.

" Put him in the cell."

The cell was a small one, with a stone pillar, to which was attached an iron ring. High up was a small window with bars ; he could hear the lapping of the lake against the wall. He sat on the wooden seat and looked about with a wry smile. Then an old grumpy gaoler came with a plate of porridge ; with a loud clang he locked the door and went away mumbling. By this time it was near nightfall. The wind began to rise on the lake and moan around the castle ; the waters dashed themselves against the grey stones and sometimes clouds of spray came through the bars.

He wondered if Tadhg were near. Always the realist, Tadhg was well able to go through with it ; it wouldn't be easy to break his spirit. Soon the rats began to scamper about ; their eyes flashed in the dark. He tried to keep awake, aiming now and again, a kick at a pair of eyes that moved noiselessly nearer.

Could a Ferriter go through with it ? Could he die like Finian died, his heart all on fire ? And how did Florence die ? It must at any rate have been brave ; for Florence certainly didn't lack courage. But it was a quick death not like the cat-and-mouse tactics of Ludlow, though Ludlow gave one ample time to review the old query—to be or not to be—to disappear into nothingness or else to live a fuller, more intense life than ever experienced here. Would he meet Florence again, Florence with wings ? (I wish I could get rid of these damned wings, Pierce !) Would he hear Sybil singing endless songs, or see his father discuss once more with his cronies the question of Spanish aid ? Why did such ridiculous thoughts come crowding on him ? Is a man responsible for his thoughts ? Do not thoughts and emotions make one sometimes feel a different being entirely unknown to oneself ? But that was going very deep indeed, far deeper than his skimpy theology or philosophy would allow. The world of sense was his domain ; for how else could a poet convey his message ? Theologians from their high altitudes might treat with scorn the tinkling of the rhyme and the dance of the numbers and frown upon sensuous imagery. But the glory of external creation as expressed in such sensuous imagery was proof of the Creator's existence ; the poet's inspiration raised him to the same level as the mystic ; whether the poet was aware of it or not, he was sharing in some stupendous mystery.

All the glory of nature he was soon to leave behind : he knew it instinctively—all the sights and sounds he loved so well —royal Desmond with the grandeur of the ocean beating round her shores ; the glory of spring and autumn in the fields and woods ; the sweet evening song of the birds. Craftmanship he loved, too, like the weaving at old William's ; the woman of the house spinning in her cabin as she crooned an air ; the potters, wedging, throwing and turning on the wheel ; the woodworkers with their settles and chests ; the perspiring coopers amidst the clattering of the keelers. The smell of good, fresh earth was sweet to his nostrils ; the waving of the silky grass in early summer ; rich autumn with her golden store ; snug winter with the blazing fires, the story-teller and the music. Now all that was going ; he felt in his bones it was. Ludlow surely meant nothing well by bringing him back and throwing him into this filthy place with rats running round him.

It all gave one to think ; surely not the time to debate academically the existence of a hereafter or to take refuge even in a vague pantheism ; but to touch upon those things which lay very deep and which neither he nor his friends seldom or ever spoke about. How was he prepared to meet death ? Was there nobody to lift their hands in blessed forgiveness over him ; nobody to say the simple words of tremendous import : I absolve thee from all thy sins ? All during the siege, all during his young life in Corca Dhuibhne, Tralee and Baile Mac Egan, he tried to be a faithful son of Mother Church. An occasional lapse, but in the main, he had woven a fairly distinct pattern into his life. It was Sybil's death which first brought him to a realisation of the complexity of life. Useless now, of course, to repeat the old question : should he have brought her thus to her doom ? Dwelling on that would drive a man to madness ; long ago he had put it from him. Had she been shriven ? Did despair grip her in its icy grasp at the last horrible moment ? Had she time to say she repented ?

Where did such thoughts get one ? What was the use of their interminable repetition ? Surely time to think instead of his own preparedness. When last had he been at Mass ? Not since before the fall of Ross. And before that ? Once or twice when the people met and worshipped in the old way. They would tramp long distances to be present at the holy supper ; to have at least a few moments' peace ; to forget the ashen features of the land ; to talk with blessed Erc and Brendan and Carthage ; to pray for their dead, especially the dead who died against Cromwell ; to forget for a while Cromwell and his doings and commune instead with quiet, restful things, things which the greatest Poet of all spoke about, lilies, the lilies of the field. The phrase for some might have almost become a cliché, but beholding a lily in the freshness of May one sees things in a new light. What a lovely thought ! See how tall and straight they were ; see the sparkling whiteness as no whiter on earth could make them ; and then think of Solomon in all his cloths of gold and diamonds and gems ; yes, they were more beautiful ; no denying that ; more beautiful with neither labour nor spinning ; and yet they fitted perfectly into the design destined for them by the great Poet. They without demur, gave themselves to be the instruments in a divine plan.

Like the lilies, he must serve. So easy, yes—in theory. But when his hopes had all faded like the mist ; most of his friends laid low ; the cause for which he had deserted his own class trampled in the dust ; and a blood-soaked ruffian to rule the Commonwealth—not easy then to bow one's head and say " serviam." He would pray not to become sour, sour from frustration and defeat ; sour from the loss of all he possessed, materially and spiritually. Even suppose he had remained loyal to Denny's crew ; what then ? It could scarcely have mattered ; for even staunch old Lady Kerry, with her " beeves, garrons and acres of somer corne " had been bundled off to Connaught.

If Pierce but knew it he was typical of the mediaeval world wholly taken up as it was with the twin problems of sin and death. The Renaissance, or the interest in the new learning, had, of course, altered much of that ; but this new learning barely touched the fringe of Anglo-Irish life and never at any time did it penetrate into Gaelic thought.

CHAPTER XXXVI

IF ONE HAD to die, however, one might as well get used to thinking about it ; but it was so difficult to leave this lovely world. Even as a child perched on the battlements of Castle Ferriter, he loved to listen to the ceaseless roll of the ocean and watch the flocks of birds flitting in the evening sunshine. He loved winter, too, with the huge fires and the splendour and the feasting. It was again that far distant day in November when his father, the Chieftain Ferriter, crossed the courtyard to receive his guest.

" Pardon my lateness, Eamon, the mist at Dingle delayed me," the Knight of Kerry said.

" Not at all, Maurice, you're the first : come in and have a cup of wine."

The Chieftain led the way down the stone passage to the anteroom.

" Whiskey, I suppose ? "

" You keep a good cellar."

" Glad you think so."

He poured out two pewter cups from a decanter.

" Here's to the boy : how old is he now ? "

" Seven "

" Well, here's to Pierce."

" Slainte, Maurice."

" What plans have you made for him ? "

" An ollamh here, and afterwards the seminary at Tralee."

" And then ? "

" A bardic school, perhaps."

" Few left ! "

" But Flann Mac Egan is still in Tipperary."

" I didn't think you were interested in poetry."

" Neither am I ; but if the boy wants to mix with the chieftains, it would be useful."

" How many of them are left ? Denny and his likes will never take to the Gaelic."

" I wonder."

" Never, Eamon."

There was knock.

" Yes ! "

It was Robert, the steward.

" Master Walter Hussey, sir."

" Excuse me, Maurice."

Shortly the steward announced O'Donoghue of the Glens and immediately after, Mac Elligott from Bally Mac Elligott. Then O'Falvey and the Mac Carthy Mor arrived ; and finally, Fitz Gerald from Castle Gallarus.

The crystal candelabra with its twinkling lights made the dining-hall a cheery place. At the door, a little boy looked up shyly.

" Well Pierce, here are your guests ! "

The light gave a golden sheen to his curls.

" Welcome, gentlemen."

" Thank you, Pierce : many happy returns."

All sat down, the boy in the place of honour.

" I hear, Pierce, you are a splendid scholar," said the Knight.

Pierce was not used to visitors, let alone a banquet : he said very little. To-night he seemed paler than usual in his black velvet suit and white lace collar. Like the prince in the story, he thought only of the day when he would be a knight in shining armour going forth to slay the fiery dragon and woo the princess of his dreams.

" What do you think of the latest rumours, O'Donoghue ? " asked O'Falvey when they were all in their places.

" I haven't heard any."

" But everybody talks about them ! "

" Listen, O'Falvey, Dun an Oir finished me with foreigners."

" Indeed ! "

" We never do a thing of ourselves but wait with folded arms till the Spanish ship sails in : I'm tired of this talk of foreign help."

" Wine, gentlemen ? "

Robert stood behind with a flagon.

" Please ! "

The rich ruby sparkled in the soft light.

" To Pierce ! " said the Knight.

" And may he be worthy of his ancestors," said Hussey.

When they were reseated, O'Falvey returned to his argument.

" But why not accept help, no matter what the reason for its being sent ? "

" Because, I will repeat, such dependence leads to want of confidence in ourselves."

" But surely there are men still left ? "

" True enough ; but none like James Fitzmaurice. Alone of all he tramped from court to court looking for ships ; for money ; for men. He got them, got them O'Falvey, after begging on bended knees ; but what happened ? What happened, O'Falvey ? Nobody bothered at home."

" And why can't somebody rouse them now to a last rally ? "

" I am older than you, O'Falvey, and I have seen preparations for many campaigns : I have seen plans mislaid, plans miscarried, excellent plans brought to nought. I, too, was an ardent advocate of foreign aid. As I watched Fitzmaurice flit from court to court, I longed for the day when the Spaniards would sail over the seas and crush the English heretic. But I was young then, O'Falvey, and I knew little of men. Fitzmaurice was a great and noble soul who tried to do the impossible : he thought they were all as great and noble as himself. He little dreamt they would murder him on a cold winter's night ! I am sick of it all, I tell you : if this new expedition comes, it will be the same old story."

Then a harp began to play, a harp, beautifully soft, at first scarcely audible, like elfin music on a moonlit night. A harper had entered unobserved, and sat on a dais at the end of the hall. It was blind Nicholas from Clanmaurice.

The guests held their breath for the sheer artistry of his skill. Slowly the melody became louder and more agitated, like the wind about Dun an Oir on a stormy night. One seemed to hear the screams of the dying, the wail of the children, and see a ruined and wasted land, but soon it became soft and sweet like angel choirs.

Afterwards, Pierce retired and the others climbed the spiral stairway to an oak-panelled chamber. The logs blazed in the

stone fireplace ; and the candles shone in silver sconces. Some
played backgammon while others sat about the fire and smoked,
in the lastest fashion, the tobacco plant from the Indies. When
they had said all that could be said about the Spaniards, they sang
with such lustiness that Câit overhead feared they would disturb
the sleeping child.

*   *   *

Before Pierce was many more years, the meagre Spanish
help came. O'Neill and O'Donnell marched to Kinsale, and
to the doom of the Gaelic nation. However, children do not
think of such things. Pierce became more and more the delight
of his father, and the beloved of the tenants from the parish of
Moore to Marthain and from Clochar to Dun Chaoin.

He would play for hours among the red rocks of Dun an
Oir, hearing the ring of the restless sea and feeling the salt kiss
of the spray : tumbling amidst the brown bracken, climbing
slippery paths into tiny coves and caught sometimes by a sudden
wave.

About the small peninsula where the castle stood, the greenish-
blue waters churned themselves into a creamy surf. Here and
there lichen-covered rocks jutted over the cliff edge. Often
he would sit and listen to the roll of the breakers making endless
war with the broken coast, and watch the clouds of spray rise
above the rocks. North of the castle stretched a dark, sandstone
promontory, brooding over the waters like a gloomy giant ;
and away to the east rose Brandon, mighty and cloud-capp'd.

As he grew older, he visited the farmers when work was at an
end ; and everybody sat about the glowing fire listening to
melodies played sweetly in tune. Seamus, the seanchai, told
tales of knights in shining armour who braved the terrors of
the deep : then about the wreck, the Jenny Lynd, seen at low
tide on Smerwick Strand, the mysterious lands whence she
came and the stormy seas she ploughed. The boy, with his
dark eyes rivetted on the story-teller, drank in the magic of the
tale ; sometimes he would tell him about Dun an Oir for often
the other boys and himself pretended to be Grey, Raleigh or

Spenser butchering the prisoners and throwing their heads over the cliff.

But it was the story of the sailor-saint, the holy Brendan, that made him gaze in tongue-tied wonder at the seanchai. To think that a man born in his own very Kerry could so sail into the unknown and leave behind him a tale that would enthrall Europe for centuries, was indeed a wonder past all recording.

CHAPTER XXXVII

PIERCE WOULD NEVER take his eyes from the face of old Seamus while he told this story ; no matter how often he heard it he would always want to hear it again. The Isle of Birds in particular with their tinkling bells fascinated him, and he would ask the seanchai to repeat it many times, as also the incident where Brendan said Mass in the boat while all the monsters of the deep encircled the holy brethren as would a phalanx. And sometimes he might wake in the early hours thinking he had come to the island of evil where the hideous hairy smiths banged unceasingly on their anvils.

And so Pierce grew up : riding to Dun Chaoin with his father : sailing out with the nets and lobster pots : going with Robert to shoot plover and petrel, snipe and stare ; plodding up Marthain to view the pagan altar—and even once climbing in the footsteps of the sailor saint to the summit of Brandon.

One beautiful Sunday when the sun sparkled in the bluest of skies, he stood watching, with the other lads, a game of hurling in the public pitch not far from the Castle. Perhaps the scene was not so splendid as that before the King's Majesty at Whitehall. No bugles blared but none the less, no courtiers ever heard such nimble wit. Sometimes the eye might wander past the golden corn to the blue of Béal Bán, and thence across to the grandeur of Brandon. The ollamh, Domhnall O Dalaigh and Blind Nicholas stood in a far corner ; Father Micheál, the old philosopher-priest, strolled among his people ; Seamus, the seanchai, revived old memories with his cronies ; the tenants jostled one another for a better view. The parish of Ferriter had challenged that of Moore.

Pierce joined with the other lads in the tremendous burst of applause when Ferriter scored ; still his eyes held a wistful look, for on the morrow he would leave for the seminary at Tralee.

His friends were sorry to see him go especially Seainin and Tomás. Next afternoon, when mounted on his dark pony, Seainin came forward and, without speaking, handed him a hurley on which Pierce had often thrown longing eyes.

" Thanks, Seainin," he said, doing his best to be brave, " I shall be back again at Christmas."

" Good-bye, Pierce, lad," said his father, " and come back a great scholar : Robert will take good care of you. I have made all arrangements at the school ; and Robert has full instructions. As you shall stay in Dingle to-night, perhaps you may see some of the fair. Good-bye ! "

That day Dingle sang gaily ; for it was the yearly fair of St. James. The travellers found difficulty in picking their way through the throngs. Pierce never before saw so many jugglers and showmen ; and several times Robert had to turn back.

In a short while, Pierce and Robert joined the jostling crowds. Pretty maidens gathered round the fortune-tellers : trick-o-the-loop men waved their hands in their mysterious way : women haggled over a piece of fine linen or Hollands lace : men bought and sold and went into taverns : musicians played, and sang of doughty deeds in royal Desmond.

Pierce never ceased asking questions, and even that night at dinner, he still wanted to know more.

Afterwards they went to the tap-room in The Rose where there were a few customers seated. Candles burned in the bronze brackets about the walls ; and the red plush curtains were drawn across in the usual way. Tom bustled to and fro, with a smile and a word for everyone. Robert and Pierce sat near the door. Many glanced their way and most recognised the prim steward and the boy ; but few felt bold enough to be familiar. Robert sipped his wine in silence while Pierce fidgeted and fumbled.

They were not long thus when two men entered who on looking about for a seat, recognised the steward. They had frequently been to the Castle to advise the Chieftain on the sale of stock. They seated themselves near Robert much to the delight of Pierce for Sean had unlimited stories. Often when he stayed at the Castle he had enthralled the young lad with tales of the Black Earl's raid.

Then he told him about the old Countess of Desmond who had died some time before that at the age of seven score. She danced with Richard III, got married in the reign of Edward IV and held her jointure from all the Earls of Desmond from that onwards. When the old Earl was attained in the late Queen's day she lost her fortune too and was in great distress for some years but nothing daunted, at the age of one hundred and forty, she travelled to Whitehall to ask a little help of King James. This the monarch graciously granted but the dear old lady did not enjoy her gratuity for very long, not on account of old age, however, but through a fall from an apple tree where she had been picking apples.

Sean in his younger days had been a sailor in the Spanish service and thus knew a little of that great civilisation. The final routing of the Moors by Ferdinand and Isabella was a tale that always captivated the boy and now once more he insisted on hearing how the Cross finally came to victory in the peninsula—how on that great day, with flags waving, pennants flying and with all the glitter and gorgeousness of the Court, both of the Sovereigns accepted the surrender of Granada and thus began a new era.

Next he told him about the great navigator, the Very Magnificent Lord Don Cristobal Colon, commonly called Christopher Columbus and of his voyage into the unknown to reach the sun-kissed islands in the west; his meeting with the Indians; his search for gold; his return to Europe in triumph and finally his downfall.

But nearer their own days was the story of the Armada, which within living memory had been scattered as autumn leaves before the west wind. Down it came past the coast of Kerry, sixty galleons still left out of the original one hundred and thirty one. The Duke himself passed so far out that he did not see the Irish coast but one of his officers, with two large ships besides his own, came round by Dunmore Head ; his crews were dying for want of water so he made straight for Dingle Bay, but in passing through the Blasket Sound, the Santa Maria de la Rosa went down with all on board. Out of the seven hundred who originally manned her she still had two hundred left, but of these there was one only to swim to safety.

That was at the end of August. Slowly the stragglers made their way back to Corunna, that same Corunna from which they had set out only the month before, bounding over the waters, the mightiest fleet of the mightiest monarch in Christendom.

Then Sean told once again the story of Dun an Oir and all the subsequent happenings ; and so thus it was that when Robert returned with Micil some two hours later the boy was sitting quietly on the bench near the fire, sipping his cider every now and again, and in his dark eyes a faraway look. Would it always be defeat, defeat ? he was thinking. Would there never be a morning, a glorious morning of victory, when we too with Don John of Austria would go riding to the wars ? Or must we accept as inevitable an existence, where " a nettle-wild grave was Ireland's stage ? "

After chapel next morning, they prepared for the road. Soon they took their leave of Tom and in a short while were on the mountains. The horses ambled at their leisure. Higher they climbed, past a horseshoe bend, with cliffs like columns of a temple. At the summit, Robert paused to show Pierce the Shannon and the headlands of Clare, and on the other side Uibh Rathach and the Skelligs.

As they descended, the horses found it difficult to pick their steps, but they reached level ground without mishap. They rode at a brisk rate. After a time, they saw Gregory Hoare's castle near the sea's edge. Once, when the Elizabethan soldiers were on the way to Smerwick, they stopped the night here. The wine ran short and Gregory Hoare sent his lady down to the cellar for more. But she, being a proud Desmond, preferred to see it running waste over the cobbles than used by Denny, Raleigh, and Spenser. So she pulled out all the stoppers and left it flow. Gregory, wondering what delayed his lady, came down. He was so mad with her that he plunged his sword through her breast.

Sunshine filled the vale. To the left, the ocean rolled in white rings round the rocks of Kerry head. In a short while they trotted through the town of Tralee—the great distant town of Tralee where he had come for Latin learning and English graces. Here he was to spend many years and meet many friends, friends who would be true even in that far distant day when one of them would stand with him on the scaffold on Cnocán na gCaorach in Killarney town.

The travellers went slowly through the narrow, cobbled streets. As it was market-day, they sometimes had to stop to let sheep or bullocks pass. They followed the river along Bridge Street into Burgess Street, where, turning to the left, they came to a square where there was a tavern painted in blue. Over the doorway hung a large golden key.

CHAPTER XXXVIII

IN THE BEGINNING he felt homesick at the school of Doctor O'Connell, especially when the clang of the morning bell brought the meaningless ritual of another day. But in a few weeks he found his feet; and life began to take on a pattern again. He who had been reared amidst the loneliness of the mountains found mixing with the boys the hardest task. There were so few he could confide in, except perhaps young Thaddeus Moriarty from Castle Drum. They had much in common and from the start they became fast friends; Thaddeus, though not as tall as Pierce, had the same dark eyes.

Also in the first year was Florence Mac Carthy, then a pug-faced hardy youngster who always knew what he wanted and was in complete contrast to the other two.

After school the boys would walk along by the river, and on fair days they would dodge in and out between the crowds Once when Pierce and Thaddeus, (then Tadhg), were together, Pierce overthrew a cask of apples. Tadhg was never exactly able to say whether it was deliberate or not ; for Pierce sometimes did the most irresponsible things. Old Sam Jones, the proprietor, with a warlike whoop set after them ; but they were too quick for him. They ran up by Brogue-Maker's Lane towards the Parish Church.

The boys, seeing that Sam had given up the chase, strolled down the bank of the river towards the castle. When they came to the bridge, they saw Daniel O'Daly on the other side ; they halloo'd him and he turned to them, smiling. Daniel was a day pupil and lodged in the town. He was four or five years older than the boys and would soon be leaving the school. He was a lad of considerable promise, the Doctor taking no pains to conceal his admiration for his brilliant verse composition; but, withal, he was no bookworm and was good at games and none loved a prank more than he. He was tall and had a pleasing countenance with a Roman nose. The O'Dalys were a very old and honoured sept and it was Dan's proudest boast that they had been traditional bards to the Mac Carthys. He had taken a liking to the lads and they in their turn regarded him with the hero-worship of the schoolboy ; he had a veto in everything they did and nothing was finally decided till he had spoken. Even that night when Tadhg hid the spectacles of the Master of Studies in the clock, it was Dan who found them and discreetly restored them. He lived at the western end of the town and often the boys came home with him to partake of his mother's venison pies.

" Well ! and where are you for ? " he queried.

" Anywhere but within reach of Sam Jones," answered Pierce, as they laughingly told of their encounter. Dan smiled for poor old Sam was a peculiar character.

As they strolled down the Mall, many of their fellow-students passed them. The town was busy as it usually was on the eve of the Sabbath. Carts of all kinds rumbled past on the narrow roadway, sometimes bespattering an indignant coxcomb.

A tall, whitehaired figure approached who bore a slight stoop but unmistakeably he must have been of commanding presence in his younger days. It was Dean Comane, now in his seventieth year. His features were well-chiselled and his eyes were kind and held a depth of tenderness. It was indeed extraordinary how the Dennys tolerated him in the town. He was attired in a saffron jerkin over which was a dark cloak and he had a small, black hat. He spoke to the boys for some time and then went his way.

Tralee was also in those days a town of many shops : book shops, apothecaries' shops, shops for trinkets, clothiers' shops and even a shop kept by Manuel Gabriel who dabbled in the hermetic sciences.

Old Gabriel had a white wrinkled face and wore a black skull-cap, from which escaped his unkempt locks. Thirty years ago he came with Sir Edward and when the wars were over, bought a house on the river facing the castle.

Nominally he was an apothecary. On the shelves gleamed hundreds of bottles. But unknown to most he spent whole nights with his bubbling retorts, mixing feverishly, pouring from phial to phial, bending closer over the weird concoction, hoping against hope for the precious transmutation.

" If only I could find it ! Ah, if only I could ! " he would murmur as, with the coming of dawn, he pushed aside his retorts in despair.

Dan knew him well ; and his was the first shop they visited.

Pierce had never before been in such an interesting shop. The shining bottles fascinated him. Now and again, he would glance at Manuel with ill-concealed admiration. The alchemist, like an old hag, would press his thin lips into an acid smile and cackle :

" You like my shop, my young friend. He, he ! Have you anything like it where you come from ? "

" Why, no, sir : I've never seen so many bottles in my life."

" He, He ! Probably not, probably not."

" What of the philosopher's stone, Mr. Gabriel ? " asked Dan.

" Ah, my young friend, you natives always ask awkward

questions. Listen, I will tell you a secret ; but you must promise not to give it away."

" We promise," Dan replied, trying not to smile. Alchemy was surely going to poor Manuel's brain.

Lowering his voice and looking solemnly at Tom, he said :

" I've discovered a special element among the red rocks of Slieve Mish : in a cave by a stream I came upon it. See, it glitters like a diamond. Look ! " and taking from a drawer a large semi-transparent bluish stone, he held it before them triumphantly.

Dan nearly burst out laughing.

" But that's a Kerry diamond, Mr. Gabriel."

" A what ? "

" A Kerry diamond : these stones are quite plentiful in Kerry."

" Master O'Daly, I'm afraid you will severely strain our friendship. I surely know more about these things than you. I am certain that this stone will supply the missing element : there's no doubt of it. Imagine," he said, opening wide his eyes and giving a deep sigh, " imagine when His Majesty hears that in the wilds of Ireland an alchemist has transmuted metals to gold."

" It will be truly wonderful, Mr. Gabriel," said Dan.

They bade him good afternoon and continued on their way. A few doors further up Nathaniel Harrison kept his bookshop. No sooner did they enter when Nathaneil, with a smile, said :

" Ah, Master Dan, I haven't seen you for a long time : I have some new books."

" Thank you, Mr. Harrison ! By the way, these are two friends of mine."

" How do you do, young gentlemen ? "

" Master Ferriter is an authority on Gaelic lore, Mr. Harrison."

" Indeed ! son to the Chieftain, I presume."

" Yes, sir," answered Pierce.

" I've sold many books to your father, young man. I've just got a few things from Louvain : do you know if he has a copy of O'Hussey's poem to Miler Magrath ? "

" Yes sir, I am sure he has : I've heard him speak of it."

" And what about Archbishop Conroy's ' Mirror of Religion ' ? "

" I'm not sure about that one, sir."

" I'd better let him know I have it : copies are rare, you know."

Nathaniel had also come with the Dennys, and afterwards set up shop. He married a girl from near the town and thus had sympathy with the old race.

" But see my fine shelf of the dramatists'," he continued, " they've only just arrived : here's rare Ben Jonson."

Dan took an exquisite volume with gilt edges.

" They say this old Jonson was a merry fellow, Dan : he used to sit in the Mermaid Tavern in London town with a throng of poets about him, laughing and quaffing the hours away."

The talk opened a new world to Pierce : hitherto his idea of a poet had been the bard with his dignities and privileges. To him a poet was a priest of the muses who sat next the chieftain at the board, rejoiced with him in gladness, wept with him in sorrow. He was the family historian, too, and his knowledge of royal pedigrees profound. Small wonder, then, that Pierce could scarcely visualise a throng of poets so bereft of dignity as to carouse in a cheap tavern.

" And there is Sir Edmund Spenser," went on Nathaniel. " Did I ever tell you I spoke to Spenser ? No ! Well, he was in this very shop : it was after Dun an Oir and he was staying with Sir Edward across. One morning as he walked about the town, he saw a few volumes in the window and came in : of course I didn't know him.

" ' Ah, a bookshop," he said, his bearded lips curling into a smile, ' and what books might you have, Mr. Bookseller ? '

" ' In Latin, sir ? I said.

" ' No, in the English tongue.'

" ' Well I have poems by Master Chaucer and Master Langland.'

" ' Anything else ? '

" ' The poems of Sir Philip Sidney, sir, and some copies of the latest poem, The Faerie Queene.'

" ' What do you think of it ? '

" ' Well, sir, to tell you the truth I haven't read a lot of it ; but the little I have read I like very much : it has an unearthly sweetness entirely new to me. It is a fairy world, sir, where crystal streams sparkle and knights in shining armour ride past.'

" ' True, I suppose ; but do you know where the poet got this unearthly sweetness, as you call it ? '

" ' No, sir.'

" ' In the woods and meadows near his castle at Kilcolman.'

" ' I never imagined his scenery could be Irish scenery, sir.'

" ' About this question of English written in Ireland, people can never see the wood for the trees : they don't stand far back enough. Of course my scenery is Irish.'

" ' I beg your pardon, sir.'

" ' I said my scenery—oh, I'm sorry, Mr. Bookseller : I must introduce myself. I am Edmund Spenser.'

" ' Edmund Spenser ! '

" ' Yes, Edmund Spenser : are you surprised ? '

" ' Why this is an honour sir : won't you sit inside ? ' "

" Yes, he came in, Dan, and we spoke for a short while ; and then he went away. He left the Castle that day ; and I never saw him again."

" Very interesting, Mr. Harrison : did he say anything about the massacre ? "

" Not a word, Dan, nor I to him : he looked so courtier-like that I couldn't associate him with bloodshed."

" Some call him the gentle Spenser."

" Yes, I know : seems very hard to reconcile with Dun an Oir ! "

And Pierce, though scarcely more than a child, thought the same. His early years had so dinned into him the guilt of Grey, Spenser and Denny, that he could scarcely believe them to be of flesh and blood. It was strange to hear that a robber like Spenser could possess such brilliance of intellect, and as well, the traits of a gentleman. It was a puzzle, the poisonous puzzle of English-Irish relations.

But the boy said nothing. The talk was too far above himself and Tadhg. Some day, perhaps, he would be able, like Dən, to speak to Mr. Harrison as man to man : for the present he could only listen.

When they were going Mr. Harrison said :

" Now young gentlemen, don't be afraid to come along any time you like : I'll be delighted to see you, and show you any books you wish."

" Thank you, sir ! "

" And now let's walk further down the river," said Dan, " we've more than a half hour yet : I want to show you where the black friars live."

Pierce gave him a startled look.

" The black friars, Dan : I don't want anything to do with them."

" Why ? That old story ? "

" Because, I heard Mr. Ware say they walk in the abbey every night."

" Nonsense ! These are real friars ; they've only lately come back."

And when they had seen the friars' thatched cabin almost hidden among the trees, they returned to school.

CHAPTER XXXIX

SOON MANY IN TRALEE knew of Dan's going to Spain. It would not do, of course, to talk openly about it, for though there was little active persecution ; yet one must beware of sleeping dogs. King James had just issued a proclamation warning those who had received orders in foreign lands not to dare appear in the Kingdom. Those found transgressing would be placed, in close confinement, at the pleasure of the Viceroy.

One evening towards the end of October, Mistress O'Daly gave a farewell supper. Old friends came. Among them were Dean Comane, the Doctor, Manuel Gabriel, Walter Ware sitting near Pierce and Tadhg, and, of course, Nathanial Harrison beaming upon everybody.

Dan himself, trying to look as if nothing were the matter, sat at the head of the table. When it was time for the toast, Nathaniel proposed it.

Daniel left on a Spanish wine-ship next morning from Curra Graig. As he passed over the plank that served as a gangway, he wondered when he should step on his own beloved soil again. Perhaps never ! He brought his belongings below and then came on deck again to chat with his friends. There was much to do about getting away, as some barrels which Peter Cambridge, the cooper, had promised the evening before, had not arrived. The captain decided to sail without them, so with much heaving and creaking, the little vessel, the "José," left the grey, misty shores of Ireland. His comrades cheered him till he could hear them no longer, but he could still see them waving, waving him away to unknown climes and other ways of life. It was only then that the tears came, wet salt tears of loneliness and a sense of vast, empty void. It was easy enough for one to say he would go to Spain, easy enough till the final parting came. The south-westerly breeze fanned his cheek and the seagulls hovered about the rigging. The crew heaved barrels, threw ropes about and finally unfurled the topsail; but the boy scarcely saw them. He was staring at Slieve Mish. He thought of the last time he had climbed it with Tadhg and Pierce to see Cu Ri's fort. And over there was Brandon. What fun they had when Pierce and he left Castle Ferriter to make the ascent. Now they were at the Maherees and straight across was Kerry Head. Soon the ship was rounding the bend of the peninsula and heading straight for Spain. Ireland was fast disappearing.

" Whereas the peace of this kingdom has been imperilled by seminarists and priests, who go beyond seas for the purpose of education, and on their return teach doctrines calculated to imbue the minds of the people with superstition and idolatry, we strictly prohibit all, save merchants and sailors, from passing over to other countries———"

Pierce and Tadhg missed him much at first. They had their classes each day as usual and romped and played in the afternoon ; but it did not seem the same without Dan. When they called on Manuel Gabriel, they missed Dan's half-cajoling, half-serious tone as he used to question the old man on his alembics and crucibles, and on the planetary signs.

The boys could look forward however to the festival of Saint John, the patron of the parish. This year it coincided with the granting of Tralee's charter. They were full of excitement especially as the Doctor promised a free day.

It was indeed a gala day. Crowds thronged the streets. Players and mummers, jugglers and showmen were scattered amongst the gaping groups. Harpers and singers went from inn to inn.

Robert Blennerhassett with his twelve burgesses marched in procession to Saint John's. Denny, to give him his due, did not spare the wine. There were barrels and barrels along the river. Also he had had oxen roasted and distributed. For weeks after, the boys still talked of Sam Jones trying to dance, or Peter Cambridge pledging a health to the King in Latin.

CHAPTER XL

SHORTLY AFTER this Tadhg also sailed away to Spain. Pierce was very lonely for a bit. He would wander towards the mountain when the catkins came. He was now almost sixteen and he was beginning to see Nature not as in the hours of thoughtless youth, but rather as a mysterious force whose beauty is the shadow of another and happier state. He began to feel a stirring within him, a response to beauty which was at first bewildering. He used to jot down notes on the landscape. The putting of one's thoughts into language was not easy, as he well knew ; besides, he had to remember the intricate rules of Gaelic poetry.

That was his last year at the Doctor's. From thence he went to the great school of poetry and of the feineachas, taught by Flann Mac Egan at Baile Mac Egan, in the County of Tipperary.

Flann's school was a long building of one storey, constructed

of limestone and having a thatched roof. Most of it was divided
up into a large number of cells without any window whatever,
each cell containing a trundle-bed with a straw pallet. At the
southern end, however, there was a large assembly hall having
many windows.

In all there were about two hundred students. From the
slopes of Errigal and the Mourne Mountains ; from Carn
Tuathail and the peaks of Cill Manntain they came ; from the
deep rich soil of Loch Garman and the luscious grass of the
Golden Vale scholars of all ages trooped to sit at the feet of the
master and drink in the old lore grown mellow with the
centuries.

Pierce found the school very strange at first after the " renaissance " curriculum at Tralee. There were many young
men from Desmond there, Domhnall Mac Taidhg an Gharain,
Diarmuid Riabhach O Dalaigh, Maurice Fitzgerald and Richard
Hussey being among his particular friends. Often when they
were supposed to be " tossing on their beds " courting a smile
from the muses, two or three might be found in a cell quietly
comparing the hounds of Ormond with those of Desmond, or
speculating on the hurling match for the coming free day.
Sometimes, too, they would discuss how far the system of
the darkened cell contributed to the desired result. For centuries
this procedure was an integral part of the apprenticeship to
the craft of Gaelic poetry.

It is obvious, however, human nature being what it is, that
such schools of Gaelic lore were by no means the mirthless and
solemn assemblies that one might gather from much that has
been written about Bardic poetry. They were, after all, the
equivalent of our modern university, and thus it is not stretching
probability too far to imagine some of the students now and
again in a mood for gossip rather than work.

Thus Pierce and his friends would sometimes gather in
one or other of the cells and talk of everything, from the pirates
on the high seas to the wisdom of King James. They would
decide, and perhaps rightly so, that the system of the darkened
cell was admirably suited to the student of first class ability,
as well as to him of prodigious capabilities for concentration on

his theme, but that for the rank and file it was obviously un-suited.

And soon, perhaps, the bell would reverberate throughout the building and everywhere there would be movement—servants bringing the lights and the students rising from their beds and committing their thoughts to parchment. An hour would be given them to fashion the verses and then at the sound of the second bell they would all assemble in the great hall for the nightly session.

On this particular night Flann was seated in his usual oaken chair on the rostrum behind a small table upon which lay a few sheets of manuscript as well as other writing materials. There were innumerable rows of deal benches reaching to within a few yards of the rostrum. Seated over by the wall were the three assistant ollamhs. The tall one with the dark countenance was Maghnus O Caoimh, who lived with his wife and lovely daughter Maire about a mile further up on the river. He was quick to note Pierce's considerable proficiency in poetry and often invited him to dine at his home. The others were Seamus Mac Giolla Phadraig, medium sized and turning grey, and Michael Mor O Nuallain, who, true to his name, was a fine figure of a man and had graduated at the school a few years back.

Candles burned in the bronze holders about the oaken walls and heavy sable curtains had been drawn across the windows. When the last student had seated himself Flann rang a bell. Immediately the hum of conversation ceased, he began :

"Last evening I set for you a subject which I feel sure gave splendid scope to your muse. You remember I warned you of the pitfalls and above all I told you that when writing of Ireland nothing is more difficult to avoid than false sentiment ; it is always better to err on the side of under-praise. For example, when speaking of the Shannon, the subject of this evening's session, the majestic sweep of the waters can first be described by a few delicate strokes. There is one such poem, a splendid example of its kind and written by a graduate of this school, Diarmuid O Briain. See the skilful manner in which he etches his background. Many of you would perhaps waste—I deliberately use the word 'waste'—a few stanzas describing the glories of Brian; but not so the poet. Notice how the artist in him gives us a picture of the glittering freshness of the river. And finally we hear the soft roll of the waters. That is what I require of you and I shall never be content till I get you to cut away every unnecessary syllable and to trim a stanza till it is well nigh perfect.

"Another important point is to remember the irony that is rarely far distant from the Irish scene. This may be observed to perfection in the learned and fantastic love poems which originated in Provence and which were practised here by, among several others, Gerald the Earl, and Maghnus O'Donnell; and among our brothers in Scotland, by the Earl and Countess of Argyle and Duncan Campbell of Glenorguhy. There is beauty, no doubt, in this type of verse, a beauty of gossamer-like sheen, but a beauty, nevertheless, interspersed with ironic comment which prevents the least contact with that false sentiment, which besides being bad art is repugnant to the Irish character in any form; for you must have observed before now among our people a tendency to react against any form of sentiment or even mysticism and to look upon life objectively and in a humorous vein. This characteristic can also be seen in our literature, besides the love poetry alluded to, from the epic tales onward.

"These few observations may, perhaps, assist you in your search for the beautiful and the true—the truth of substance and the form of the beautiful, or if you will the splendour of form of which the great Aquinas spoke. But I'm afraid some of you are infected by the new poetry, they dare to call it 'song metre.' All that is necessary we are told is a certain number of feet in each line. I wonder what Tadhg Dall O Huiginn would have thought of it or Giolla Brighde Mhac Con Midhe! We are living, indeed, in strange times, gentlemen," and with that he shook his old grey locks with a despairing sigh.

"But now let us hear some of your attempts. Master Domhnall Garbh O Suilleabhain; what have you got to say on the River Shannon in ae freislighe metre?" and Domhnall stood up in the third row, confused-looking, and began to read.

But it was just as well, perhaps, that the old master, sitting to-night so solemn on his rostrum, was unable to penetrate the future and see to what a sorry pass his noble calling would come. No doubt, the poets of the eighteenth century kept alive among their people the spirit of hope, the vision beautiful, when the Stuarts would come back over the sea and claim their bride Caitlin, the daughter of Houlihan ; but it would be a state of things so completely at variance with all Flann's previous ideas and accepted standards that, perhaps, it were better not to compare them further.

When Domhnall Garbh O Suilleabhain had read his poem there was a good deal of applause and then the master called on Tomás Rua O Coinceanainn, who was a brilliant scholar and whose reading of his verse in an easy measured tread was generally much appreciated. During the auditions Flann usually said little but kept taking notes and at the end of the session, which lasted an hour, delivered judgment.

Then supper was served in the refectory. There was wine and mulled sack ; sweet oaten cakes and wheaten bread with toasted cheese. Seldom, indeed, were the rations short at the school of Flann, son of Cairpre. On the contrary, he received such a supply of provisions by way of gifts from the countryside about that his students were sometimes hard put to consume them all. Besides, when each student arrived at Michaelmas he brought a sack or two of flour or a couple of beeves or some mountainy sheep. The school year was short—it lasted only till March—and often at breaking-up time the buttery was so laden with provisions that several days feasting followed for the people of Baile Mac Egan.

Every Saturday and the eves of festivals the students dispersed themselves among the gentlemen and rich farmers of the surrounding countryside, where they were well entertained and made much of till it was time to return. During the other days at free time when not playing hurling or the old game of football called caid, they would wander along where the long reeds and water lilies lined the Shannon's banks or perhaps sail over the blowing billows to the tiny island of Baile Mac Egan, or further still to the opposite bank which was the County

Galway ; then back again, taking care to steer carefully up the tiny channel through the rushes near the shore. At other times, they would go in the opposite direction to the village of Lorrha, the site of the monastery of St. Ruadhan, who with holy Brendan was one of the twelve apostles of Eireann and who tradition says pronounced that curse against Tara which has ever since left it in solitude.

Afterwards they returned to their cells and trundle-beds and thus the years slipped quickly by. Four years in all Pierce spent there until at length there were few metres he could not handle with consummate mastery or few themes he could not bend to the rhythm of each metre. Flann always held up his compositions as an example to the others. " I've often told you," he would say, " the better the poetry the less conscious one is of the metrical rules. When reading that piece of Piaras Mac Eamuinn last week "—he always called him " Piaras Mac Eamuinn "—" to Maghnus O Caoimh, I could not help being struck by its easy flow."

Pierce had become a frequent visitor to the house of Maghnus. It was a snug building and the Mistress O Caoimh, a gracious lady, always received him kindly. Maire, her daughter with the gentle features and dark eyes, would now and again look up from her embroidery and give a shy glance at the young scholar. And on fine afternoons, Maghnus and he would tramp for miles over the long white dusty roads.

What a contrast, thought Pierce, and how true it is that one never properly appreciates a gift until deprived of it— health, wealth, contentment—it's all the same. Life was ever thus. He remembered when he would grumble and complain about things that seemed so trivial now ; how he would become cross with Robert when he did not instantly fetch his horse, or when the servants would not readily do his bidding. Even that time when he left Baile Mac Egan for good he would go about morosely and sulk because he could not find the companionship of Flann's school in that lonely old castle on the rim of the world. For years he had looked forward to this time, but now being freed from what he had imagined were the shackles of discipline, he found it was far otherwise. He would stroll by Smerwick stand till he came to Dun an Oir, and sit and think of happier days.

Affection fared ill in loneliness. A truism. A good subject for a poem ? Maybe ! A poem to Richard who had opened his own school at Inis Ce in Mayo ? It would at least get his mind off brooding. What would he say ? " This valiant scion comely as Goll "—" the honey of his words "—" the well of knowledge "—" the doorway to learning," and so on. He would start on it when he got back. He didn't want to go back ; since Eoin O Callanain had said his father's heart was weak, the old man had got more and more irritable.

It was a bad autumn. The wind whistled and shrieked through Smerwick ; across from Marthain the rain beat with unusual ferocity. The chieftain had had another heart attack ; however, during the periods of watching by the bedside, he wrote a tolerable poem to Richard.

CHAPTER XLI

ONE DAY A few weeks afterwards came the news of the death of King James. Sir Edward proclaimed King Charles from the battlements at Tralee ; in Dingle, Pierce heard the Constable read the announcement. They had a merry night in The Rose, for few regretted pedantic Jamie.

Lord Kerry gave a ball for the accession. Pierce was there as well as most of the county. The river reflected the rows of lanterns that crossed the lawn and crowds watched the coaches rumble up to the main gates. Lady Kerry, in white satin, beamed upon Pierce.

While he danced a Spanish pavanne, a pretty girl with brown eyes nodded to him and try as he would, he could not recall where he met her. Afterwards she came up to him. She was Meg Russell and they had been children together.

Afterwards they sat and talked of the days when they went nutting along the Feale ; he would steal shy glances towards her and think to himself how beautiful she had become.

Then her partner came and claimed her; even if she had stayed, he couldn't have said much. There was a better way: he would write her a poem. Never was his muse so active as in these first years home from Baile Mac Egan.

When he went to his room, he began. At first he jotted down a few phrases at random. *None more pitiable than hidden love—love for her stately mien and features lily-white—for her flashing teeth and swan-like neck.* Then the verses began to take shape. He sealed and addressed the paper, and ringing for a servant, gave it to him.

After breakfast, he strolled down the river. It was a hard, spring day with a northerly wind. The primroses peeped shyly along the grassy banks; and the breasts of the goldfinches gleamed in the sun.

On his return, as he crossed the lawn, Lord Kerry came out.

" Morning Pierce, how did you like the ball ? "

" Couldn't be better, Lord Kerry, thank you; you certainly spared nothing."

As he went to collect his belongings, he met Meg in the corridor. She was smiling but this time with impudence and he knew then her heart was cold; he cursed himself for a fool. She said, or rather hissed:

" Pierce, don't be an ass: after all, we talked only of childhood days," and she disappeared before he could say a word.

He returned home. His father was still in bed; the cold, he said, but anyone could see he was not well. Pierce told him about the night.

" Ah, young men aren't the same as in my time: I often danced for seven nights in turn all over Desmond and was none the worse."

When he saw his father was weary of talk, he went outside; it was a beautiful afternoon all mellow with the tints of autumn. He was thinking of Meg. Perhaps he didn't sufficiently embellish the poem; or maybe she was indifferent to such things. Wasn't she the " London-woman " ? Didn't she come of a tribe of foreigners. Maybe if he wrote another, a longer one, she would listen. He again jotted down a few phrases.

My heart it was that loved her, but loved her without my leave—a *puzzle it is that she could so charm me and still remain so cold—her features so white—*how shall I put it ? *Beside her even the swan seems less white, and the sparkle in her eyes makes the crystal dull.*

He sent it by the next coach. For days, weeks, months, he waited but there was no reply.

Then news came of the death of the beautiful, shy young Maire Ni Chaoimh whom he used to love to sit with at Baile Mac Egan and watch her deft fingers fashion her lace and embroidery. A fever she got in that damp, unhealthy season and taking to her couch, made a poor struggle. Maghnus, they said, was disconsolate. " Take courage, Maghnus, dear and generous friend," Pierce wrote him, " for all sing your praises. O manly one of the weeping countenance, whose hand revenges treachery, take courage and forget your sorrow."

But it was easy to bid one forget his sorrow, a mere gesture of convention, manners, call it what you will. Even he himself found it difficult to forget the sweet fragrance of Maire's memory though he never professed his shy young love for her—except in verse, but unlike the jade Meg Russell, Maire never even saw it ; for it was merely to ease the burden of his heart that he wrote the lines that came to him in the darkness of his trundle-bed in Flann's school.

But looking back on it now he saw that in comparison with his love for Sybil these former sentiments were merely a temporary infatuation written with all the prettiness and irony which went to the making of the scores and scores of love poems, which, having their origin in the Provence, found their way into Gaelic verse and established there a tradition lasting hundreds of years. Love perhaps, yes, of a kind, but in its expression so given to stock themes as to be rarely convincing, themes which could do such little justice to the surge of joy which filled his whole being when first the hazel eyes of the Lady Sybil looked into his own.

Then one day shortly after his father sent for him ; that was the time when, all propped up between the pile of pillows, he had that fateful talk with his son, which set Pierce on his long trek to the Corrib—into the arms of the Lady Sybil.

*   *   *

Yes, if one had to die one might as well get used to it. No
more would he romp the hills with Sceolan, the huge jet-black
hound, and Sighle the red setter ; and come tramping and
slashing through the bogs with their riot of greens, browns,
purples and blues. He loved June when the feileastroms filled
the fields ; and the soft scent of the new-mown hay added to
the glory of summer. Then he would creep under cover down
by Gallarus to wait for the duck after dusk, or look for woodcock on the side of Marthain. In the pride of his youth and
strength he would repeat again and again as he tramped home :
" Yes, I with my own right hand shall keep the foreign devils
from you, proud Dun Urlan." But how hollow the words
sounded now. Instead here he was at the mercy of that same
foreigner who, no doubt, would never let him free again—never
again to see Spring days ; the quiet roll of the sea on Smerwick
with Brandon's huge bulk behind ; the soft brown bog with
little pools mirrowing the sky ; the gold of sunset like the gold
of Paradise, the gold of the burnished throne of God ; and
the blue, that deep blue of the mountains coming down to
rest in the silence of the sea.

Next day they brought him again before Ludlow. The
General's face seemed to have got harder and his smile of yesterday had gone.

" Captain Ferriter, we've decided it would be dangerous
to let you go among your people again. It may be the cause
of royalist sedition, for, I hear many gather at your castle."

" Many gather at my castle, General, but they are mainly
poets discussing poetry."

" A quibble, Captain."

He paused for a moment, and becoming even more stern,
continued :

" Since we are leaving here soon and manifestly can't take
you with us, I've decided you shall die."

" You surprise me, General."

" If you think so, Captain."

" Besides, General, you've broken your word : a safe conduct
was one of the terms of surrender."

" That does not apply to dangerous rebels."

" A quibble, General."

" Be that as it may, Captain. Be ready, then, to-morrow at midday."

" Might I ask what form of death ? "

" Death by hanging."

" But I'm a soldier, General."

" Captain Ferriter, we've wasted enough bullets on the Irish already."

He turned to the guard.

" Take the prisoner to his cell."

As Pierce was going out, Ludlow halted him.

" By the way, Captain, it may interest you to know you shall have company to-morrow. Your friend, the priest, Moriarty, will also wear the hangman's noose."

*   *   *

Cnocán na gCaorach lay to the east of Killarney. It was a commonage where markets and fairs were held. There, too, public events like executions took place.

It was a bright October morning when the friar, Thaddeus Moriarty, and the poet, Pierce Ferriter, came forth to the gibbet. A crowd collected and stood silently under the trees. The soldiers looked smart in their trim tunics and shining sabres. A row of drummers stood to the south, and behind them, a battalion. To the west was a troop of cavalry, and in front of them, the prisoners.

The crowd came nearer as the prisoner Moriarty slowly mounted the scaffold. His face was pale and drawn and his back bent. It was whispered that he had been in a cell where he could neither stand nor lay at full length. But his voice was still clear.

" I only did my duty," he said, " if I got my freedom, I'd do the same again."

He glanced down at Pierce.

"——these soldiers know not what they do : they are only the tools of Cromwell——"

The hangman stood behind, waiting. The October wind sighed round the trees : the brown leaves fell about the scaffold.

Down below, Pierce could see the deep blue of Torc and Tomies etched against the pale sky. What a lovely world to leave behind!

Still he was ready to go. Even the poet in him sensed that the grandeur of Loch Lein was but a shadow of the glory to come. Ready to go—for though his faults were many, yet he seemed buoyed up with unusual courage. Perhaps Tadhg had given him that. For if a Moriarty, with his wan pale face could die like a man, why couldn't a Ferriter do the same?

He thought of a grave in Dun Urlan where Sybil lay. Then his mind went back to his boyhood days—the hunting on Slieve Mish, the swimming at Béal Bán.

"——my friends, I forgive everybody who has done me any wrong, and my last words to you——"

Father Thaddeus looked down on the tense, silent crowd. If he had wished, he could have remained in Spain, and might now be with the friar O'Daly, the ambassador of Kings and the confessor to Royal Houses. What a contrast? From the glittering court at Lisbon to the sighing wind round the scaffold at Cnocán na gCaorach!

"——never be false to those holy things which we learned as soon as we were able to understand. The Puritans have tried to take these things from us. You in your hearts will preserve them and will hand them on. Some day, in God's good time, the faith will return. Then the bells of Muckross will ring out over the silvery lake, echo across to the Reeks, and re-echo through the vales and glens of Desmond."

His voice was steady to the last. Many of the people were now on their knees. He raised his hand in blessing. Pierce bowed his head and his friend, looking down on him once more, lifting his hand slightly, murmured the words of absolution. Having performed his last duty, he turned to the hangman and said:

"I'm ready now!"

*   *   *

For days afterwards their shrivelled bodies still swung in the breeze. The women of Duibhne walked all the way over the stony ground to bow and kneel where their lord gave his life that Ireland might live on. Let us listen to the stream of words that comes from that tall, stately woman with the flowing robes.

"We have come to bewail him, he who was the strength of our weak ones, the renowned of our warriors, the dowry of our maidens, and the splendour of our scholars. Dun Chaoin, Dun an Oir, Dun Urla and Dun Meidhreach, his four fortresses, stand bare and gaunt without their Chieftain; even the town of Dingle, though not often sad, laments him. Never again till Judgment Day shall his like be in the land.

"The holy priest, Moriarty, too. He went to his death, like a hero would and prayed that their crime be not remembered against them. But it's wrong to grieve, for with that smile he wears he surely has no need of grief—not of our grief at any rate.

"Then came our Chieftain's turn. He said nothing at all but stood like a noble hound amid ill-bred whelps. Yes, a noble hound indeed. He was a gentleman with his equals, a judge, like to Cuchulainn even—but a very terror to the tyrant.

"He was clever, too, as clever as a hawk seeking prey on the Blaskets. There was none so generous at the board—a Guaire was he for hospitality. None excelled him either as a giver of gifts of fat beeves, and none better than he to purchase wine, silks and tapestries.

"Before all the men of Eireann he came in the art of poetry; none so able to turn the last two lines of a verse. It's no wonder the poets are in deep distress and the young men fly across the seas to Spain.

"O Pierce, you were to us as life itself,
Since from the dungeon of death there's no return,
May the Prince of the Angels call you to the Kingdom,
To the City of the Only-Begotten."